T0306046

CHILDREN IN TOURISM COMMUNITIES

This book explores how children living in tourism destinations are particularly susceptible to the impacts of tourism and how they can be included in public policies, programmes and decision-making, focusing particularly on case studies in Europe.

Children in Tourism Communities argues that for tourism to exercise its regenerative role and encourage sustainable development, it must be inclusive of all voices, especially children who represent the future generation and will soon become adults with the rights and responsibilities for engaging in and delivering tourism activities. The book is based on original, ground-breaking research assessing the views of children regarding tourism, with a specific focus on sustainable tourism and development. It includes discussion on key case study locations including Croatia, India, Ireland, Malta, Serbia and Slovenia, although the themes, issues and practices have relevance in all tourism destinations worldwide. Through child-centred research, the book evaluates the differences between those living in mass tourism destinations and smaller-scale micro tourism areas. It encourages a rethinking of sustainability as a concept and demonstrates how tourism can be utilised as a tool for achieving the Sustainable Development Goals.

This will be an important discussion text for students, academics, and instructors in sustainable tourism and development, destination management, culture and heritage, as well as practitioners engaged in continuing professional development in these areas.

Marko Koščak held the position of Assistant Professor from 2014 to 2019 and is currently an Associate Professor at the University of Maribor, Faculty of Tourism Brežice, Slovenia. He studied in Ljubljana (Slovenia), Birmingham (UK), Vienna (Austria) and in 1999 completed his PhD thesis on "Transformation of rural areas along the Slovene–Croatian border" at the Faculty of Arts, Department of Geography, University of Ljubljana. His academic interests are in the field of Sustainable and Community Tourism, Geography of Tourism and Destination Management. These topics are his research work interest fields in which he also lectures to students.

His professional career started with different activities in the field of rural development in Slovenia and abroad since 1986, when he commenced the implementation of integrated rural development projects on the local community level. He was a Project Manager of the Dolenjska and Bela krajina regional sustainable tourism initiative Heritage Trails in South East Slovenia from 1996 to 2009, under the umbrella of the Chamber of Commerce Novo mesto. Since 1986, he has been a regular consultant for the Ministry of Agriculture and from 1999 to 2001 he was also an advisor to the Slovenian government in the sector for structural policy and rural development.

In the past 30 years, he has worked as an advisor to UNDP LoSD and sustainable tourism initiative in Croatia, and the south-east Balkan countries of Bosnia & Hercegovina, Kosovo, Montenegro, North Macedonia and Serbia. He was also involved in a number of sustainable tourism projects and development initiatives in Europe and Asia.

Mladen Knežević is a full professor with tenure. He studied at the University of Ljubljana, where he obtained his bachelor's and doctoral degrees in sociology. He completed his social work studies at the University of Zagreb. After retiring from the University of Zagreb, he worked as an external collaborator at the University of Osijek, where he was part of a team that established a new social work programme at the Faculty of Law in Osijek. During his career, he worked as a social worker and a therapist for alcohol addicts within the prison system of the Republic of Croatia for nearly 20 years. After that, he spent 20 years teaching in the social work programme, progressing from an assistant to a full professor.

In addition to social work, he was heavily involved in the methodology of social research. He taught research methodology at the Faculty of Tourism in Portorož and later at the Faculty of Tourism in Brežice, both in the Republic of Slovenia. He focused intensively on research methodology, leading to the establishment of a laboratory for experimental research at the Faculty of Tourism in Brežice, where teachers from tourism faculties in three countries participated. The laboratory initiated collaboration on experimental research in tourism, resulting in several experimental studies on tourism-related topics, some of which were published in prestigious journals. His main research interest lies in the development of experimental research techniques in tourism studies, a subject he particularly emphasises as a lecturer in the doctoral programme.

Tony O'Rourke studied as undergraduate and post-graduate at the universities of Warwick, Edinburgh and Stirling. His academic interests are in the fields of Sustainable and Responsible Local Tourism, Financing of Local Tourism organisations and the long-term future of tourism in the face of climate change. His background is in management education and small business financing. He worked from 1990 to 2002 with Scottish Financial Enterprise, two Scottish universities and the European Commission on small business financing at a micro level as well as the financing of tourism enterprises in Central and Eastern European transition economies. This included monitoring EU projects in Czech Republic, Hungary, Kazakhstan, Poland and Slovenia. From 1996 to 2001, he was Secretary-General and Chief Executive of the Association of European Regional Financial Centres. From 1992 to 2004, he was a part-time Professor in micro/small business financing at universities in Ireland, Montenegro and Serbia, and at the same time an Expert Advisor to Dun & Bradstreet Country Risk Services on Bosnia & Hercegovina, Croatia and Serbia. In 2004, he returned to the University of Stirling as the Director of the programme for continuing professional development in the Scottish finance and investment sector, as well as teaching on the MSc Banking and Finance Programme. Since retiring in 2011, he has taught part-time at MSc and MBA level as a visiting Professor and also carried out advisory work. He is currently collaborating with the Green Lines Institute for Sustainable Development in Portugal. This is his fourth co-authored book with Routledge.

Tina Šegota is an Associate Professor in Tourism. She studied at the University of Ljubljana, obtaining two doctoral degrees, one in marketing communications at the Faculty of Social Sciences and one in tourism at the School of Economics and Business. Tina is a multi-award-winning academic with research and teaching experience in marketing and tourism worldwide. She received accolades for research excellence and contribution to the academic community. Before joining the Faculty of Tourism at the University of Maribor, Tina worked at the University of Greenwich for several years as a Senior Lecturer in Advertising and Marketing Communications.

In tourism academia, Tina became recognised as a researcher focused on residents' quality of life, children and destination marketing. She was invited to speak for the OECD Academy and UNESCO UNITWIN Conference and delivered numerous public presentations worldwide. Tina initiates and leads several interdisciplinary projects with authors from multiple disciplines (economics, marketing, sociology, sports science) and various countries. In addition, Tina has worked on several different consultancy and research-focused funded projects. She is leading the project Empowering the Neglected Voices of Children, selected for funding by the Slovenian Research and Innovation Agency. She sits on the editorial boards of different tourism and marketing journals.

Tina is a mom to two-year-old Tia and a four-year-old Filip. She is very proud of her children and enjoys raising them to be empowered, open-minded individuals with a strong sense of their community.

"Children are seldom identified as stakeholders in tourism development and marketing. It is refreshing to see the authors of this book take up this topic and to provide such comprehensive coverage of how to better involve younger people in community tourism. This text provides invaluable information on how children perceive tourism, how they are involved in tourism, and how they can contribute to more meaningful tourism in destinations. The authors are to be highly commended in preparing such an innovative and insightful book on children and tourism. This is a must-read for all seriously interested in community tourism development, including practitioners and students."

Alastair M. Morrison, *Research Professor, School of Management and Marketing, Greenwich Business School, UK*

"This volume provides a much-needed child-inclusive human rights approach to communities dealing with tourism. In an era of overtourism and climate catastrophes, the voices of future generations matter more than ever. This is essential reading for any researchers and destination managers willing to understand how tourism impacts children and how their young powers can be harnessed for a more sustainable future."

Heike Schänzel, *Professor, School of Hospitality and Tourism, Auckland University of Technology, New Zealand*

CHILDREN IN TOURISM COMMUNITIES

Sustainability and Social Justice

Marko Koščak, Mladen Knežević, Tony O'Rourke and Tina Šegota

Designed cover image: Tina Šegota

First published 2024
by Routledge
4 Park Square, Milton Park, Abingdon, Oxon OX14 4RN

and by Routledge
605 Third Avenue, New York, NY 10158

Routledge is an imprint of the Taylor & Francis Group, an informa business

© 2024 Marko Koščak, Mladen Knežević, Tony O'Rourke and Tina Šegota

The right of Marko Koščak, Mladen Knežević, Tony O'Rourke and Tina Šegota to be identified as authors of this work has been asserted in accordance with sections 77 and 78 of the Copyright, Designs and Patents Act 1988.

British Library Cataloguing-in-Publication Data
A catalogue record for this book is available from the British Library

ISBN: 978-1-032-44876-3 (hbk)
ISBN: 978-1-032-44874-9 (pbk)
ISBN: 978-1-003-37429-9 (ebk)

DOI: 10.4324/9781003374299

Typeset in Sabon
by Taylor & Francis Books

CONTENTS

ILLUSTRATIONS

Figures

Tables

Boxes

PREFACE

This book explores how children living in tourism destinations are particularly susceptible to the impacts of tourism. It sees tourism as a sector that affects their socialisation process and represents an imminent future as an employment opportunity or a force that shapes their quality of life once they reach adulthood. It is suggested that tourism communities are required to embrace their role as enabling environments in which children's voices, needs, priorities and rights are integral to public policies, programmes and decision-making. Importantly we view this as a book for use by academics, researchers and advanced undergraduate and postgraduate students as recommended reading on related and applicable courses. At the same time it is also highly appropriate and a natural fit for professionals and practitioners in the field. We are seeking to embrace sustainability across every chapter, but always from a different perspective. Sustainability is the concept of this book but has a clear and determined focus on children and their relationship to tourism with a sustainable purpose.

We would at the same time suggest that:

a Children in tourism communities have been socialised in tourism all their lives: firstly, in the process of primary socialisation (i.e. in families where other members are employed in tourism); secondly, in the process of secondary socialisation in which the two most essential socialisation agents are the education system and peer groups; and thirdly, in the process of tertiary socialisation which is the socialisation of adulthood in which a critical factor is the work environment but also their newly created family, the role of parents.

b Of course, this whole socialisation circle from child to adult is in areas of intensive tourism activity at the same time and several levels of different involvement in tourism activity, because socialisation in such areas is nothing but tourism.

c   The authors are cognisant of the fact that there is almost no research on children as an active factor in tourist destinations – particularly in regard to sustainable tourism. Nonetheless, the authors have been engaged in original and ground-breaking research to assess the views of children regarding tourism and more specifically sustainable tourism. This research examined the role of children in assisting tourism to exercise a regenerative role and encourage sustainable development and was a dynamic impetus in the development of this book.

d   We see the important lens of social justice as part of the sustainability paradigm and seek throughout to expose and discuss this.

It is important also to explain the structure of the book, as a guide to all readers. It is divided into five main parts, which each explain important features affecting the role of children in tourist communities within the concept of social justice.

In each part, there is a brief introduction to the topic followed by two chapters that explore critical elements of the topic including relevant research and material drawn from real-world situations. This is followed by a third chapter in each part, which reflects on the issues in those preceding chapters. This is initially based on an analysis of:

- Key Concepts – those issues in the two chapters that are of concern and that require examination.
- Critical Factors – here the authors examine those critical elements that have a fundamentally decisive impact on success or failure.

Thereafter we propose issues raised in each part that reflect on the potential engagement of:

- Students by posing questions which may assist the connections between teaching and learning.
- Researchers (graduate or professional) where we suggest some guidelines for further research – with particular emphasis on the role of children in tourism communities and the need for evidential research.
- Practitioners where there is now an impelling requirement to seek to balance the short-term demands and conflicts apparent in the current post-pandemic environment with the long-term need to meet and counter the looming climate crisis.

Fundamentally, it must be clear to all of these groups that we are required to create strategies which realistically and substantially face the impending climate disaster and the socio-economic effects this will place on global society. Within that society, today's children are an important group whose voice should not be neglected.

ACKNOWLEDGEMENTS

The authors would wish to take this opportunity to thank all our families for supporting us, encouraging us and, most importantly, tolerating our time spent on writing this book instead of on them. However, we hope that we have used this time to open the minds of students, researchers and practitioners to improve our future. Hence, we are dedicating this book to our loved ones – to Branka and family, to Mladen's family, to Elizabeth and family and finally to Jožef, Filip and Tia.

Also, thanks to Matt Shobbrook at Routledge for his continuing encouragement and most helpful support through the publishing process.

Hopefully, we have started and extended the creation of a community of similar-minded individuals who see the value in socially just tourism for children, with children.

Marko Koščak, Mladen Knežević, Tony O'Rourke and Tina Šegota

ABBREVIATIONS AND ACRONYMS

BoP	Balance of Payments
bn	billion
CPI	Consumer Price Index
EC	European Commission
EU	European Union
EUR	Euro area currency – euro
GBP	UK pounds
GDP	Real Gross Domestic Product
G7	Group of 7 advanced economies
G20	Group of 20 advanced economies
HICP	Harmonised Index of Consumer Prices
IMF	International Monetary Fund
ILO	International Labour Organization
km	kilometre
LSIs	Large Scale Industries
m	million
m-o-m	month-on-month (i.e. comparative monthly data)
MSEs	Micro & Small Enterprises
OECD	Organisation for Economic Co-operation and Development
pp	percentage points
SDGs	UN Sustainable Development Goals
SMEs	Small & Medium Enterprises
trn	trillion
UN	United Nations
UNEP	United Nations Environment Programme
UNESCO	United Nations Educational, Scientific and Cultural Organization

UNWTO	United Nations World Travel Organization
USD	US dollars
WB	World Bank
y-o-y	year-on-year (i.e. comparative annualised data)

PART I
Sustainability

INTRODUCTION TO PART I

This part is integral to the book as the focus is on rethinking the concept of sustainability and using tourism as a tool for achieving sustainable development goals whilst opening discussion on the role of children in community sustainability. This involves the search for new development paradigms, as well as examining best practice in sustainable tourism communities. At the same time there is consideration of the complex interaction between Sustainable Development Goals, the socio-economic system and community planning for sustainability.

Chapter 1 considers how Covid-19 and the events in the aftermath of the pandemic were harrowing for the tourism sector; unfortunately, predicted trends show that more negative events will continue crippling the industry in future. However, tourist destinations, which provided individual safety and distance, quality natural environment, and remoteness from the masses, were more successful survivors of this crisis. Having experienced such a unique crisis in the modern world, we reached the point of thoroughly rethinking the concept of sustainability. This also entails the transformation of development strategies and the search for new development paradigms, which can no longer bypass the principles of sustainable and responsible tourism or be allowed to move away from them. Hence, in the chapter, we provide a selection of good practices from tourism destinations that we believe may help to illustrate how a sustainability paradigm could be rethought for destinations worldwide. Already struggling to recover from the pandemic, tourism businesses face rising energy and food prices and other costs, labour shortages and skills gaps. This is compounding a cost-of-living crisis that puts pressure on household budgets, with discretionary items such as engaging in tourist activity on the front line of potential cuts.

In Chapter 2 we evaluate how the interaction between tourism and the globally accepted norms defined by the UN's Sustainable Development Goals is so complex. We have to face the problem of tourism's existence as a

DOI: 10.4324/9781003374299-2

significant source of pollution and environmental damage through transport and excess numbers. This leads us to question how tourism is able to re-focus itself economically, socially and environmentally to meet the UN goals. Yet, at the same time, when we add the role of children in tourism, we have laid down a further layer of complexity. Furthermore, the issue becomes much more complicated when we seek to differentiate tourism at the individual and community levels. Local tourism communities are at the front line of the negative aspects of modern tourism in terms of their sensitivity to excessive footfall and cultural and environmental damage. Children's role in local tourism communities will likely be the most affected in the longer term. This poses a fundamental question – where do children in local tourism communities fit into sustainable development goals?

In Chapter 3 we summarise the Key Concepts and Critical Factors in the two preceding chapters, as well as examine the most appropriate Connections for students, researchers and practitioners.

1

RETHINKING SUSTAINABILITY IN THE POST-COVID ERA

Introduction

The Covid pandemic was a moment of sobriety for our society, and it presented the most severe crisis experienced by the tourism sector overall. The disruption caused by the pandemic has been far more powerful than previous crises, such as SARS in 2011 or the 2008/09 financial crisis, and has brought fundamental changes to the travel industry worldwide. Since March 2020, many governments faced a public health emergency, struggled to support their economies and stopped non-essential activities, especially those that were tourism-related (Koščak & O'Rourke, 2023). According to Tourism Economics reports, global international travel declined by over 50% in 2020, with 2019 levels not achieved until 2023. The fundamental nature of tourism has changed, and the sector's recovery was expected to be as gradual as the re-opening of different economies (ETC, 2020).

The expectation that pre-crisis levels of tourism demand would not bounce back before 2023 was correct for some tourism destinations and also provided them with an opportunity to reshape the industry towards a sector that was more sustainable, more innovative and equally benefited travellers, local communities and the environment. The pandemic emerged as a universal challenge; thus, global support, collaboration and understanding are required to mitigate the social and economic impact of the pandemic (ETC, 2020).

As if the pandemic was not a very difficult challenge for the tourism industry, the current energy crisis, the cost-of-living crisis driven by inflation, and problems with a lack of resources in many tourism destinations (e.g. financial, managerial and structural) seem like never-ending issues obstructing further development of sustainable tourism. A loop of multi-crises has positioned tourism planning and management in a non-enviable position that demands rethinking and renegotiating strategies for sustainable tourism development.

DOI: 10.4324/9781003374299-3

Conflicting interests must be examined and resolved with mutually acceptable solutions, be based on participative planning, and ensure the compatibility of different strategies and the long-term satisfaction of all destination stakeholders. Tourism destination residents and their quality of life should be the torchbearers of sustainable development, as they are the most critical stakeholders who share local resources with visitors and thus engage in a social exchange that posits economic, social, cultural and environmental benefits and costs. Hence, appropriate returns on the resources utilised by tourists must be achieved. Measures should be taken to rationalise, regulate and legislate economic, social, cultural and environmental impacts. Therefore, appropriate tourist activity types and levels should be determined according to the goals and objectives established through a coherent and well-orchestrated planning process that examines all vulnerabilities and involves all stakeholders (Buhalis, 2000).

Therefore, we are at the point of thoroughly rethinking the concept of sustainability. Pre-pandemic keywords bestowing the concept were, for example, responsible management, seeking added value for local products and services, safety and social responsibility, accessibility for all, assessment of the carrying capacity of the environment, excessive tourism or "overtourism", participatory planning and partnership approach (Koščak & O'Rourke, 2020). All these remain highly important for the future development of sustainable tourism. However, the post-pandemic discourse of sustainability has shifted towards developing understanding of how new and potentially experiential approaches in such areas as product design, security and "green" values might be designed and managed. This would then lead away from mass tourism and towards protecting the human, physical and cultural environment and thus building sustainable tourism in the long term. Of course, this also entails the transformation of the development strategies and the search for new paradigms, which can no longer bypass the principles of sustainable and responsible tourism or be allowed to move away from them.

Pre- and post-pandemic tourism until 2022

Each year, between 2010 and 2019, travel and tourism grew faster than the global economy. It enriched local communities and destinations more quickly than other sectors, accounting for 10.3% of global GDP and providing one in ten jobs in 2019 (UNWTO, 2020c). Hence, travel and tourism as a sector has been emphasised as a driver of growth, job creation and prosperity for destinations and communities worldwide.

The knock-on effects of the Covid-19 pandemic have been unprecedented in scale and duration. In 2020, global international travel fell by 74% over the previous year, while Europe's decline reached 70%. Europe's path to recovery will be gradual, with pre-pandemic levels only reached fully by 2023 and beyond. The recovery requires a strong adaptation in fast responses from the tourism sector and a more substantial commitment among society, businesses and institutions at a local, regional and international level. Travel demand is becoming a complex variable to predict, considering the number of external factors that are involved (e.g. economic conditions, natural disasters, terror attacks, fuel prices, geopolitical environment, etc.) (ETC, 2021).

Before the pandemic, travel and tourism (including its direct, indirect and induced impacts) was one of the world's largest sectors, accounting for 1 in 4 of all new jobs created in the world, 10.3% of all jobs (333 m) and 10.3% of global GDP (USD 9.6 tn). Meanwhile, international visitor spending amounted to USD 1.8 tn in 2019 (6.8% of total exports). Travel and tourism enabled socio-economic development, job creation and poverty reduction. This has driven prosperity and significant positive social impact and provided unique opportunities to women, minorities and young people. The benefits of travel and tourism spread far beyond its direct effects in terms of GDP and employment, with indirect gains extending through the entire travel ecosystem and the supply chain linkages to other sectors (WTTC, 2022).

However, in 2020, 62 million jobs were lost, leaving just 271 million employed across the sector globally. This 18.6% decrease was felt across the entire industry, with small and medium-sized enterprises (hereinafter SMEs) being particularly affected alongside women, the young and minorities. Meanwhile, the sector suffered losses of almost USD 4.9 tn, with its global contribution to GDP declining by 50.4% year-on-year, compared to a 3.3% decline of the global economy. The pandemic has altered how we live, work and travel and shifted traveller requirements, expectations, and preferences (WTTC, 2022).

Some key characteristics and reactions of national tourism organisations (hereinafter NTOs) in some EU countries to minimise the pandemic impacts were the following (ETC, 2020):

- During the recovery phase (approximately from July 2020 onwards), NTOs focused primarily on stimulating demand from the domestic and neighbouring markets, supporting tourism businesses in adapting to new social distancing and hygiene measures, and promoting products and experiences associated with nature, health and well-being. They actively promoted outdoor activities and supported DMOs with strategic guidance and funding to meet the needs of local businesses and communities.
- The pandemic caused changes in how NTOs are perceived, with diverse stakeholder groups relying on NTOs for data, insights, guidance and an amplifier effect to spread key messages. NTOs have had to adapt to the challenging situation caused by lockdowns being imposed, with staff often switching roles at short notice to focus on delivering business support advice or switching from international to domestic marketing. As with many organisations, the process of digitalisation has accelerated within NTOs.
- Some changes in consumer travel preferences were already evident in 2020. These include more significant concern around personal well-being, air quality and human impact on the environment; a strong preference for

domestic travel; a desire to spend time in open spaces, outdoors and private accommodation; and a preference for active holidays involving fitness activities or following hiking and cycling routes. Many NTOs expressed hope that these patterns of behaviour would become more permanent.

In addition to these, Table 1.1 below shows a summary overview of the response measures taken by NTOs to mitigate the impact of the Covid-19 crisis on the tourism sector, divided into two broad groups based on the "scope of responsibility".

However, some positive trends were also identified despite more or less negative figures from 2020. For instance, Europe's tourism sector's contribution to GDP was 47.1% below the pre-pandemic level in 2020, and the gap reduced to 32.3% below the 2019 level in 2021, showing a strong rebound. The sector's performance in Europe is estimated to surpass those levels of 2019 in 2024, when travel and tourism contribution to the region's GDP may reach 4.1% above the pre-pandemic amount. In 2022, as travellers' confidence improves, the global travel and tourism sector is estimated to hasten its pace of recovery to 43.7% compared to 2021 and add a further ten million jobs. The industry is likely to return to pre-pandemic levels around the end of 2023, and the preliminary data for the first half of 2022 supports this forecast (WTTC, 2022).

In 2021, booking trends showcased a domestic rediscovery, with ongoing restrictions compelling consumers in search of travel experiences to explore within the borders of their home destinations. The concept of a staycation has taken on new meaning in this era, as consumers create work-cations and increasingly stay longer in destinations, given the normalisation of remote work. While continued restrictions have limited international travel, wanderlust remains. Although domestic travel has been a critical factor in the recovery to date and remains essential, the full recovery of the global economy will require the total return of international travel.

While projections are positive overall, there are continuing downside risks to recovery, described by the IMF as a "rocky road" (IMF, 2023). This includes the negative impacts of the conflict in Ukraine, with supply chain disruptions and rising energy prices propelling inflationary pressures. There is clear evidence of a fall in disposable incomes in key tourism outbound markets. This is driven by expectations of faltering growth in the advanced economies, where real growth is unlikely to reach above 1.8% in 2025 (authors' estimates). Even in 2023, IMF projections indicate that real wage growth will fail to reach the expected level of inflation at 4.7% (IMF, 2023).

The pandemic has demonstrated the importance of tourism as an economic force and a provider of livelihoods, raising awareness of this at the highest levels of government and amongst the public at large. However, it has also thrown light on the fragility of the sector, which is highly fragmented and interdependent, with a heavy reliance on micro and small enterprises. Furthermore, it has shown that tourism development can be imbalanced, leading to an over-dependence on the

TABLE 1.1 Overview of response measures

RESPONSE MEASURES: NTOs *directly responsible for implementation and/ or coordination (Areas 1 and 2)*	RESPONSE MEASURES: NTO *is in a position to influence / measure effects on the tourism sector (Areas 3 and 4)*
<ul><li>Set up COVID-19 tourism crisis response group</li><li>Provide information to tourism businesses about support schemes online and with direct business support hotline</li><li>Support tourism sector with representation to central government, relaying specific requests for support</li><li>Waive or postpone collection of fees (e.g. membership fees or operator licences)</li><li>Liaison between the government and the tourism sector</li><li>PR and communication recovery planning (market monitoring and prioritisation)</li><li>Monitor impact of the crisis on tourism businesses (e.g. with B2B survey)</li><li>Monitor impact of the crisis on consumer sentiment in key markets (e.g. consumer confidence surveys, travel search patterns, media coverage shaping consumer perceptions of destination country)</li><li>Relay official information to visitors about public health measures through NTOs' social media and NTOs' websites (translated into languages of key markets)</li><li>Roll out inspirational campaigns e.g. 'Dream now, visit later'</li><li>Support visitors needing to be repatriated (e.g. arrange emergency accommodation for passengers awaiting repatriation, facilitating repatriation flights, cooperation with embassies and consulates)</li><li>Tourism infrastructure planning and investment (e.g. providing finance for renovating and restoring hotels and attractions or fast-tracking planned transport and hotel construction works)</li><li>Coordinate national pre-purchase voucher system to support business liquidity</li><li>Set up official online training courses for inactive/furloughed employees</li></ul>	<ul><li>Fiscal measures to support affected tourism sector employees (e.g. furlough schemes, waived taxes or social security payments)</li><li>Fiscal measures to support affected tourism sector businesses (e.g. waived rent collection or business taxes or VAT submission)</li><li>Support packages for specific sectors (e.g. airlines, cruises) or individuals (e.g. self-employed guides or artisans)</li><li>Reimbursement of fees for cancelled events</li><li>Financing for national voucher system with voucher redemption guarantee against business failure</li><li>Reconstruction funds for specific infrastructure upgrades</li><li>Skills training programmes</li><li>Transport and accommodation provision for visitors in need of repatriation</li></ul>

Source: European Travel Commission (www.etc-corporate.org 2020)

sector in some economies. Despite tourism's clear potential as a driver for positive change, it is widely accepted that rapid or unplanned tourism growth can result in a range of negative impacts, including in the use of land, water and other non-renewable resources, the generation of waste and a significant contribution to global greenhouse gas emissions. Pressure on local communities has occurred, arising from high visitor volumes and weak management, and the quality of jobs in the sector can be inconsistent. Many businesses and destinations have been unable to develop and manage tourism to their full advantage due to a lack of planning, coordination, skills and resources and a failure to make the most of new opportunities digitalisation offers. The fundamental changes in tourism demand and supply and their responses since March 2020 point to a need to rethink and reshape tourism policy moving forward.

Three essential requirements and opportunities that should guide changes in tourism demand and supply are (OECD, 2021):

- Restoration of confidence and enabling recovery;
- Learning from the pandemic experience; and
- Prioritising a sustainable development agenda for future tourism.

Following a period of lockdowns and isolation, travellers preferred to travel to less crowded and unfamiliar destinations. Indeed, there has been increased interest in exploring secondary destinations and nature. During this period, travellers have become more committed to sustainability, which in turn is affecting their travel choices. The lockdowns have also shone a brighter light on wellness and overall health, driving more consumers to seek out further wellness experiences. From domestic travel leading the recovery and younger generations being the first to travel again to an increased demand for extended stays, fee-free cancellations, and enhanced health and hygiene measures, consumers have made their preferences clear through bookings, enquiries and surveys forecast (WTTC, 2022).

View to the future – 2023 and beyond

Before the pandemic, many researchers and tourism institutions had noted a growing demand for unique and authentic travel experiences and a desire among tourists to positively impact the places they visit. This trend is likely to accelerate. This can drive the sustainable development of rural communities, creating jobs and other opportunities outside of big cities while protecting and promoting the cultural and natural heritage. It may not always be obvious, but the Covid-19 pandemic is allowing the travel industry to rebuild itself more ethically, responsibly and considerately, and be regenerative for the planet and people (Euronews.travel, 2020).

The abrupt decline in global travel has also given a foretaste of a world without the possibility of travel, a possibility that is gradually becoming more realistic as climate change accelerates. The decline in tourism arrivals across Europe has also exposed the extent to which some neighbourhoods, towns or regions have become heavily dependent on tourism as a source of revenue, demonstrating the need for more diversified economies and stronger local supply chains.

The pandemic has changed consumer behaviour around the world in unprecedented ways. Lockdown restrictions and concerns around the economy and personal health have led to many short-term changes in spending behaviour that may become more permanent. Key trends observed by NTOs to date include (ETC, 2020):

- Greater concern around personal well-being, air quality and humans' impact on the environment.
- A strong preference for travel domestically or to neighbouring countries with easy access by car.
- A desire to spend time in open spaces, outdoors and in private accommodation.
- A desire to avoid high-density accommodation facilities and activities or mixing too closely with strangers (e.g. hotels, cruises or long-haul flying).
- A preference for active holidays involving fitness activities or following hiking and cycling routes.
- A long-term increase in precautionary savings, as well as falling consumption rates and increasing frugality among consumers, potentially leading to a fall in discretionary leisure spending.
- A desire for consumers to be seen (through social media images) as safe and responsible, with travel plans scrutinised through the lens of what is safe rather than what is popular.
- Greater awareness of the impact of Covid-19 on SMEs and the livelihoods of local communities, leading to prioritised spending with SMEs to support the community.

If we elaborate further on the above points, lessons learned from previous crises and the early stages of Covid-19 point to the need for destinations to be well prepared to take swift action. This requires advanced planning, engagement with key stakeholders, strong alignment between the public and private sectors and excellent communication. Specific actions are needed to address the immediate needs of visitors, businesses and local communities, contain the impact and take initial steps to stimulate recovery. Actions taken during the crisis and beyond may include marketing programmes, incentive schemes for selected market segments and general communication to maintain destination brand values and visibility (OECD, 2021).

Resilience priorities differ between destinations and at different points in time. These other priority areas depend on location, climate, visitor mix, reliance on travel and tourism as an economic driver, typology of visitors, political vision and prioritisation of tourism, among other activities. Typically, destinations most exposed to climate risk and/or extreme weather focus on environment and infrastructure. Those with a high reliance on travel and tourism receipts tend to focus on economic resilience, and particularly the ability of the destination, its businesses and its workforce to quickly pivot in case of crisis. Societal support and acceptance are key priorities for destinations with the most seasonal or concentrated demand, with the balance between visitor and resident value being a key ingredient to resilience (WTTC, 2022).

Some possible priorities should be addressed by destinations, including (WTTC, 2022):

- Maintaining travel and tourism jobs in the face of travel shut-downs.
- Swiftly adapting to new visitor markets to keep accommodation occupancy high.
- Implementing effective processes for responding to natural disasters protecting local populations and natural assets, and re-opening for tourism as soon as it is safe to do so.
- Ensuring community involvement in tourism activities to build greater connection and information flow.

The most critical areas to be addressed with resilience measures are the natural environment, infrastructure, energy and water, economy and society. Table 1.2 below summarises some of the actions that destinations can take to build both resilience and longer-term sustainability across five main groupings (WTTC, 2022).

Here are some key actions that the OECD (2021) suggested in their G20 report guidelines for the future of tourism:

- The Covid-19 pandemic has shown the importance of government assistance in retaining the essential structure and framework of the tourism value chain through prolonged crises so that crucial parts remain in place to enable a successful recovery. Tourism businesses should also be encouraged and helped to adapt their services during the crisis, such as providing services within the local community. Support for workers may include job retention schemes, social protection and security and supplementary unemployment benefits. Training and skills development can help to retain and strengthen capacity. Support should be sufficiently flexible to meet changing conditions.
- Experience from the Covid-19 pandemic points to the need for a more strategic integration of the tourism sector into the broader economy. Too many destinations have been over-dependent on tourism, which might have been avoided by seeking tourism growth within the context of more comprehensive economic and regional development planning. Tourism value chains become less vulnerable if the businesses involved have access to a range of sources of income. Policies should seek to diversify and spread risks within the sector. Destinations and businesses with a diversified market base (including a mix of domestic and international tourists) are generally less exposed to potential market failure.

TABLE 1.2 Summary of the actions for destinations to build resilience and longer-term sustainability

	Understand the risks	Prepare for shocks	Respond to shock	Longer term strategies
The natural environment	• Climate risk assessment. • Biodiversity risk assessment. • Ecological risk assessment.	• Hazard mapping, vulnerability assessment and risk mapping by area. • Physical as well as non-physical measures to safeguard vulnerable assets.	• Assess loss and damage. • Prioritise repairs and recovery.	• Tourism development plans aligned with climate adaptation plans and bio-diversity/ecological conservation plans to ensure decreasing overlap of tourism burden, bio-diversity conservation and climate impacted areas
Infrastructure	• Physical infrastructure assessment (accommodation, transportation, residential); Identify key vulnerabilities and risk areas for different types of hazards, shocks and stresses.	• Plan based on maximum capacity and ability of infrastructure in case of evacuation scenarios. • Practice drills involving residents, businesses and tourists in case of shocks and stresses.	• Close collaboration between various agencies and private sector to ensure infrastructure safety following shocks and stresses.	• Future / new development based on climate risk assessments and climate adaptation strategies. • Close public-private sector collaboration in developing future infrastructure for tourism, aligned with sustainability and resilience goals.
Energy Water	• Water and Energy systems resilience assessments.	• Create or enhance back-up generator capacity in key tourism locations.	• Follow established protocols for crisis management.	• Diversified sources for water and energy; for energy sources, where possible, including local generation and renewables.

	Understand the risks	Prepare for shocks	Respond to shock	Longer term strategies
Economic resilience	• Tourism reliance assessment. • Source market assessment. • Visitor profile and typology.	• Scenario planning for short/mid-term cessation of arrivals, including alternative markets / activities.	• Federal/state/local support for destinations and tourism stakeholders. • Risk transfer mechanisms such as insurance.	• Capacity building to support versatility of tourism workforce. • Food security.
Social resilience	• Community and other sta-keholder surveys (e.g. local businesses and institutions) to understand areas of resistance, vulnerability and risk.	• Implement policies and procedures aimed at safeguarding working conditions and visitor experiences ahead of time.	• Balance the needs of the local and visitor communities in responding to crises through clear and consistent protocols and communications.	• Improved monitoring and implementation of health protocols. • Robust community and tourism communication frameworks to ensure community engagement, correct information transfer and help rebuild traveller confidence.

Source: World Travel and Tourism Council: Enhancing Resilience to Drive Sustainability in Destinations 2022. All rights reserved.

- During the Covid-19 pandemic, a re-focus on domestic tourism, when possible, has occurred in many countries. Domestic and neighbouring markets may play a significant role in tourism strategies relying on building resilience faced with increasing restrictions, costs, safety concerns and climate change associated with long-haul travel. The tourism offer and product base may need adaptation to meet new market profiles. Irrespective of specific market requirements, innovation and related product diversification can also contribute to resilience in their own right.
- Covid-19 has revealed the fragility of many tourism businesses, some of which have closed or struggled to survive. Government emergency support programmes have often provided an essential lifeline. However, they cannot be maintained indefinitely. Even with a return of tourism markets, many enterprises will continue to struggle until the sector recovers. Relevant action to address this could include programmes to support skills acquisition, digitalisation, reinvestment and new forms of targeted funding.
- The effects of the Covid-19 pandemic on tourism have been asymmetrical, with some countries, destinations and people more exposed than others. Even under normal circumstances, destinations with a high reliance on the tourism sector are more vulnerable to the effects of such crises. This disparity is likely to be significantly exacerbated following the pandemic, and developing countries are likely to be disproportionately impacted due to limited or slower access to vaccines and an often limited ability to rely on domestic tourism.
- In many countries, experiences during the pandemic have emphasised the importance of the relationship between tourism and local communities. Many tourism businesses have diversified their portfolios by providing services within their local areas. These have been highly valued by consumers who have indicated that they may be more aware of local products and community engagement in their future travels. On the other hand, some rural communities have felt vulnerable in the face of an unmanaged and sometimes unwelcome influx of new visitors seeking outdoor and nature-based recreation.

Additional inclusiveness issues arising from Covid-19 include enhanced concerns about the availability and quality of jobs and the viability of small businesses. A different but important point, which is less frequently raised, is equitable access to holiday opportunities in the face of possible supply shortages and price increases (OECD, 2021).

The European Travel Commission presented the results of the research conducted between European national tourism organisations at the beginning of the Covid-19 pandemic. Figure 1.1 shows their responses and level of agreement with different strategic approaches to tourism.

As seen in the previous figure, most NTOs agree that the pandemic represents a turning point for making tourism in their country more environmentally friendly. There was also a strong willingness (among 85% of respondents) to work with the relevant stakeholders to find new ways to reduce the negative impacts of tourism, while 32% indicated that they might reduce or withdraw funding from sectors or businesses with high carbon emissions. There is also scepticism about mass tourism being essential to achieving the levels of growth seen before the crisis (perhaps because it may take some significant time to return), and just over half of respondents indicated that budgets and priorities in the future could be rebalanced to pursue more environmentally or socially sustainable initiatives (ETC, 2020).

The longer-term perspective

At the same time, in possible contradiction to the aims stated above, more than half of NTOs surveyed wished to see a return to the levels of tourist arrivals seen in their country in recent years. This may be due to the strong economic reliance on tourism in some survey-participating countries or based on a desire to disperse similar levels of tourist arrivals more evenly throughout the year and throughout

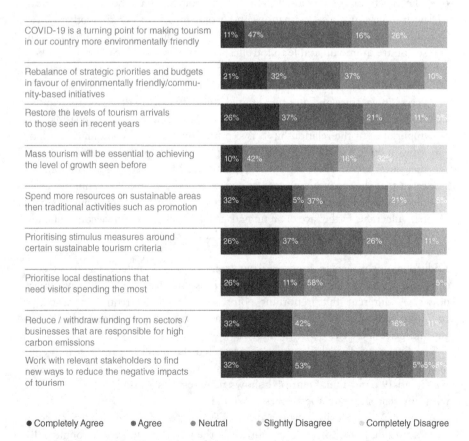

FIGURE 1.1 Responses and level of agreement on different recovery priorities
Source: European Travel Commission (www.etc-corporate.org 2020)

the country. At this stage, there was also a strong willingness not to declare whether specific local destinations within a country, most in need of visitor spending, may be prioritised in the future or whether resources would be spent on more sustainability-oriented activities rather than traditional NTO areas such as promotion. This perhaps reflects NTOs' ongoing uncertainty about the budgetary environment for decision-making in the coming years (ETC, 2020).

Against the backdrop of Covid-19, the One Planet Vision for a Responsible Recovery of the Tourism Sector provides a valuable framework for building a vision and a roadmap for recovery. The vision recommends six lines of action to guide a responsible tourism recovery for people, the planet and prosperity (UNWTO, 2020c):

- Public health – the need to connect epidemiological indicators with tourism monitoring mechanisms, connect health with sustainability and restore trust through transparent and proactive communication on the public health measures put in place.
- Social inclusion – the need for long-term support to SMEs to ensure that destinations maintain a diverse and attractive offering, the provision of targeted support for vulnerable groups such as youth, women and rural and indigenous populations, and repurpose tourism as a supporter for the community, capitalising on the new services that tourism businesses and creative industries have been providing to destinations in times of crisis.
- Biodiversity conservation – aimed at improving the management of scarce natural resources such as water and fostering disaster resilience in urban and natural environments by capturing the value of conservation through tourism, supporting conservation efforts through tourism and investing in nature-based solutions for sustainable tourism.
- Climate action – the necessity of monitoring and reporting CO_2 emissions from tourism operations, accelerating the decarbonisation of tourism operations (including through investments to develop low-carbon transportation options) and supporting the engagement of the tourism sector in adaptation to climate change and carbon removal, through both natural and technological methods.
- Circular economy – investing in circular economy processes such as reducing and reusing, repairing, refurbishing and recycling, prioritising sustainable food approaches such as local sourcing and reducing food waste, and addressing plastic waste and pollution.
- Government and finance – focusing on measures "beyond the economic impacts of tourism", steering recovery funds towards better tourism (i.e. achieving the goals presented above) and enhancing collaboration between key stakeholders along the tourism value chain, internationally and at destination level.

UNWTO (2020c) also provides some guidelines for action in the tourism sector in the post-pandemic period as follows:

- Enhance international cooperation through tourism, particularly in support of the recovery from Covid-19 through programmes that support inclusive community development through tourism and build sector resilience.
- Position inclusive community development at the core of tourism policies to contribute to inclusion through socio-economic development, poverty alleviation and rural development while promoting community, national and regional integrations.
- Adopt a holistic and integrated approach to inclusive community development through a whole-of-government approach and effective cooperation and coordination at all levels – community, national, regional and global.
- Enhance tourism governance through public–private–community partnerships (PPCPs), enabling the collective development of tourism products and services and the management of community resources for mutual benefit through jointly assuming risks and responsibilities while sharing resources and competencies and attracting new investments.
- Facilitate and improve tourism value chain development and management to empower local communities, particularly vulnerable and marginalised groups, to promote authentic experiences and preserve natural and cultural resources.
- Support the development of smart destinations with essential technical support to optimise resource allocation and consumption and direct tourist flows in the master planning process to mitigate the negative impacts of tourism flows on natural and cultural resources and social fabrics.
- Align inclusive community development through tourism with the 2030 Agenda for Sustainable Development by actively engaging in national Sustainable Development Goals (SDGs) processes, strengthening SDG engagement and commitment from all stakeholders: communities, civil society organisations, local/municipal authorities, private sector, financiers and investors.
- Adopt and develop evidence-based tourism policy and management while emphasising the need for a comparable international statistical framework for the impacts of tourism in its three pillars – economic, social and environmental – in line with the UN-supported Measuring Sustainable Tourism (MST) framework, emphasising the need for gender-disaggregated data to promote gender equality.
- Promote human capital development through targeted policies and programmes for education and capacity building for communities focusing on women, youth and other marginalised groups in the tourism development process, including self-governance within communities that enable efficient decision-making and leadership concerning tourism.

- Assist communities in accessing funds to help set up priority supporting facilities, including healthcare, sanitation, communication, accessibility, education and infrastructure, and develop necessary tourism infrastructure and services.
- Strengthen the role of tourism in inclusive community development through official development assistance agencies and international and regional financing institutions.
- Promote decent work through reducing social and economic barriers and increasing social protection within extant (inter)national legal frameworks.
- Mainstream gender in community development by integrating a gender perspective into the preparation, design, implementation, monitoring and evaluation of policies, regulatory measures and spending programmes, focusing on empowering women.
- In this process, engage with all stakeholders, including the public sector at national, regional and local levels, private sector, civil society and communities.
- Engage in consultative processes with communities on the planning, design and management of tourism projects, products and services, which includes a dialogue between the community residents and other stakeholders (governments, destinations, tourism companies and others), as well as among community members whose consent to and support for any tourism development is crucial.
- Promote and encourage entrepreneurial innovation and digital transformation, particularly for micro-, small and medium-sized enterprises (MSMEs).
- Support equitable enterprises and sustainable business practices, which ensure enhanced economic benefit and contribute to protecting cultural and natural resources and intellectual property, fostering community development and improving livelihoods.
- Promote resilience through product diversification, social and environmental protection schemes and crisis management mechanisms that enable destinations to be more prepared to manage crises and minimise their impacts effectively.

What kind of sustainability and responsibility do we need?

The role of tourism in the transition towards a green economy has again come to the forefront. Limited mobility, amongst other restrictions, has led to a series of temporary positive impacts, such as improved air quality, while global CO_2 emissions are estimated to have dropped by 7% compared to 2019 levels (ETC, 2022). Wildlife regained its territories, marine ecosystems underwent regeneration and landscapes started to recover from decades of overuse. Furthermore, residents of destinations that suffered from overtourism before the pandemic reclaimed their living space as noise pollution, overcrowding and other nuisances dropped. Overtourism describes destinations where hosts or guests feel that there are too many visitors and that the quality of life in the area or the quality of the experience has deteriorated unacceptably. Overtourism is the opposite of responsible tourism, which is about using tourism to make better places to live and visit. Often, both visitors and guests experience the deterioration concurrently.

The severe impact of the Covid-19 pandemic on the broader tourism economy has forced the tourism sector to emerge in a more sustainable, innovative and resilient way to build back better. As the European tourism economy navigates the path to recovery, it has become crucial that the sector considers its present and future economic, social and environmental impacts. Supporting sustainable tourism recovery requires a systemic approach involving not only all parties in the tourism value chain, the supply side, but also the active participation of consumers, the demand side. The turmoil brought on by the Covid-19 outbreak has fundamentally shifted people's lives, how they live and work, their education, social interactions and travel as we know it. Although consumers' adoption of sustainable tourism behaviour has grown recently, research has shown that the global pandemic has driven more sustainable travel trends. Generally, travellers seem to be adopting greener options and paying closer attention to their impact on the environment and local communities. Travelling closer to home, avoiding crowded destinations and seeking more authentic and immersive experiences have become some of the emerging trends driven by the pandemic. However, consumers' willingness to adopt a more sustainable travel behaviour does not always materialise, and these changes are still difficult to predict. Therefore, it has become imperative to understand the gap between people's sustainable values and their related actions, and explore approaches to minimise this discrepancy (ETC, 2022).

Overall, travellers are most likely to adopt sustainable practices in the behavioural category of interacting with the local community and immersing in local life, learning about the local traditions and trades, buying local products and choosing locally owned restaurants while in the destination. The travellers generating the lowest carbon footprint are most aware of environmental pressures and are most willing to change their behaviours; however, as their footprint is already low, focusing on behavioural change in this segment is the least impactful.

In light of the identified range of concepts and actions which can support destinations in becoming more resilient and sustainable, some of the common themes identified point to the importance of the following concepts (WTTC, 2022):

- Destinations looking to ensure that this key ingredient is in place should follow these steps:

  a *Identify the critical resilience and sustainability issues relevant to the destination (e.g. environment, economy, energy supply, etc).*
  b *Define the key stakeholders linked to each priority area.*

c Prioritise goals and initiatives to ensure those priorities are manageable and sensibly sequenced.
d Identify gaps in the desired state, including finance, data and knowledge, ownership and policy.
e Define and implement governance mechanisms, including structure, responsibilities, oversight, reporting and communication.

• This includes the need for travel and tourism providers to be empowered to be truly responsible for their environmental, economic and social impacts. This, in turn, requires legitimacy, as a specific form of leadership is needed to establish such a framework of responsibility. This framework must incorporate the travel and tourism assets across all relevant stakeholders – from residents to employees, SMEs to large corporates, as well as policy-makers and governors to travellers – to strengthen ties and engagement, and thereby adaptability and ingenuity – two key factors in resilience.

Transparency is another key element; stakeholders need to have clear rules and requisites to enable success in achieving resilience goals. Steps that can be taken to establish this approach include:

• *Enhancing public–private–community collaboration between governments, trade unions and civil society to identify common pool resources and ensure that the governance structure (above) addresses these.*
• *Addressing regulatory/policy frameworks to encourage/incentivise innovative and creative approaches that support resilience goals.*
• *Implementing comprehensive and transparent communication to demonstrate the value of travel and tourism and encourage dialogue and trust through the DMO and/or dedicated resilience governance body.*

Public–private collaboration models should convert sustainability priorities into practical initiatives. To do this, governments and DMOs can support designing and implementing destination-shared value projects. This approach should now be applied to destinations, with the participation of numerous companies and key stakeholders, proving to be a successful tool to achieve these same objectives at a larger scale. Destination-shared value projects are action-oriented exercises carried out jointly by various companies in destinations to expand beyond corporate social responsibility on an individual basis, accelerate the sustainability process and produce a meaningful impact. The model requires the involvement of the local population and solid partnerships with governments and institutions. It includes specific actions to be implemented by each group of stakeholders (see Table 1.3).

The shared value ecosystem summarised in Table 1.3 gives protagonism to visitors as travellers play a central role in creating a successful shared value project. Their incorporation into the overall vision allows them to connect with the destination and amplify the benefits of travel and tourism by creating a positive impact via their trip. This element is also an emerging consumer demand, contributing to positive change with daily gestures in the consumption process. Shared value project examples include:

- *Collaborating with travellers in conservation, regeneration and heritage preservation through beach clean-ups or participation in social programmes, enhancing the visitor's experience and creating a win-win for visitor and destination.*
- *Channelling part of the receipts from travel and tourism back into nature conservation, infrastructure and social programmes in local communities.*

Change is the only constant. Future shocks are highly likely, particularly with climate change, and those destinations that learn not only from their own experiences but from those of others will find their resilience "muscles" develop rapidly. A culture of continuous improvement, a growth mindset that focuses on learning from crises rather than apportioning blame for any failings and careful knowledge management are all necessary for crisis preparedness and resilience. The lessons from Covid-19 must not be forgotten. Every destination should follow a clear framework for cataloguing learnings and start to prepare for the next event that will inevitably disrupt its travel and tourism ecosystem. Destinations need to be especially mindful that the sector works within the local capacity for water and energy and ensure that future development and infrastructure plans consider resilience and are built with any stresses to these essential systems in mind. Risk and disaster management disciplines provide clear

TABLE 1.3 Specific actions for specific group of stakeholders

Stakeholders	Actions to be implemented
Public sector	• Design the schemes and coordinate / incentivise participation.
Tourism companies with local presence	• Incorporate the SDGs into every level of the business strategy. • Leading collaboration with other companies in the sector by launching joint activities.
Global companies with no local presence	• Participate through sponsorships or by channeling donations from clients.
Suppliers	• Follow sustainable processes. • Respect the environment.
Local population and employees	• Volunteer.
Travellers	• Donate. • Participate in joint projects.

Source: European Travel Commission (www.etc-corporate.org 2020)

guidelines for cataloguing lessons from previous experience to ensure that these are learned and applied. Having periodic cross-sectoral public–private dialogue on resilience themes will help to keep these issues front of mind and can help to ensure that the best ideas are captured, irrespective of where they come from.

Foster integrated, agile, forward-looking policies to shape a brighter tourism future:

- Promote forward-looking tourism strategies to boost recovery, accelerate the green and digital transition and build capacity across government to prepare, react and adapt to future shocks.
- Build on the innovative approaches to design and deliver Covid-19 response measures, in cooperation with the private sector and civil society, to address the structural transformation needed to build a stronger, more sustainable industry and tackle future tourism policy issues.

Build resilience in the tourism ecosystem:

- Foster a business environment where tourism SMEs can succeed and strengthen by improving access to finance, building skills and capacity, and promoting greener digital practices.
- Encourage collaboration between actors across the tourism ecosystem to respond and adapt to events, share information and experiences, and develop an understanding of risks and opportunities.
- Support sustainable and diverse destinations with flexible, tailored and adequately resourced destination management plans, effective monitoring mechanisms and engagement of actors.
- Build robust and comparable data and tools to measure and monitor tourism resilience, fill data gaps, and inform quick response and effective decision-making for future crises.

Promote a green tourism recovery:

- Develop long-term integrated strategies with a sustainable tourism vision, goals and targets, with action plans and mechanisms to leverage resources and coordinate across government.
- Implement a mix of evidence-based policies prioritising high-impact interventions along the tourism value chain to raise awareness, regulate and incentivise green practices and investment.
- Promote carbon literacy and build the capacity of tourism actors to develop innovative solutions, empower sustainable travel choices and help businesses reduce their environmental impact.
- Leverage the role of government in catalysing the green transition, and organise publicly funded or procured tourism infrastructure to contribute to environmental and climate-resilient development.

Some possible trends in the post-pandemic period

The choices consumers make about how to live their lives are clearly impacting how they choose to travel. Some of these changes will prevail in the short to medium term, as Covid-19 management policies continue to dictate how most of the world travels, while other changes may transform travel and tourism in the longer term.

Travellers are remembering all the things they love about exploring the world while also considering how their travel habits impact that world. Specific existing trends have accelerated, and new ones have emerged. All of us have had to transform how we live our lives to manage the outbreak and keep each other safe. With these changes and restrictions, consumer travel habits have shifted and will continue to evolve. In a world where travel restrictions can change overnight, and substantial rules are often implemented to maintain public health, consumers are even more concerned about the cost implications of changing travel plans and what kind of health and hygiene protocols they could encounter during their travels. From domestic travel leading the recovery and younger generations being the first to travel to increased demand for extended stays, fee-free cancellations and enhanced health and hygiene measures, consumers have made their preferences clear through bookings, enquiries and surveys, and the sector is responding.

Booking trends have showcased a domestic rediscovery, with ongoing restrictions compelling consumers in search of travel experiences to explore within the borders of their home destinations. The concept of a staycation has taken on new meaning in this era, as consumers create work-cations and increasingly stay longer in destinations, given the normalisation of remote work. In the short term, however, even with the flexibility to work from anywhere, consumers are weary of booking too far in advance for fear of travel restrictions causing cancellations. Following a period of lockdowns and isolation, travellers prefer to travel to less crowded and unfamiliar destinations. Indeed, there has been increased interest in exploring secondary destinations and nature. During this period, travellers have become more committed to sustainability, which in turn is affecting their travel choices. The lockdowns have also shone a brighter light on wellness and overall health, driving more consumers to seek out further wellness experiences. However, consumer concerns around Covid-19 circulation and infection persist, making it crucial for their chosen travel partners to provide knowledge of virus prevention measures (WTTC, 2021).

The allure of secondary destinations

In the wake of the pandemic, consumers increasingly seek secondary destinations, rural areas and nature-based destinations for their travels. Modern travellers increasingly seek adventure to satisfy their pent-up wanderlust, with 40% of travellers exploring unfamiliar destinations. Similarly, American

Express found that 69% of travellers were interested in visiting lesser-known destinations, 72% hoped to support local communities through their travel and 59% were interested in "philantourism", specifically choosing an experience or vacation to support a destination through tourism. Moreover, 52% of consumers are more likely to take an outdoor trip than before the pandemic, and 47% of travellers want their next trip to be in nature (WTTC, 2021). While there is pent-up demand for travel, consumer criteria evolved during the pandemic, significantly impacting purchasing decisions. Implementing enhanced health and hygiene measures remains a top priority for consumers worldwide. Indeed, while price still drives bookings, consumers are now equally focused on health and safety.

Responsible together and sustainable forever

While sustainability has been a priority for the travel and tourism sector for some time, it became even more prominent through the pandemic. Indeed, consumers pay closer attention to their human impact on the environment and seek more sustainable options in how they live and travel. Increasingly, the private sector offers sustainable alternatives, and the public sector is more eager to finance sustainable tourism and development. From the UN Sustainable Development Goals (SDGs), the Paris Agreement, and the UNFCCC's Climate Neutral Now initiative to action on diversity, inclusion and illegal wildlife trade, the public and private sectors are working towards a more sustainable future for people and the planet. The trend toward sustainability will remain long-term, with more consumers intending to travel more responsibly and sustainably. Consumers will likely continue to behave more responsibly with the support and continued work of the public and private sectors and local communities and increasingly clear information on more sustainable options.

While travellers are still concerned about Covid-19 transmission, their growing confidence is enabled by the public and private sectors, whose overt virus management measures are present throughout their travel journey. Indeed, consumers are more conscientious than ever; they increasingly pay attention to how travel organisations protect their health and that of the staff that help make their travel possible. Traveller booking habits show continued concerns around rapidly changing restrictions, amplifying demand for easy and free cancellations. However, this has not hampered consumers' desire to travel with a rise in domestic travel in the short term and with lengthening stays. In this new context, travellers are increasingly taking responsibility to help protect the environment and support local communities. They also plan to cultivate healthier lifestyles and maintain good mental well-being. Indeed, younger travellers are leading the recovery, and the luxury travel segment will see new travellers in the short term. As travel recovery accelerates, consumers and the public and private sectors are responsible for rebuilding a more sustainable and inclusive travel and tourism sector for our people and planet. Yet, travellers' desire to discover the world remains unabated, giving us hope for the future of travel and tourism and its ability to make a meaningful difference in people's lives and livelihoods. Understanding the changing context, emerging trends and consumer expectations will support businesses, governments and communities to adapt, pivot and deliver authentic experiences whilst prioritising sustainable, inclusive and resilient growth (WTTC, 2021).

References

Buhalis, D. (2000). Marketing the competitive destination of the future. *Tourism Management*, 21 (1), 97–116.

ETC (2020). *European Travel Commission: Handbook on Covid -19 recovery strategies for national tourism organisations*. ETC & Toposophy, Brussels, September 2020.

ETC (2021). *European Travel Commission: Handbook on tourism forecasting methodologies 2021*. ETC & Inzights & Silverbullet research, Brussels, February 2021.

ETC (2022). *Sustainable Travel in an Era of Disruption – Assessing the impact of the Covid-19 pandemic on travellers' sustainable tourism attitudes and projected travel behaviour*. ETC & CELTH, EFTI and Breda University of Applied Science, Brussels, January 2022.

Euromonitor (2020). *The Implications of Covid-19 for the Global Economy*. www.euromonitor.com.

Euronews.travel (2020). *Travel Report October 2020*, Euronews. www.euronews.com/travel.

International Monetary Fund (2023). *World Economic Outlook – A rocky recovery*, April 2023.

Koščak, M., & O'Rourke, T. (2020). *Ethical and Responsible Tourism – Managing sustainability in local tourism*, 1st edition. Routledge.

Koščak, M., & O'Rourke, T. (2023). *Ethical and Responsible Tourism – Managing sustainability in local tourism*, 2nd edition. Routledge.

OECD (2021). G20 Rome guidelines for the future of tourism: OECD Report to G20 Tourism Working Group. *OECD Tourism Papers*, 2021/03, OECD Publishing, Paris. http://dx.doi.org/10.1787/d11080db-en.

Porter, M.E., & Kramer, M.R. (2011). Creating shared value. *Harvard Business Review*, 89 (1), 2–17.

Smart Travel Lab & Kantar (2020). *Anticipating the Future of Travel*. www.smarttravellab.org.

UNWTO (2020a). *International Tourism Growth Continues to Outpace the Global Economy*. https://www.unwto.org/international-tourism-growth-continues-tooutpace-the-economy.

UNWTO (2020b). *One Planet Vision for a Responsible Recovery of the Tourism Sector*, June 2020. www.unwto.org.

UNWTO (2020c). *Global Guidelines to Restart Tourism*, 28 May 2020. www.unwto.org.

WTTC (2021). *World Travel and Tourism Council: Travel & tourism economic impact global trends 2021*.

WTTC (2022). *World Travel and Tourism Council: Travel & tourism economic impact global trends 2022*.

United Nations (2015). *Transforming Our World: The 2030 Agenda for Sustainable Development.* https://sdgs.un.org/goals.

2

TOURISM AND SUSTAINABLE
DEVELOPMENT GOALS AT PRESENT

Introduction

Children are the defining factor, whether active participants in tourism communities or passive spectators. Either way, they (knowingly or unknowingly) represent destination stakeholders who succumbed to economic, socio-cultural and environmental tourism effects. Relatively recent research has indicated that the role of children in tourism may be differentiated by the type of tourism activity that takes place within their tourist communities. An example of such differentiation is between children in mass tourism destinations and those in rural tourism destinations (Knežević et al., 2020). It is also essential to consider the role of local tourism communities – bringing the context towards the local rather than the regional or national level.

Local tourism communities are, therefore, a critical factor in our considerations; it is understood that local tourism communities may have the following characteristics (Koščak & O'Rourke, 2023):

- Peripherality – e.g. rural, coastal, islands or areas with poor transportation links.
- Numerical dominance of small and medium enterprises (SMEs).
- Potential for an intimate relationship with the specific local culture, history or environment.
- Challenged by complex environmental and/or socio-economic issues.

The impact and effects of the macro-economic climate 2023–2025

The "rocky road"

Tourism activity is conditioned, to a great extent, by the individual tourist's ability to participate in the activity. This is based on their choices of tourism

DOI: 10.4324/9781003374299-4

activity concerning type and format, duration, destination, travel mode and level of comfort desired. Inevitably, the choice will depend on individuals' purchasing power. When Covid-19 restrictions were lifted in 2022, there was a surge in tourism demand, particularly as spending on non-domestic tourism for the best part of two years had been limited by health restrictions and border closures. However, the post-pandemic environment changed as tourism spending and participation were affected by real growth flatlining, increasing inflation, rising interest rates and declining consumer confidence. In addition, there was:

- Falling business confidence in the key tourism output economies (OECD, 2023a) – declining confidence severely impacts investors' willingness to participate in tourism investment.
- The effect of higher energy pricing on service industries – all of the tourism sector is affected by the cost of energy.
- Restoring profitability for hotels and airlines – vacation costs in many advanced economies have risen as prices are boosted to recover the lost profitability in 2020–2022.

Therefore, the macroeconomic climate is important to tourism, and the broader picture is less than optimistic over the short and medium term. Indeed, Pierre Olivier Gourichas, Economic Counsellor at the International Monetary Fund (IMF), stated that the post-pandemic recovery "was never going to be an easy ride" and spoke of the "rocky road" to recovery (IMF, 2023). Table 2.1 indicates real GDP growth.

This table indicates the year-on-year changes in real GDP for 2019 and then 2022–2024. In general, it can be seen that 2022 was a year of recovery for the major economies except for the USA. Similarly, except for Japan, 2023 is, according to IMF projections, set to be a period of lessening growth; for 2024, whilst the euro area and the UK see reasonable growth, the overall figure for the advanced economies indicates only a marginal level of growth.

Another important set of data regarding tourism is the level of real private consumer expenditure (see Table 2.2).

TABLE 2.1 Real GDP growth (% *y-o-y change*)

Economies	2019	2022	2023 (p)	2024 (p)
Advanced economies	1.7	2.7	1.3	1.4
USA	2.3	2.1	1.6	1.1
Euro area	1.6	3.5	0.8	1.4
Japan	-0.4	1.1	1.3	1.0
UK	1.6	4.0	-0.3	1.0
Canada	1.9	3.4	1.5	1.5

Source: IMF, World Economic Outlook, April 2023

TABLE 2.2 Real private consumer expenditure (% *y-o-y change*)

Economies	2019	2022	2023 (p)	2024 (p)
Advanced economies	1.5	3.6	1.5	1.4
USA	2.0	2.8	1.5	0.9
Euro area	1.4	4.3	1.1	1.6
Japan	-0.6	2.1	1.7	1.0
UK	1.1	5.4	-0.6	0.6
Canada	1.5	4.8	3.3	1.9

Source: IMF, World Economic Outlook, April 2023

Note: Personal spending of households on goods and services.

In many advanced economies, personal spending fell between 2019 and 2023, with the exception of Japan and Canada. For 2024, a further decline is generally visible. Table 2.3 indicates an additional feature regarding consumers' overall confidence in the future. This suggests that consumer confidence has fallen since September 2021, although less in the euro area than in the USA and globally.

Undoubtedly, lowering economic growth indicates less consumer spending capacity on tourism. The assumptions that consumers will switch from cross-border or international travel to domestic destinations do not necessarily play out, as domestic destinations increase accommodation costs to match demand shifts. Consumers will then look for lower-cost destinations to fulfil their demands, implying higher transportation costs, as such destinations will be in third-world locations.

Cost sensitivity and interest rates

It is clear that for sustainable and ethical tourist activity, the cost sensitivity of tourists may be significantly less important than those seeking mass-tourism packages (e.g. cruises or sun–sea–sand locations). Sustainable and ethical tourism

TABLE 2.3 Consumer confidence in September 2023 (*projection*) over September 2021

Economies	September 2021	September 2023 (p)
World	100	93.5
USA	100	95.5
Euro area	100	97.0

Source: Authors' projections (July 2023)

Note: This consumer confidence indicator provides an indication of future developments of households' consumption and saving, based upon answers regarding their expected financial situation, their sentiment about the general economic situation, unemployment and capability of savings.

is based on an experience that satisfies tourists' needs and concerns about sustainability and puts ethical practices in the destination at the forefront. Nonetheless, tourists will be concerned about the level of costs. If prices, which are expected to reach an average of 4.7% year-on-year growth across the advanced economies in 2023 (IMF, 2023), indeed reach such levels, then this will impact consumer spending (i.e. shrinking budget available for travel, food and accommodation). The view of the OECD for the period of October 2022 to the end of May 2023 was that across the advanced global economies, headline inflation continued to fall, standing at 6.5% in May 2023, down 0.9 percentage points against April and 4.2 percentage points down from the high point of 10.7% in October 2022 (OECD, 2023b).

Nonetheless, persistent core inflation (this is inflation that excludes food and energy) continues. It dropped to 6.9% in May 2023 in OECD countries – only 0.9 percentage points from its peak of 7.8% in October 2022. Among the G7 countries, only the US and Canada recorded lower core inflation in May than in October. It remains above 5% in the UK, US and Germany (OECD, 2023b). In the euro area, the June 2023 data indicated that inflation, as measured by HICP (Harmonised Index of Consumer Prices), fell to an annual rate of 5.5% against an 8.6% annual rate in June 2022 and 6.1% in May 2023. However, food stood at 11.7% annually in June, compared to 8.9% in June the previous year; energy, on the other hand, fell by 5.6% in June 2023 year-on-year compared to the rise of 42% annually during the previous June (Eurostat, 2023). Undoubtedly, OECD countries' wage growth is unlikely to match 4.7% (authors' projections), which implies a real negative income growth. Does this impact the ability of local and sustainable destinations to attract a new class of traveller?

Interest rates provide a further uncertain variable. Between June of 2022 and June of 2023 – a perfect post-pandemic period – euro area interest rates rose by 3.9 percentage points, UK interest rates by 3.8 percentage points and USA interest rates by 2.8 percentage points (authors' calculations based on ECB, 2023). The effect on MSEs operating in local tourism destinations was severe, given that commercial lending rates rose more rapidly and began almost to mimic inflationary pressures as credit institutions sought to create lending costs at real levels. Globally, after a relatively lengthy period of relatively low actual lending rates, the cost of lending to higher-risk small enterprises is rising as credit institutions factor in inflationary pressures on interest rate margins between what they pay to savers and what they charge borrowers. Credit risk will likely increase over the short term (i.e. into 2025) in the local tourism sector as credit institutions will also avoid any potential for default by MSEs. This means there will be credit shortages in a sector that already suffers from low access to finance. As many tourism SMEs are family businesses, this will also impact the lives of family members and their lifestyle and entrepreneurial activities.

The costs of sustainability

In such an environment, local tourism is faced with two pressures:

- The need to create and maintain sustainable, ethical and responsible tourism practices in order not only to retain existing customers but also to penetrate new markets.
- The costs of sustainable development.

Thus, marketing and cost pressures conflict in a sector that frequently lacks the resources, capacity and knowledge to manage such conflict. We may suggest that the pressures of attaining sustainable development ambitions have the following features:

a   Economic/enterprise costs have become an overwhelming feature due to the rapid increase in energy and food costs at a global level. Amelioration of such expenses is apparent in the latter part of 2023, but the medium-term sustainability of such decreasing inflationary pressures is questionable due to international security and climate security shocks.
b   Meeting sustainable development targets requires a continuing level of financial commitment. How can local tourism communities have the ability to maintain such obligations in the face of global uncertainty and heightened levels of socio-economic risk?
c   Commitment to sustainable goals also requires resource shifting and resource categorisation. Local tourism businesses are frequently short of human resource inputs, which have increased cost and reduced availability post-pandemic. Financial and strategic management skills have been a severe restraint on tourism SMEs.

The World Tourism Picture

The World Tourism Picture encompasses the following elements, which will be considered in this section:

- The return to normality – what recovery has there been? What has driven the post-pandemic tourism market?
- How successful has the green recovery been?
- Is there resilience in tourism against future shocks?

The return to normality?

The UNWTO reported in May 2023 that, according to their data, international tourism arrivals reached 80% of pre-pandemic levels in the first quarter of 2023 compared to the same quarter in 2019. Some regions had recovered above Q1

2019 levels in Q1 2023, namely Southern Mediterranean Europe (+1%) and North Africa (+4%). In addition, four regions came close to their Q1 2019 levels – Central America (98%), the Caribbean (94%), Western Europe (92%) and Northern Europe (91%) (UNWTO, 2023a).

Data was also released on global international tourism receipts, which in real terms reached the USD 1 tn level in 2022, which is 64% of the 2019 level. International visitor spending in real terms reached 64% of pre-pandemic levels in Q1 2023 compared to the same quarter in 2019. More specifically, Europe pushed receipts to 87% of pre-pandemic levels at USD 550 bn, Africa 75%, the Middle East 70% and the Americas 68%. Source markets also showed a more substantial level of spending, with three countries reaching above pre-pandemic levels – Saudi Arabia (+6%), Germany (+2%) and France matching the 2019 level. The USA, Italy, the Netherlands and Sweden all came close to pre-pandemic spending levels at 92% (UNWTO, 2023a).

What does this mean? The pent-up demand in 2020–2022 was being released from late 2022 into early 2023. In Europe, travel and tourism providers were discounting capacity to attract travellers through 2022 despite the ability to handle problems in airports and frontiers due to post-pandemic staffing shortages. Whether a full recovery occurs globally after 2023 is a matter of speculation. In the advanced economies' key source markets, high inflation and fragile real growth will likely weaken demand and cause a shift to lower-cost tourism solutions. In addition, many travel and tourism operators seek to recover the financial resources lost through the pandemic by significantly raising prices.

The green recovery

A key policy message from OECD (2022) focuses on promoting a green tourism recovery to address past structural weaknesses and avoid unbalanced tourist development. Promoting green recovery is based on four critical areas:

- Developing long-term integrated strategies with a sustainable tourism vision, goals and targets, with action plans and mechanisms to leverage resources and coordinate across government.
- Implementing a mix of evidence-based policies prioritising high-impact interventions along the tourism value chain to raise awareness, regulate and incentivise green practices and investment.
- Promoting carbon literacy and building the capacity of tourism actors to develop innovative solutions, empower sustainable travel choices and help businesses reduce their environmental impact.
- Leveraging the role of government in catalysing the green transition and organising publicly funded or procured tourism infrastructure to contribute to environmental and climate-resilient development.

Revisiting resilience

> We may comment that resilience arises from preservation and renewal and that "future viability and resilience are also leitmotifs in the competition of political ideas on various levels ... in the European house and in the global village. What decisions must be made today to preserve that which has been achieved, and to initiate desired developments and work towards resilience of nature, the economy and society against disruptions?" ... "For the most part, there is no lack of (scientific) knowledge, but rather it is about overcoming implementation deficits and building trust in the fact that the democratic constitutional state will master the fundamental change."
>
> *(Konrad Adenauer Stiftung, 2023)*

The rebuilding and restructuring of tourism should occur within the overarching development of resilience in the tourism system. It is clear from the past that tourism is not only "vulnerable to exogenous shocks" but that the pandemic also heightened "endogenous weaknesses" (OECD, 2022). Time and time again, we saw mass tourism effectively crippled by terrorism (e.g. Lockerbie, 9/11, the North African terror attacks), climate (e.g. the Eyjafjallajökull ash cloud) or a disease (e.g. SARS). The Covid-19 pandemic was the defining event that saw mass tourism coming to a grinding halt and what appeared to be a shift in how tourism operates and affects communities. We believed the "new normal" would be different; the period from mid-2022 as final restrictions were lifted showed that the "old normal" has re-appeared. Even the vast threat inspired by climate change – desertification of many tourism areas by 2050, water scarcity and the potential for mass migrations – seemed to have slipped from the agenda (Koščak & O'Rourke, 2023).

Other issues for tourism destinations are connected to product or market-oriented identities. These may include heavy reliance on a specific:

a   Tourism season (e.g. April–October) due to a relationship with climatic conditions.
b   Market (e.g. country or visitor segment).
c   Product (e.g. "sun–sea–sand").

Sustainable Development Goals

The 17 UN Sustainable Development Goals (SDGs) are:

1. No poverty
2. Zero hunger
3. Good health and well-being
4. Quality education
5. Gender equality
6. Clean water and sanitation

7. Affordable and clean energy
8. Decent work and economic growth
9. Industry, innovation and infrastructure
10. Reduced inequality
11. Sustainable cities and communities
12. Responsible consumption and production
13. Climate action
14. Life below water
15. Life on land
16. Peace and justice strong institutions
17. Partnerships to achieve the goal

The problems in attaining these goals are, however, significantly tricky and to a degree, the effects of the pandemic have compounded those difficulties. A report to the UN Economic and Social Council (2023) indicated that many SDG targets were off track at the midway point towards 2030. Of the 140 targets, 12% were on the way to be achieved, almost half were off track, and 30% had shown no progress since 2015. Whilst this level of progress was global, the most significant problem was the difficulties for the developing countries in achieving target compliance due to the pandemic's effects and the general economic situation since 2019.

The goals and tourism

The UN viewpoint on the application of Tourism SDGs in tourism is that sustainable tourism development guidelines and management practices apply to all forms of tourism in all destinations, including mass tourism and the various niche tourism segments. Sustainability principles refer to the environmental, economic and socio-cultural aspects of tourism development, and a suitable balance must be established between these three dimensions to guarantee its long-term sustainability. Thus, sustainable tourism should (UNWTO, 2023):

1. Make optimal use of environmental resources that constitute a key element in tourism development, maintaining essential ecological processes and helping to conserve natural heritage and biodiversity.
2. Respect the socio-cultural authenticity of host communities, conserve their built and living cultural heritage and traditional values, and contribute to intercultural understanding and tolerance.
3. Ensure viable, long-term economic operations, providing socio-economic benefits to all fairly distributed stakeholders, including stable employment and income-earning opportunities and social services to host communities and contributing to poverty alleviation.

Sustainable tourism development requires the informed participation of all relevant stakeholders and strong political leadership to ensure broad participation and consensus building (Šegota et al., 2017). Achieving sustainable tourism is a continuous process, and it requires constant monitoring of impacts introducing the necessary preventive and/or corrective measures whenever necessary. Sustainable tourism should also maintain high tourist satisfaction and ensure a meaningful experience, raising awareness about sustainability issues and promoting sustainable tourism practices.

The critical goals for sustainable tourism

We may imply that of the 17 goals, eight are directly linked to sustainable tourism. These are:

6. Decent water and sanitation
7. Affordable and clean energy
8. Decent work and economic growth
11. Sustainable cities and communities
.12. Responsible consumption and production
13. Climate action
14 & 15. Life on land and water

The importance of these goals concerning tourism may be evaluated as follows:

Goal 6: Ensure availability and sustainable management of water and sanitation for all

Tourism is an industry with significant water and sanitation use. Climate change is creating a massive crisis for water supply in tourist regions where rainfall is in progressive decline and where tourists compete against local communities over water use. Sanitation is an equally difficult challenge, as tourism numbers put pressure on inadequate disposal systems and climate change in the form of flooding often leads to the outflow of raw human waste into oceans and rivers and onto beaches.

Goal 7: Ensure access to affordable, reliable, sustainable and modern energy for all

Tourism energy use impacts local communities and is made more critical mainly by mass tourism. Tourism competes for a share of a scarce resource in developing economies, and economic pressures will likely result in prioritising tourism. In advanced economies, tourism represents just one of the many other players seeking access to resources, but its access is equally affected by unexpected disruptions (i.e., crises).

Goal 8: Promote inclusive and sustainable economic growth, full and productive employment and decent work

The stall of economic growth in the advanced economies is likely to impact sectors such as tourism, where employment is more precarious and sensitive to external forces. In particular, as tourism consumption may decrease due to higher interest rates imposed by the central banks and consumers' concern about a decline in actual earnings, the propensity to achieve sustainable economic growth and full employment becomes more problematic.

Goal 11: Make cities and human settlements inclusive, safe, resilient and sustainable

Tourism and environmental planning deserve to be closely inter-connected, but in such a way as to protect the environment and heritage of tourism communities. Planning has frequently been overridden by the pressures of capital and large-scale tourism economies, resulting in an exponential growth of excess tourism in heritage cities, of which Barcelona, Dubrovnik and Venice are key examples. Rural destinations have not escaped – Cinque Terre in Italy and Skye in Scotland are examples of excess tourism in fragile rural destinations.

Goal 12: Ensure sustainable consumption and production patterns

The high level of economic growth in the tourism sector before 2020 had a profound effect on reducing consumptive sustainability. The high levels of food waste created by tourism alone, even when households and children are without adequate levels of food in the advanced economies, go against this SDG.

Goal 13: Take urgent action to combat climate change and its impacts

As the Glasgow Climate Conference indicated, meeting the Paris Climate commitments continues to be a slow process with a lack of uniformity. There are now only six years until 2030 to achieve the reduction of emissions by half. Tourism is a significant driver of emissions – cruise ships, aircraft and road transport use levels are likely to return to pre-pandemic levels in the EU by 2024.

Goals 14–15: Conserve and sustainably use the oceans, seas and marine resources for sustainable development, and protect, restore and promote sustainable use of terrestrial ecosystems, sustainably manage forests, combat desertification, and halt and reverse land degradation and biodiversity loss

Changes in the climate and increased rates of human activity have a substantial impact on the land and marine environments. Economic pressures will frequently seek to change land or marine use from traditional functions with an integrated level of sustainable tourism (e.g. agro-tourism or marine tourism) towards large-scale tourism (e.g. building seaside resorts, aqua-parks and marinas or rural holiday complexes). Apart from the effect on the cultural heritage, such actions may also damage or destroy the land or marine environment (e.g. footpath erosion or plastics in the sea bed).

Degradation in tourism communities and the effect on children

There are many examples of this form of degradation created by tourism activity, which affects communities and has a specific and potentially harmful impact on children in those communities. Prime examples are:

- The intrusion of large numbers of foreign visitors with high consumption and waste habits into natural areas or towns with inadequate waste management infrastructure can change those areas more significantly than residents.
- Such tourism-related changes are particularly deleterious when residents rely on those natural areas for sustenance.
- Additionally, such economic losses can encourage socially harmful economic activities such as prostitution, crime, the use of illegal migrants and the intrusion of both child labour and the trafficking of children for exploitative purposes.

Negative aspects of tourist activity

We can define four aspects of the adverse effects of tourism, particularly felt by local communities, where the balance between positive and negative is fragile. These aspects are samples of the types of problems encountered in the Scottish rural tourism sector.

(i) Impact on employment

Many jobs are seasonal, while there may be problems in getting other work out of season. This also makes access to living accommodation complicated (see 2nd homes below). There are problems with the continuity of the contract and lack of security (e.g. pension contributions). In addition, particularly in local community-based tourism, access to training and development may be difficult.

(ii) Cultural destruction

Unmanaged and high tourism footprints in rural, coastal and island communities have a destructive effect on the cultural heritage. Traditional rural skills (e.g. weaving and spinning wool) will be overwhelmed by the need to meet the demands of tourist groups. There are examples of linguistic damage affecting children and youths in Gaelic-speaking areas (the *Gaeltacht*) where the distinctive cultural heritage and history are swamped by Anglo-centric language and culture, which is at odds with local communities.

(iii) Economic impact of 2nd homes

Between 2010 and 2022, low-interest rates attracted the purchase of second homes in rural destinations from those who had resources to outbid people in local communities. These homes were then only inhabited occasionally or used for Airbnb-type accommodation. In both cases, economic input into communities was negligible. Therefore, housing for young people from the local community (e.g. to remain in the local tourism workforce) was lost. They could not afford the property purchase cost, and rented housing was unavailable. As a result, they were left with the decision to move to an urban centre or travel daily. This has a powerful effect on retaining their native language and cultural identity. Their children will be unable to have this rich cultural and linguistic heritage.

(iv) Environmental destruction and desecration

In mountain areas and national parks, footpaths have been seriously eroded by excessive visitor numbers. Huge waste disposal issues have arisen through large visitor groups (e.g. coach parties) arriving in fragile areas. Resources and planning requirements often limit parking and toilet facilities in rural areas, yet frequent visitor numbers far outpace capacity. Littering and human waste have become a major issue.

The critical factor is the degrading impact on people, communities, their environment, their culture and their economic future. A decisive element in the overall environmental picture is waste – which implies excessive use of water, the impact of waste on water resources, health hazards from human waste, tourist-driven littering and the costs of removing/converting waste products. Therefore, looking at the waste issue is essential, mainly because of the effect on children.

Waste

According to the UN Environmental Programme (UNEP), despite tourism contributions to global GDP, global exports and employment, such benefits are not without their impacts. The research has indicated "that the tourism sector's consumption of key resources – energy, water, land and materials ... is growing commensurately with its generation of solid waste, sewage, loss of biodiversity, and greenhouse gas emissions" (UNEP, 2023). In the current operational mode, we may estimate that by 2050, tourism will account for increases of 160% in energy consumption, 120% in greenhouse gas emissions, 162% in water consumption and 276% in solid waste disposal (authors' estimates). Indeed, this is probably one of the most compelling arguments for sustainable and responsible tourism – to mitigate the excessive demands of tourism activity on communities, especially for children whose futures are being fruitlessly impacted and undermined.

It is now helpful to look at an example of the type of degradation that tourism may impose on communities, in this case in a country in which tourists outnumber the population by 4.85 times (Koščak & O'Rourke, 2023):

BOX 2.1 CASE STUDY: MALTA

The island of Malta, with a size of 316 km^2 and a population of 475,000, has a density of 1,503 people per 1 km^2. Most residents live in the capital, Valletta, and its suburbs. Adding 2.3 million tourists (excluding cruise ship visitors) imposes a heavy environmental strain on the national infrastructure and emissions from road traffic, shipping and over 4,000 aircraft movements in an average month alone. Malta has the highest population density in the EU.

The appearance of 2.3 million tourists yearly also imposes problems on the transport network. The most recent data indicates that Malta has the sixth highest level of motorisation in the EU (600 cars per inhabitant) (Malta National Statistics Office, 2023). As with many islands lacking fixed road or rail connections or well-developed ferry services, 98% of all tourist arrivals are by air. The environmental considerations of tourism growth have been in Malta for some time, as the structure of tourism has generally inhibited the development of ethical and responsible tourism. Tourism is based on the mass market model, directly or via travel agents, selling flights and accommodation in bulk.

Furthermore, the average tourist in a Maltese hotel produces 1.25 kg of waste daily, compared to one person in a Maltese household producing 0.68 kg. Roughly, the tourism industry is creating 1,300 tonnes of excess waste. In addition, Malta has problems with water provision. It is currently estimated that by 2025, 70% of the water will be produced from four desalination plants and the remainder from groundwater and bottled water. Tourism obviously is a high water user in hotels, for example – in swimming pools, toilets/showers and catering. Climate change will aggravate Maltese water scarcity as temperatures increase and rainfall declines, to the potential extent that by 2050, Malta will suffer desertification.

Regarding tourism degradation, Malta is now at a unique tipping point, with mass tourism affecting elements of Maltese life and culture. It is, therefore, somewhat difficult to see a clear path ahead; but there is a definable community of interest in creating higher levels of ethical and responsible tourism in Malta. At the same time, large-scale commercial interests wish to retain the mass tourism, low-cost model based on inbound air passengers and mid-range hotels in large tourism complexes.

Malta is thus a tourism paradox, and there is a growing demand for ethical and responsible tourism based on a rich cultural heritage with solid roots in the villages and small localities of the island. But against this is inexorable pressure from large corporations with engagement in the mass tourism sector to move ahead with significant tourism developments and marina projects in highly sensitive local communities. This division is reflected in the size of enterprises in each of those two contrasting sectors – on the one hand, large internationally connected corporations and, on the other hand, micro and small enterprises. The issue is that the former have significant economic and political resources, while the latter do not.

How do we combat the situation of many tourism destinations linked to the toxic effects of waste, of which Malta is a prime example? How do we halt children and youth in tourism communities facing the waste tourists impose on them? This second example may be of relevance (Koščak & O'Rourke, 2023).

BOX 2.2 CASE STUDY: THE LEAVE NO TRACE MOVEMENT IN IRELAND

Leave No Trace is an outdoor ethics programme which was established internationally (Fág Gan Lorg Éire, 2023). In 2004, the Irish government was concerned about the lack of operational rules for access to the countryside to help prevent conflict between local populations and tourists. It established a semi-state organisation (*Comhairle na Tuaithe*) to progress these rules, given the continuing expansion of domestic and international tourist activity with its consequent impact on the environment and rural communities. It was decided to use the internationally recognised Leave No Trace initiative from September 2008 in Ireland's uplands and lowlands, urban parks, lakes and rivers, and local neighbourhoods.

The Leave No Trace initiative has devised a series of guidelines for outdoor recreation to ensure visitors have a minimal environmental impact by promoting and inspiring responsible outdoor recreation through education, research and partnerships. Its seven principles, which are applied educationally as well as in communities, are:

1. Plan ahead and prepare.
2. Be considerate of others.
3. Respect farm animals and wildlife.
4. Travel and camp on durable ground.
5. Leave what you find.
6. Dispose of waste properly.
7. Minimise the effects of fire.

The Leave No Trace initiative in Ireland is a not-for-profit company comprising partner organisations with a shared interest in encouraging responsible enjoyment of Ireland's natural environment. The programme strives to inspire those who enjoy outdoor recreation to take personal responsibility and reduce their environmental impact by conveying simple skills and techniques. Its focus on children through the national school system is an important component of its work. Their target is to reach 60% of schools in the state at primary and secondary levels through the programme "Sharing Outdoor Environmental Ethics". A similar programme is also aimed at youth groups and organisations. The objective is to influence and advocate for the next generation of environmental stewards – today's children and youth. At the same time, they continue to work with local communities and voluntary groups to deliver core training programmes through training courses and online methods. This includes the development of the trainer's network and designing programmes in continued professional development projects.

Community tourism development

There are many examples of community-driven tourism. The example we present next reflects on a tiny community in population terms and a geographic locality that is very small in global terms but has significant resonance regarding community success in managing tourism. By community, we mean a considerable number of children and young people. Finding the correct balance between environmental sustainability, cultural and natural heritage protection and ensuring economic development for the benefit of inhabitants is a highly delicate task (Koščak & O'Rourke, 2023; Inishbofin Development Corporation, 2023).

BOX 2.3 CASE STUDY: COMMUNITY AND TOURISM ON A MEGA-PERIPHERAL ISLAND

Inishbofin (*Inis Bó Finne* – "the Island of the White Cow") is one of the 24 inhabited Irish offshore islands located 10 km from the west coast of Galway. Our denotation of a tiny island is reflected in it being 5.7 km by 4 km. The main activities are tourism and farming, with fishing declining over recent years, represented by only two full-time fishing vessels.

Inishbofin has three official looped walks of varying difficulties, each offering spectacular views of the island's wild Atlantic scenery. It has EU Blue Flag status, with sandy beaches perfect for swimming, snorkelling and diving. Two beaches on Inishbofin have been awarded a "Green Coast Award" to denote their exceptional water quality and natural, unspoilt environment. Inishbofin is also a special conservation area, a breeding area for many species of rare and threatened species of bird.

The population stood at 1,404 in 1841 (before the Great Famine of 1845–1847), falling to 909 in 1851. A century later, the 1951 census revealed a population of 291. By 2011, it had dropped to 160 but grew to 175 by 2016, with the current number of permanent residents estimated at 220. During summer, the population tends to expand to around 450. There is a passenger ferry connection from the mainland port of Cleggan; however, there is no passenger car ferry access, which limits the capacity of traffic to the island.

Tourism background

The island's history of tourism dates back to 1969 with the opening of two hotels. In 2023, the island hosts three hotels, six bed and breakfasts, a hostel, a campsite, 25 self-catering holiday homes, and an estimated 40 privately owned holiday cottages. Inishbofin tends to operate from Easter until the end of October, with most visitations from fellow Irishmen. Most visitors tend to be the great-grandchildren of original summer visitors from five decades ago, e.g. third and fourth generations of visitors, and they mostly tend to stay in private accommodation. On the other hand, visitors from the UK and France prefer staying in hotels, which also house around 80% of domestic visitors. The island is also famous among daily visitors, mainly from Ireland, followed by France, Germany, Italy, Spain and the United States.

It appears that word-of-mouth and personal referrals are significant in generating tourist flows. The island has not had to resort to expensive marketing campaigns, although it participates in national tourism marketing activities through Fáilte Ireland (http://www.failteireland.ie). Clearly, tourist influx is limited by the capacity of the ferry service (90) and the total capacity of the island's accommodation facilities. This ensures that carrying capacity will not reach levels at which damage could be made to a relatively fragile ecological environment.

Tourism organisational structure

In 1989, the existing island's Community Council and the crowd-funding group formed to build a Community Centre merged to create the Inishbofin Development Association, a voluntary organisation tasked with assisting in a wide range of tourist, ecological and community development plans. In 1993, this was replaced by a not-for-profit entity, the Inishbofin Development Company, which has the mission of improving 1) the quality of life for the island through the establishment, development and provision of support and services and 2) the island's socio-economic, economic, infrastructure, environmental, cultural, heritage and administrative requirements.

It is clear that on Inishbofin, the community seeks to take a different approach to tourism, aiming to develop its tourism sustainably so that it does not negatively impact the island's natural environment while benefiting and supporting the local community. This precarious balance between ethical and environmental engagement over the longer term and shorter-term socio-economic needs of inhabitants reflects the central dilemma numerous rural and peripheral communities face.

External events and its peripherality have driven the island to maintain its existence. The abandonment of a nearby island (Inishark) in the 1960s shocked the inhabitants of Inishbofin and created an urgent need to ensure that the island remained populated and viable. Notably, the island did not await the provision of government or EU grants before seeking to improve and structure its tourism and related offers. Instead, it relied on a process of self-resourcing, and then when it had achieved viable products, it began to seek grants and financial support. This is an exciting learning point, as it indicates that tourism-driven communities can be self-sufficient, independent of grant/loan support, and only apply for such aid once they have developed a tangible project. The focus on tourism activity from Easter to October has traditionally been part of the socio-economic model for the island population. It has then enabled a focus on other economic activities from November to March (e.g. farming, fishing, marketing and development). However, it has become clear that there was surplus capacity in the "shoulder" periods (mid-April to end-May and end-August to end-October). Whilst the Irish school holidays occupy eight weeks from the beginning of July to the end of August, there are periods outside that peak season which are being exploited. The shoulder seasons have now become a primary area for the development of outdoor cultural and natural heritage activities that are not weather-dependent by nature.

Ecotourism developments

Inishbofin was the first Irish offshore island to have international EcoTourism status; it is tourism car-free. It achieved Gold Certification from EcoTourism Ireland for its *Cultúr na nOileáin* tours, with the Community Centre offering walking ecotourism experiences. This has led to EcoTourism being viewed as a significant force in the "greening" of the island – with EcoTourism Ireland certifications covering more than 23 tourist activities. This includes such diverse activities as historical tours and studies, equestrian activities, stand-up paddle-boarding, self-guided walking, horse riding, nature photography, birdwatching and sailing. In addition, the community is also engaged in a number of festivals – food, Fair Trade, walking, arts, yoga, sailing, dancing and a half-marathon. Importantly, the Inishbofin Development Company has operated to a reasonably tight schedule in developing these actions. Utilising grant aid from the state's environmental protection agency, it gained certification for the main ecotourism activities.

The positive power of community engagement

Despite the issues of location (e.g. peripherality, lack of developed infrastructure and dependence on a single transport link), this community appears to have built cohesion in its efforts to attract sustainable and environmentally friendly tourism activity. This task has been done through self-reliance and self-support, using the island community's cohesion and the islanders' skills. The Community Centre is the island's activity hub, providing tourism information, developing and delivering cultural/heritage activities, and providing community support (e.g., nursery/childcare). There are two critical success factors for the island:

- The first is the engagement of the permanent community, who see build-ing a sustainable tourism product and extending the tourism season as helping to ensure the long-term survival of the island. Connected to that has been embracing environmental and ecosystem controls to ensure that the flow of visitors does not damage a fragile environment. Carrying capa-city is effectively restricted to the size of the passenger vessel, which effec-tively, even in high season, can only transport around 200 passengers per day in each direction – some will stay, and others will visit only for a day.
- The second is community cohesion, which has been bottom-up driven to reflect the boundaries in a peripheral island environment. The driving force of self-reliance and self-support has underpinned this.

Community development structures

This example enables us to understand how community development struc-tures evolve and how they meet the challenges of the environment in which they operate. It focuses on the potential for community cohesion and self-generated funding rather than over-reliance on public financing – whether regional, national or international.

The role of the development company, a community-generated social enter-prise, is crucial. Its tasks were to oversee tourism businesses seeking to improve the residents' quality of life and visits for tourists. Hence, establishing, developing and providing support and services through the Inishbofin Development Cor-poration has been crucial in enhancing the island's social economy, infra-structure, environment, culture, heritage and administration. At the heart of sustainable tourism development were environmentally appropriate policies that harness the island's natural environment while benefiting and supporting the local community. This has resulted in the wide range of tourism providers in Inishbofin seeking methods of achieving this goal and, equally importantly, con-veying the message of sustainable tourism to all visitors. The EcoTourism Ireland and LNT Ireland awards for sustainable tourism development evidence this.

Undoubtedly, Inishbofin is a tiny tourist destination. However, it presents a microcosm of the situation affecting Europe's many offshore island tourism facilities; to a substantial degree, restricting tourism access minimises the potential of excessive and potentially damaging tourism flows and severely limits the environmental effects of car use.

Communities benefit from bottom-up-driven tourism development in that it better represents a wider range of local actors – individuals, families, local enterprises and children. Children are closer to the tourist through family tourism businesses; in the Inishbofin example, local children help parents with guests whilst older youths act as hotel workers, guides or other support roles during the peak summer tourism period. Thus, they have a very close commit-ment towards and a sense of engagement with their local tourism community.

Such closeness is not always possible in large resorts where employment hierarchies are established, and there is a distance between participants and customers.

Moving towards all-year-round tourism also benefits the community; as rural/island activities such as fishing diminish, maintaining a flow of non-weather-dependent guests helps businesses and the community. What is important about the Inishbofin tourist development model is that the primary driving factor has been a community that has built cohesion to attract sustainable and environmentally friendly tourist activity. This task has been done through self-reliance and self-support, using the island community's integrated aspect and the islanders' skills. In this case, tourism as a socio-economic activity is an organic part of the community.

Where do children fit in?

Children are frequently viewed as a neglected topic in tourism. Dallari and Mariotti (2013) expressed the view that "tourism for children and adolescents is a neglected topic in tourism research, despite the importance of a child's life trajectory up to the age of 17/18 in terms of the psychological and social impact it has on their formation of subjectivity". Their case study focused on the Romagnola coastal destination of Emilia-Romagna, which had some 20% of tourist visitors up to 17 years of age.

Nonetheless, the presence of children in local tourism communities may be viewed as a multi-faceted engagement and distinctively apart from their role as tourists – individually or within a family. Multi-stakeholder structures undeniably require the input of all community actors in tourism destinations, including children. Knežević et al. (2020) expressed that "children are not only 'residents' in tourist areas, towns and villages, but also participants in events in these areas and careful observers of the events around them." Moreover, they stated that, despite the enormity of tourism research, "no one ... has ever asked children and young adults their views about tourism and the impact tourism may have on their lives and their future" (Knežević et al., 2020).

We may, for example, see them in the following perspectives:

1. They may have a role as economic actors in tourism communities as consumers.
2. Equally, they also may be economic actors in tourism SMEs; in agro-tourism, for example, children will frequently have an active role in the business.
3. They may have a valuable role in community culture and heritage as participants in actively maintaining the heritage. This may include using a specific local dialect, dress forms and involvement in cultural performances.

This indicates that children are participants in local tourism labour markets and may have an important role in those markets (see Chapter 8); unfortunately there is a lack of realistic evidence about that role as many of those under 16 do not appear in statistical data. But we can predicate that in many European tourism economies, children under 16 have a frequent role in underpaid and demanding tasks in the tourism industry. This may include working as kitchen porters and bar staff in cleaning service facilities and hotel rooms. Such roles mean they are frequently employed at pay levels below national fair-pay structures and generally do not receive social benefits (e.g. unemployment, sick pay and pensions).

This sector also excludes those who work in family tourism businesses; in general, we may presume that there is a degree of engagement in the family business and the potential prospect of inheritance. The reality is that those children who work in family tourism businesses may not ultimately continue to engage in those family functions and may move geographically to larger communities or cities for higher education. The engagement of children and how they fit into the local tourism community as players in the longer term will be contingent on pressures for older children to migrate to cities or other countries for work purposes and then not return. Ideally, whilst accepting that children will often be required to leave for education, work or training, their return at some stage (as entrepreneurs or specialists in specific fields) will bring strong and consistent future benefits. What is clear is that we have no concrete and reliable data on the role of children who are active in family tourism businesses.

Taking the long-term strategic approach to SDGs

As progress in attaining the 2030 SDGs shows, governments generally have not made as rapid a level of improvement as was agreed in 2015. The COP26 Glasgow summit also indicated the varying approaches to the crisis and underlined the predilection of many governments to (a) take a short-term strategic approach and (b) fail to begin building resilience to climate change. The former reflects the nature of politics, where strategies relate to electoral cycles rather than facing the reality of long-term planning; the latter indicates an almost wilful disregard for current conditions. A May 2023 OECD report on "Net Zero+: Climate and Economic Resilience in a Changing World" stated that:

> Net Zero+ is … about not only making sure climate policies are as ambitious as they need to be but also resilient in a world of overlapping disruptions. This means building resilience to the impacts of climate change itself, as well as designing policies that fully take into account socio-economic implications and considerations of fairness and equity.
>
> *(OECD, 2023c).*

We live in a world that has had overlapping disruptions during and since the pandemic. Yet events in July 2023, e.g. 48°C temperatures in Southern Europe and forest fires in Canada, displayed that the effects of climate change are becoming closer and that our state of resilience in the advanced economies is significantly less than might be expected. Indeed, the OECD (2023d) is seeking:

a   A more systemic approach to climate policy-making for building economic resilience whilst maintaining resilience to climate impacts.

b   The accelerated net-zero transition must be resilient for the long term – this requires an increase in the scale and speed of policy action with a focus on resilience.

c   Businesses such as tourism have an essential role in turning climate policy commitments into resilient action across the real economy, and avoiding greenwashing.

d   Building systemic resilience to climate impacts – creating synergies in reducing emissions is vital in minimising climate risks and adapting to climate impacts.

The climate crisis, the SDGs and children

We have already discussed the nature of the UN SDGs. Let us now discuss how these SDGs affect children and young people:

- Goal 6: Exposing water and waste resources to tourism can create stress for children and young people in tourism-dependent local communities. Where tourism is highly seasonal, visitation often peaks in the hottest months when the water supply may be challenging.

- Goal 7: Energy is a similar resource for which residents and tourists compete. For example, children and young people may be impacted when schools have to minimise air-conditioning or heating due to energy savings, whilst tourism facilities must ensure high operations. Children and young people's learning may suffer due to excessively high or low temperatures.

- Goal 8: A tourism slowdown impacts family incomes and employment. This indirectly affects children with family members working in tourism, directly affecting young adults holding part-time tourism jobs. In any slowdown or slump, jobs done by young people are the first to go. This also removes the potential for training and expertise acquisition by these young entrants into the tourism industry.

- Goal 11: Lack of cohesion and synergy between tourism and planning may create problems that affect local populations and children. For example, new mass tourism developments could create environmental damage or remove child or youth facilities in favour of tourism. Poor planning allowing property owners to switch from long-term housing for locals to short-term accommodation for tourists (e.g. Airbnb) will affect the future socio-economic prospects for children needing affordable housing in their community.

- Goal 13: Emissions generated by transport (public or private) continue to be hazardous. Removing fossil fuels from transport, domestic heating and power generation does not appear to be moving at the pace envisaged in the 2015 Paris Accords. The pollution thus created has proven long-term effects on children and young people.

- Goals 14 and 15: The pressures of tourism expansion, especially in fragile rural communities, create issues for children and young people. Large tourism numbers can damage both the tangible physical environment and the intangible cultural environment.

Achieving the SDGs has the potential to benefit children and young people in tourism communities; nonetheless, we can observe that the climate change crisis poses one of the most urgent and complex challenges to children and young people in those communities. Today's 13-year-old "new teenagers" will be 20 in 2030, when the SDGs should be met, and will be 40 in 2050, when 100% of the 2015 Paris Accords should be operative. We are therefore looking at the role of children who will effectively spend their early and developing adult stages in the shadow of a climate crisis. For these children, the shadow of non-compliance with the SDGs looms over them. A potential scenario for Europe is that an over-heating planet would create an arid semi-desert in Mediterranean Europe in which tourism activity would only be possible in the winter months. Furthermore, countries would be impacted by severe droughts and lack of water for the population, let alone millions of tourists. In Northern Europe, severe storms, flooding, and above-average temperatures would lead to water shortages in summer. These and similar doomsday scenarios loom over tourism; and not only tourism but our collective future.

References

Dallari F., & Mariotti, A. (2013). *Le pratiche turistiche dell'infanzia: una prospettiva rinnovata?* https://doi.org/10.4000/viatourism.1398.

ECB (2023). *Key Interest Rates*, 6 July. https://www.ecb.europa.eu/stats/policy_and_exchange_rates/key_ecb_interest_rates/html/index.en.html.

Eurostat (2023). *Flash Estimate HICP Inflation in the Euro Area.* https://ec.europa.eu/eurostat/documents/2995521/17075124/2-30062023-AP-EN.pdf/230735d1-74e6-4d30-2039-c9ed1e660296.

Fág Gan Lorg Éire (2023). *Leave No Trace Ireland*, July. www.leavenotraceireland.org.

G20/UNWTO (2023). *G20 Goa Roadmap for Tourism as a Vehicle for Achieving the Sustainable Development Goals.* UNWTO for OECD G20.

IMF (2023). *World Economic Outlook – A rocky recovery*, April 2023.

Inishbofin Development Corporation (2023). *Report*, July. http://www.inishbofin.com.

Knežević, M., Koščak, M., O'Rourke, T. & Šegota, T. (2020). Chapter 9. In Koščak, M., & O'Rourke, T. *Ethical and Responsible Tourism – Managing sustainability in local tourism*, 1st edition. Routledge.

Konrad Adenauer Stiftung (2023). *Resources & Environment*, July. https://www.kas.de/en/resources-and-environment.

Koščak, M., & O'Rourke, T. (Eds) (2020). *Ethical and Responsible Tourism – Managing sustainability in local tourism*, 1st edition. Routledge.

Koščak, M., & O'Rourke, T. (2021). *Post-Pandemic Sustainable Tourism Management – The new reality of managing ethical and responsible tourism.* Routledge.

Koščak, M., & O'Rourke, T. (2023). *Ethical and Responsible Tourism – Managing sustainability in local tourism*, 2nd edition. Routledge.

Malta National Statistics Office (2023). *Data on Motor Vehicle Ownership*, June. https://nso.gov.mt/motor-vehicles-q1-2023.

OECD (2022). *The Green Recovery*. https://www.oecd.org/coronavirus/policy-responses/assessing-environmental-impact-of-measures-in-the-oecd-green-recovery-database-3f7e2670/.

OECD (2023a). *Business Confidence Indicators*, 6 July. https://data.oecd.org/leadind/business-confidence-index-bci.htm.

OECD (2023b). *Inflation (CPI) Indicators*, 6 July. https://www.oecd.org/sdd/prices-ppp/consumer-prices-oecd-updated-4-july-2023.htm.

OECD (2023c). *Net Zero+: Climate and economic resilience in a changing world*, Executive Summary, May. https://www.oecd-ilibrary.org/search?value1=Net+Zero+:+Climate+and+Economic+Resilience+in+a+Changing+World.&option1=quicksearch&facetOptions=51&facetNames=pub_igoId_facet&operator51=AND&option51=pub_igoId_facet&value51='igo/oecd'&publisherId=/content/igo/oecd&searchType=quick.

Šegota, T., Mihalič, T. & Kuščer, K. (2017). The impact of residents' informedness and involvement on their perceptions of tourism impacts: The case of Bled. *Journal of Destination Marketing & Management*, 6 (3), 196–206.

UN Economic and Social Council (2023). *Report A/78/50 to UN General Assembly*. UN.

UNEP (2023). *Situation Report*, July. https://www.unep.org/publications-data.

UNEP/UNWTO (2005). *Making Tourism More Sustainable – A guide for policy makers*. https://wedocs.unep.org/handle/20.500.11822/8741;jsessionid=935E49BF041D706A85DC065215
1CF2E2.

UNWTO (2023a). *World Tourism Barometer* (Vol 21, Issue 2). UN.

UNWTO (2023b). *Tourism on Track for Full Recovery*, 9 May. https://www.unwto.org/news/tourism-on-track-for-full-recovery-as-new-data-shows-strong-start-to-2023.

3
REFLECTIONS ON PART I

The Key Concepts

This chapter discusses and examines the Key Concepts from each of the preceding chapters in Part I.

Chapter 1

The Key Concepts may be categorised as follows:

- *Understanding that pre-Covid global tourism developed at a rate above the actual growth of the global economy.* For decades, travel and tourism have been drivers of growth, job creation and prosperity at a global level, enabling economic development, job creation and poverty reduction. This has driven prosperity and made a significant and positive social impact, providing unique opportunities to women, minorities and young people. The benefits of travel and tourism have spread far beyond the direct effect on GDP and employment, with indirect gains extending through the entire travel ecosystem and the supply chain linkages into other sectors.
- *During the pandemic between 2020 and 2022, there was strong growth in an alternative tourism model.* Domestic and "safe" tourism was supported by state intervention through vouchers and other promotional schemes. Tourism destinations that provided individual safety by enabling social distancing and delivered outdoor activities in a quality natural environment tended to be more successful survivors of the global health crisis. The latter brought us to the point of thoroughly rethinking the concept of sustainability.

DOI: 10.4324/9781003374299-5

- *The post-pandemic new challenges were either finding the "new normal" or slipping back to the "old normal".* It is clear that, to some extent, we have slipped back towards the "old normal" in terms of the return of mass tourism. There are new challenges for sustainable tourism, not only those that surfaced with the Covid-19 pandemic but also to the current energy and cost of living crises driven by inflation, as well as problems with lack of resources in many tourism destinations (e.g. financial, labour, managerial and structural). Therefore, tourism planning and management should provide a strategy for sustainable tourism development.

- *Rethinking sustainability.* Before the pandemic, much of the shift towards sustainability was "greenwashing", e.g. promoting green credentials with little substance. Rethinking sustainability means giving realistic attention to incorporating solid sustainable factors into the tourism model. Conflicting interests must be examined and resolved with mutually acceptable and participative planning solutions. This ensures the compatibility of differing strategies and the long-term satisfaction of all stakeholders in tourism destinations.

- *New development paradigms.* Residents in tourism destinations are the most crucial tourism stakeholders, given that they provide local resources to visitors in exchange for economic benefits and an improved quality of life. Measures should be taken to rationalise, regulate and legislate economic, socio-cultural and environmental impacts. Therefore, appropriate tourist activity types and levels should be determined according to the goals and objectives established through a coherent and well-orchestrated planning process that examines all vulnerabilities and involves all stakeholders.

- *Acknowledging the fragility of tourism.* The pandemic was a massive shock in exposing how tourism relied on a stable socio-economic and physical environment. The post-pandemic discourse of sustainability has shifted towards understanding experiential approaches in product design, security, general and personal hygiene, social distance and "green" – away from the mass visit and towards the preserved environment, conditions for guests' well-being, and market proximity. These factors may be considered for sustaining tourism in the longer term. Essentially, this entails the transformation of development strategies and the search for new development paradigms, which can no longer bypass the principles of sustainable and responsible tourism nor be allowed to move away from them.

- *Uncertainty.* Lack of clarity in the global future, whether short-, medium- or long-term, inspires uncertainty. This affects investment, business and consumer confidence. These factors affect investment and growth. The lessons learned from previous crises and the early stages of Covid-19 point to destinations needing to be well-prepared to take swift action. This requires planning, engagement with key bodies, strong alignment between the public and private sectors and excellent communication. Specific measures are needed to address the immediate needs of visitors, businesses and local communities, contain the impact and take initial steps to stimulate recovery. Actions taken during the crisis and beyond may include promotional strategies and incentive schemes aimed at selected market segments and more general communication to maintain destination brand values and visibility.

- *Promotion of human capital development.* Targeted policies and programmes for education and capacity building for communities should be focused on women, youth and other marginalised groups in the tourism development process, including self-governance within communities that enable efficient decision-making and leadership concerning tourism.

Chapter 2

The Key Concepts may be categorised as follows:

- The "rocky road" towards recovery. Lowering economic growth indicates less consumer spending capacity on tourism. Tourism activity is conditioned to a great extent by the ability of the individual tourist consumer to participate based on their choices of tourism activity regarding type and format, duration, destination, travel mode and level of comfort desired.
- Cost sensitivity. From the consumer perspective, the objective is a vacation experience that satisfies needs and concerns about sustainability and the ethical scope of the destination. Nonetheless, consumers will be concerned about the level of costs, and this may dampen concerns by tourist participants to indulge in genuinely sustainable tourism activities.
- Interest rate pressures on tourism SMEs. Most tourism SMEs are affected by commercial lending rates, which mimic inflationary pressures as credit institutions seek to create lending costs at real levels. Tourism SMEs will likely suffer the hardest as credit shortages in an industry already suffering from lower access to finance will exist. As many tourism SMEs are family businesses, this will also impact the lives of family members and their lifestyle and entrepreneurial activities.
- The costs of sustainability matching. These are undoubtedly heavy for SMEs. To an extent, we may see the effect of sustainability matching costs on a sector that frequently lacks the resources, capacity and knowledge to manage such demands. Commitment to sustainable goals requires resource shifting and categorisation, which is challenging given increased cost and availability post-pandemic.
- The Green Recovery. Revisiting resilience is problematic as it is based on four critical areas: long-term strategic planning, incentivisation of green practices, building capacity to reduce environmental impacts of tourism activity and developing a climate-resilient environment. Tourism has been highly vulnerable to exogenous shocks – Covid, terrorism, climate impacts and socio-economic collapses.

- SDG goals attainment. It is evident that many of the SDG targets are off track at the midway point towards 2030. Of the 140 targets, 12% were on track to be delivered, almost half were off track, and 30% had shown no progress since 2015. Whilst this level of progress was global, the most significant problem was the difficulties for the developing countries in achieving target compliance due to the pandemic's effects and the general economic situation since 2019.
- SDG critical goals for sustainable tourism. The following goals are specific to sustainable tourism: water and sanitation, affordable and clean energy, work and economic growth, sustainable communities, climate action, and life on land and in the water. For children, the shadow of non-compliance with the SDGs looms over them; failure to achieve targets initiates a miserable future existence.
- Degradation in tourism communities and the effect on children. Many examples of degradation created by tourist activity specifically impact children. These include large visitor numbers with high consumption and waste habits producing significant environmental changes, which have a high impact where residents rely on the natural environment for food and safe living.
- Effect of economic losses on children and young people. Financial losses in local communities may encourage prostitution, environmental crime, exploitation of illegal migrants, child labour and the trafficking of children for exploitative purposes. We may observe that children effectively spend their early and developing adult stages in the shadow of a booming climate crisis.
- The role of children in tourism. They are economic actors in tourism communities and may have a valuable role in community culture and heritage as participants in the active maintenance of the local heritage. Achieving the SDGs has the potential to benefit children and young people in tourism communities. Nonetheless, we can observe that the climate change crisis poses one of the most urgent and complex challenges to children and young people in those communities. Today's 13-year-old will be 20 in 2030 when the SDGs should be met, and they will be 40 in 2050, when 100% of the 2015 Paris Accords should be operative. We are therefore looking at the role of children who will effectively spend their early and developing adult stages in the shadow of a booming climate crisis.
- Children and climate change. For children, the shadow of non-compliance with the SDGs looms over them. A potential scenario for Europe alone is that an over-heating planet would create an arid semi-desert in Mediterranean Europe in which tourism activity would only be possible in the winter months. Further countries would be impacted by severe droughts and lack of water for the population, let alone millions of tourists. In Northern Europe, severe storms, flooding and above-average temperatures would lead to water shortages in summer. This is the problem we face in tourism, but it is not its problem alone.

The Critical Factors

Identification of long-term issues

It is essential to effect a long-term strategy for local tourism that identifies critical success factors that include:

- An agile, forward-looking approach.
- Dedicated environmental responsibility and environmental capacity development.
- Embracing the circular economy.
- Ensuring transparency in planning and development and inclusion of all actors in communities – public, private and social.
- Reviewing and revising the stakeholder model in local tourism communities.
- Committing to the Green Recovery.

At the same time, in possible contradiction to the aims stated above, more than half of national tourism organisations surveyed wished to return to the levels of tourism arrivals seen in their country in recent years. This may be due to the firm economic reliance on tourism or based on a desire to see similar levels of tourism arrivals dispersed more evenly throughout the year and the place.

Resilience

There is a critical need to develop a model to create and impose tourism resilience based on critical success factors to ensure that future economic, climate and pandemic shocks are more efficiently and effectively managed. Resilience priorities differ between destinations and at different points in time. These different priority areas depend on location, climate, visitor mix, reliance on travel and tourism as an economic driver, typology of visitors, political vision and prioritisation of tourism, among other activities. Typically, destinations most exposed to climate risk and/or extreme weather focus on the environment and infrastructure. Those with a high reliance on travel and tourism receipts tend to focus on economic resilience, particularly the ability of the destination, its businesses and its workforce to quickly pivot towards alternative or substitute models in case of crisis. Societal support and acceptance are key priorities for destinations with the most seasonal or concentrated demand, with the balance between visitor and resident value being a key ingredient to resilience.

Communities, children and young people

Children and young people are undoubtedly a critical success factor for the sustainable development of local tourism communities. They have both a passive and active role, but we should disregard their role at our peril. Local communities, which include the younger generation as an essential element, should be involved in decision-making and policy-making processes to uplift local communities' trust and confidence regarding tourism development. Community involvement ensures the improvement of plans and service delivery whilst promoting a sense of involvement in sharing a common objective. Local-level participation in tourism supports upholding local culture, tradition and the indigenous knowledge of local people. It confirms the achievement of sustainability goals, the local community's welfare and the environment's conservation. Community participation should target appropriate levels of communication amongst local actors in facilitating better decision-making and more sustainable growth and development. Thus, the success of tourism development relies on the goodwill and cooperation of local communities; if their aspirations and capabilities fail to match with tourism development and planning, then the industry's potential may be destructive to both parties.

Children and youth play a crucial role in this participatory planning process concerning the future performance of tourism in their local destinations. Local community participation in tourism development that reflects the role of children and young people as participants and potential economic actors is vital in attaining sustainability goals and improving community welfare. The involvement of children and young people as future stakeholders can enhance the conservation of the local environment and culture. This underlines the inseparability of children and young people as tourism creators and consumers. Their views, attitudes and concerns should be key issues in the longer-term planning process.

Sustainability comes at a cost

Building sustainability into the tourism model requires resources – not only economic but also social and time/opportunity costs for tourism communities. It is not solely solved by the commitment of grants or funding from national or international agencies. Local actors must also commit to the cause to show resolution and willingness, not simply a capacity, to take filtered-down funding. This implies a deep level of engagement. Tourism development should provide local communities the time to adjust to new environmental, social and economic conditions and help prevent the negative results of rapid uncontrolled growth. Involving local people in determining their development will prevent conflicts, which would inevitably affect the sustainability of tourism. Sustainable tourism may have a higher prospect of success in rural tourism development, peripheral, coastal and island tourism, but inevitably requires more significant financial and human resource inputs.

Avoiding degradation

A critical issue is avoiding degradation at a tangible environmental level and an intangible cultural and heritage level. The loss of cultural heritage is often irrecoverable – overwhelming and unplanned tourism activity can affect and ultimately change the underlying heritage of a locality and region. Avoiding this through systematic planning and capacity control is an important step. There is evidence of greater collaboration between public, voluntary and private sectors to achieve a more sustainable future for people and the planet. This trend toward sustainability will continue to expand over the long term, with more consumers intending to travel more responsibly and sustainably. We also know that young people have greater commitment and better attitudes towards sustainable tourism than their elders. With the support and continued work of the public and private sectors and local communities and increasingly clear information on which options are more sustainable, consumers will likely continue to take more responsibility towards sustainable attitudes over the medium to longer term.

Connections

In this section, we suggest some elements based on the issues raised in Part I. In essence, we have stated that the movement towards sustainable, ethical and responsible tourism must engage us in transformational development strategies despite the problems of the post-pandemic environment. It should also ensure that the momentum to create more resilient, sustainable and inclusive tourism is neither diminished nor abandoned. Furthermore, we must face the problem of how tourism must re-focus itself economically, socially and environmentally to meet the Sustainable Development Goals. We see that local tourism communities are frequently at the front line of the negative aspects of modern tourism in terms of their cultural and environmental fragility. An ultimate and critical issue must be where children fit into locally oriented tourism that meets all long-term sustainability requirements. In accordance with these underlying concepts, we have sought to develop some connections for readers as follows:

- For students, we pose some questions which may assist the connections between teaching and learning.
- For researchers (graduate or professional), we suggest some guidelines for further research.
- For practitioners, we raise matters of concern for their progress in balancing economic gain with environmental and cultural fragility.

Teaching and learning

Students should comment upon the following points:

a The five-year period before the Covid-19 pandemic saw a substantial increase in tourism activity across several important and fragile destinations. This was unplanned, and the environmental consequences are generally not fully understood.

b   The pandemic showed the sensitivity of tourism to globally critical events, albeit on a far greater scale than previous man-made or natural disasters.

c   There is a strong need for sustainable development planning across all forms of tourism to protect against large-scale climate change and the predatory effects of damage to the cultural and heritage environment.

d   Any critical event inevitably seems to be followed by socio-economic consequences; again, there appears to be a lack of contingency planning for the post-event situation.

e   Children and young people will have a key role in the future of tourism, particularly in the period up to 2050, as the enormity of climate change on tourism markets begins to unfold. This indicates that we need to take a more careful and perceptively deeper understanding of the role of children and young people in tourism communities.

Guidelines for researchers

Researchers may wish to consider the following:

a   Building sustainability in tourism has a cost; given the ebbs and flows of economic growth in advanced economies, what is the role of targeted research in how sustainable development may be funded and promoted?

b   The role of children in tourism is not widely researched and has mainly been related to children as tourists. What steps can be taken to examine the position of children and young people in tourism activity as economic participants and recipients of tourism training and education?

c   We also have limited information about the role of children in tourism SMEs – e.g. children in family-owned agri-tourism. How can this be researched?

Keynotes for practitioners

Practitioners may wish to review the following points:

a   How do we radically reconsider the business case for shifting towards more ethical and responsible tourism, which meets the Sustainable Development Goals?

b   How do we fundamentally understand the delicate balance between economic gain and environmental and cultural fragility in local tourism destinations?

c   How do we create strategies to face the impending climate disaster and the current level of global warming, which may well ensure that some current tourism destinations become unviable?

PART II

What is tourism doing for children?

INTRODUCTION TO PART II

Tourism impacts on children are the top loop through which we examine and discuss the crucial and often invisible role tourism has in the socialisation of children. The following two chapters are structured around three important topics: children's socialisation intertwined with tourism, the role of parents in shaping children's (dis)affection for tourism, and the cultural, social and environmental impacts of tourism on children's quality of life.

In Chapter 4 we consider how the socialisation of children might be viewed as a difficult process, with no prescribed guidebook. It rests on parents primarily and other influential groups to do their best in children's upbringing. As if it is not already difficult to master, tourism profoundly affects the socialisation process, whether one is aware of it or not. Socialisation occurs on two levels – primary and secondary – with tourism playing a pivotal role in each level. By discussing some of the less evident negotiations of activity and space in tourism destinations, we reflect on financial restrictions, time constraints, information, values and preferences about parenting and child development, family and environmental stress, and prejudices when making decisions. Parents, community and technology inherently affect how children perceive tourism and experience a bond with the place they live in. Information communication technology (ICT) has significantly changed the organisation and activities of tourism and hospitality. ICT enables children rapid access to information about their community – including unmerciful tourist opinions about that destination. At the same time, it also assists in creating an ever-widening and deepening alienation gap between locals and tourists, where host children become invisible, missing out on essential socialisation benefits through tourism.

In Chapter 5, we investigate the quality of life in tourism destinations, which is normally linked to the satisfaction surrounding job creation, income generation, infrastructure development and raising residents' standard of living. As

DOI: 10.4324/9781003374299-7

much as these are important elements of life quality, we dare to discuss the dialectical nature of the relationship between tourism, its impacts and the quality of life in a community. Even more so, the quality of life of children is not even considered within the broader conceptualisation of tourism. Thus we discuss the environment of intensive tourism and how its activity mandates the reality in which children and parents live. This establishes a framework for their social reality, within which children seek answers to why some processes occur in a particular way and try to understand the meaning of the reality in which they live. Moreover, the economic impacts of tourism are discussed, but not in a way as traditional for the studies on resident attitudes. Instead, we highlight dialectically those factors affecting children's life quality and bring some valuable observations that have resurfaced through the Covid-19 pandemic.

In Chapter 6 we summarise the Key Concepts and Critical Factors in the two preceding chapters, as well as examine the most appropriate Connections for students, researchers and practitioners.

4

SOCIALISATION AND TOURISM IMPACTS

Introduction

Tourism research has seen strong growth in the last 20 years, and a significant part of the research effort is directed towards "the economy-centric paradigm" (Korstanje, 2018; Šegota et al., 2022). This means that the research discusses different aspects of the economic dimension of tourism, which is sometimes related to the well-being and progress of the community. Many articles provide data on the share of tourism activity in global or national GDP as well as the importance of the role that tourism plays in the employment of people, on migration movements related to tourism, and the increase in the education of the population and many other economic and social dimensions of modern tourism activity. Kompier (2006, p. 406) calls this relationship between facts (recurring and very precisely measured) and deep trust in these facts "the myth of scientific value". This focus on the environment and its connection with scientific activity diminishes the importance of content about children in the tourism industry because a large part of this role is unmeasured or challenging to measure. If there is research about children in tourism, it is not easy to fit it into how traditional tourism impacts literature, which relates primarily to the economic effects of tourism.

Among the critical yet neglected topics are children who live with their parents in tourist destinations. Very little research highlights children's perceptions and attitudes to tourism (Yang et al., 2019; Koščak et al., 2023). The contemporary literature linking children with tourism depicts children as "initiators" of tourist activities because most families plan and adapt trips or holidays to the age and interests of their children (Séraphin & Vanessa, 2020). This way, family tourism is aimed at visiting friends and relatives, one of the more stable forms of tourism (Schänzel & Yeoman, 2015).

DOI: 10.4324/9781003374299-8

On the other hand, an impressive volume of literature is dedicated to various forms of social and personal pathology associated with tourism, such as child sex tourism, its impact on the spread of infectious diseases, especially HIV, organised child prostitution, child labour, orphanage tourism and similar topics that talk about the heartless exploitation of children associated with intensive tourism activity (Yang et al., 2019). We can conclude that issues related to children in tourism move into two mutually distinct areas: 1) themes exploring the influence of children on family decisions regarding tourism, and 2) themes related to child exploitation and child abuse. There is not a significant number of systematic research and experiments on children's engagement and involvement in tourism planning and development.

Tourism impacts and children need to be studied from the perspective of socialisation. Tourism destinations succumbed to the tourist influx, and all its effects undoubtedly leave a mark on the socialisation of children as hosts. Socialisation happens on two levels – primary and secondary – with each level highlighting the most important participants in the process (Bronfenbrenner, 1979). Hence, primary socialisation involves parents and children, whilst secondary includes peers, teachers and the community.

Tourism and socialisation in the parents–children dyad

This first level of socialisation is usually called the "developmental system" (Bronfenbrenner, 1979, p. 66), whereby Bronfenbrenner emphasises the "sociality" of the socialisation process. In the parent–child dyad, the socialisation process means a learning process in which the child adapts to the people in the world around them, but the other member of the dyad (i.e. the parent) also adapts to the needs and interests of the child. This dyad is a process of mutual influence and learning, and the relationship between persons is reciprocal because neither person can create a relationship alone, although they can initiate it (Shelton, 2019).

The dyad is the initial communication element in relationships between people, so logically, it appears at the beginning of the socialisation process. On the other hand, it is also the simplest form of communication, which is also logical at the very beginning of the socialisation journey of any human being. Bronfenbrenner (1979) conceptualises the dyad in several forms, whereby three forms are the most essential for the development of each person:

a   Observational dyad in which one person carefully observes the other who shows interest in that process.
b   A dyad of joint activity in which persons in the dyad experience themselves in some joint action.
c   The primary dyad continues to exist even when the participants are not physically together.

Dyads represent individual elements of the ecosystem. In this sense, the ecosystem that is being talked about plays the role of a development ecosystem, and the nature of the relationships in which the dyad is located, as well as the activities in which the participants are involved during the development of these relationships, are essential elements of the relationship formed between participants (Shelton, 2019). If the dyad represents an ecosystem in which the participants' experiences are exchanged, these experiences are mutual. Therefore, both children and parents who are participants in a dyad exchange experience with each other. Bronfenbrenner (1979) conceptualises the result of this exchange of experiences as an assertion according to which "the developmental impact of a dyad increases as a direct function of the level of reciprocity, mutuality of positive feeling, and a gradual shift of balance of power in favour of the developing person" (p. 59). Due to the nature of the development process, the exchange of experiences in the dyad is, for a good part of the development process, asymmetrical, and this is precisely what the role of parents consists of, as those who ensure the safety of children through the transfer of their experiences with the world around them.

This means children's early socialisation practices differ significantly depending on the parents' social status. For example, if parents who raise their children in the conditions of tourism-intensive activities mainly belong to the lower social strata, the cognitive and emotional characteristics of the children will correspond to the educational model developed by the lower socio-economic strata (Kalil & Ryan, 2020, p. 33). In addition, several important factors define different educational models in different socio-economic strata. These are primarily financial restrictions, time constraints, information, values and preferences about parenting and child development, family and environmental stress, and prejudices when making decisions (Kalil & Ryan, 2020). We will reflect on all of these concerning tourism and children's socialisation.

Financial restrictions

Parents from lower social strata have less financially to invest in their children's development than those from higher social strata. This is not only an investment in children's play and entertainment, which is crucial for their development, but also in developing their learning abilities and skills, various forms of dexterity necessary for developing professional skills. Financial investments are primarily needed to ensure a higher quality of education, housing in better residential areas, a higher quality of care for children when parents are at work and higher levels of preschool care and education (Kornrich & Furstenberg, 2013).

Time limits

Parents working in labour-intensive industries such as tourism have far less time to spend with their children. This is especially true for parents employed in destinations with intensive tourist activity, also characterised by seasonality.

During the peak of the tourist season, parents who perform service jobs are often busy all day and at night. If both parents are employed in tourism, balancing their work obligations and childcare is very difficult. Very often, they do not have access to childcare at an early age, leaving them reliant on other family members for help in such situations, if available.

There is an important difference between parents of higher social circles and those from lower social circles. The paradox is that parents of higher social circles (especially mothers) spend more time in their work activities than parents of lower social circles, but simultaneously, the limited time spent with children is of higher quality. For example, mothers from lower social circles dedicate more time to maintaining a household, while mothers from higher circles spend more time in activities with children (Kalil & Ryan, 2020) that improve their emotional and cognitive development.

Information, values and preferences about parenting and child development

Research has shown that values and preferences regarding child development are very important to all parents, regardless of their social status. Even more so, parents with lesser socio-economic status attached greater importance to developing children's skills than some from higher socio-economic strata (Kalil & Ryan, 2020). Parents of all social groups know the value of education and are willing to invest in their children's education (Kornrich & Furstenberg, 2013).

Of course, it is not that the lower social classes do not know what is good for their children. The problem is that they cannot satisfy most of these needs for other reasons, determined by their socio-economic position. Parents of lower and higher socio-economic strata have the same aspirations regarding their children's education. However, parents from a higher strata can expect far better results than parents of a lower status, so it is not about different value systems or attitudes towards education but other objective possibilities linked to the duration of education and financial resources enabling that process. For example, research conducted in England shows that there is no difference between parents of various socio-economic classes in assessing the value of education; however, parents from lower social strata do not expect high results from their children in comparison to parents of higher social strata (Kalil & Ryan, 2020). This may also imply that the former are more realistic about the possibilities of success in their children's education than the latter.

Family and environmental stress

Many authors associate the development of modern tourism with stressful events affecting host families. Stress is not necessarily a destructive phenomenon, with a predominantly negative impact on family members and their lives, although it is most often perceived as such. Stress can also have positive outcomes, encouraging people to take concrete and better actions (Jordan et al., 2021). When it comes to differences in stressful events, the authors point to statistically significantly higher stress levels in families with lower incomes than in families with higher incomes. For example, poor mothers report being under stress two and a half times more than mothers from better-off families (Kalil & Ryan, 2020). According to many studies, family stress caused by the family's financial situation leads to parents focusing more on making decisions related to short-term rather than long-term goals (Kalil & Ryan, 2020).

Research examining tourism-induced personal stress found that stress affected almost 80% of host families. People from higher strata cited problems in local traffic as the most significant stressors, while people from lower socio-economic strata cited no tourists, jobs, and money as the main stressors (Jordan et al., 2021). It can be expected that parents under stress will have reduced opportunities to support their children's development, consequently reducing their capacities to improve their children's cognitive development and emotional support.

It is imperative to discuss the frequency of stress in tourism communities. Research continues to demonstrate that residents of a tourist area experience stress regardless of the level of tourist attendance, or more clearly, the stress level of residents in a tourist area does not depend on the number of tourists who visit that area (Jordan et al., 2019.). Obviously, we need to accept that tourism is a source of stress for the host community, regardless of whether there are too many tourists or not enough of them. Parents who raise their children in stressful circumstances pass on to them their stress and the stress experienced by people in their immediate and distant environment. Perhaps this is one of the reasons for the relatively low interest of children in professions related to tourism, which is observed in many tourist areas (Koščak et al., 2023).

Prejudices when making decisions

No school in any community would teach parents how to raise their children successfully. Hence, parents adapt to this process throughout time, mainly relying on experiences from their upbringing and development, the experiences of their parents, friends and colleagues with whom they often exchange parenting and family life experiences. Whilst acquiring all these experiences, people also transfer the prejudices of those whose experiences they listen to and are very often ready to accept them as part of their family behaviour model. This process also reflects the socio-economic stratum to which the family belong, hence inevitably assuming all the prejudices of the stratum.

The role of parents in shaping children's attitudes toward tourism

There are very rare situations when, for example, the development of a tourist destination is discussed with children. Very rarely children are informed and consulted about plans for the development of the destination. A large European study found that 64% of children knew almost nothing about tourism in their area – a place of intense tourist activity (Koščak et al., 2023). However, the same study showed that children observed a negative impact on the lives of their families (Koščak et al., 2023). Similarly, Chan et al. (2015) showed that working in the tourism industry did not contribute to family bonding or increase the harmony and functionality of family life, although it increased material security. This kind of analysis of family life clearly indicates that children closely follow the developments in their families and are aware of the quality and dynamics of family life linked to tourism. Moreover, although parents may not often talk to their children about the financial aspects of family life, the children are increasingly aware of it by stating that working in the tourism industry does not bring much money to employees (Koščak et al., 2023). Similarly, Canosa et al. (2019) found that children think that working in the tourist industry is only interesting for people who are temporary residents of some destinations and are ready to work for low wages or for migrant workers who actually need accommodation.

Regardless of whether these attitudes of children are the result of an exchange of attitudes between children, or whether they are the opinions of children that they have come to by listening to adults' conversations, the fact is that these attitudes are incorporated into the socialisation process that children go through, either in peer groups, groups of neighbours or relatives being part of the environment in which the socialisation process takes place. Of course, these opinions are also the result of socialisation processes in primary families.

Parents and children are social partners in tourism destinations, without often being aware of their mutual positions, or at least they are not aware of it in the full meaning of that term. Both are under the social influence of tourism, i.e. the social partnership with tourists occurs whether they are aware of it or not. Children very early show signs of interest in intervening in space to ensure some common social interests. Such attitude indicates that children perceive their environment very precisely and are eager to co-create it (Rasmussen & Smidt, 2003). On the other hand, adults generally do not notice this desire of children to participate in shaping the tourism environment. Research showed that only 1 in 5 children get the opportunity to talk about the further development of tourism in their community (Koščak et al., 2023).

Children are active listeners to conversations between adults, often even when the adults are not aware of it. Some studies have shown that children can perceive a social group as "less acceptable" if they hear negative statements about it (Conder & Lane, 2021). It is known that children carefully follow the conversations of adults, especially parents, and that they often take positions towards some people or social groups in accordance with what they hear. Such activity makes children less inclined to associate with "proscribed" group members and less willing to engage in some elements of that group's culture (Conder & Lane, 2021). Tourists are often talked about negatively within family circles. Even more so, parents employed in the hospitality and tourism industry intentionally take their children on outings where there are no tourists, as they do not wish to be reminded of tourism in their free time (van Schalk-wyk et al., 2006). With such practices, children are undoubtedly missing out on their socialisation process, which is likely to result in children's negative atti-tudes towards tourism.

Influence of peers, teachers and the community

The literature has no clear boundary between when primary socialisation ends and when secondary socialisation begins. It is often stated that there is no clear end to primary socialisation because no other social factor takes over this form of sociali-sation, as the family should never cease to be an element of protection and support.

The secondary socialisations fall under the influence of peers, with some stating that this influence begins somewhere in the middle of childhood and lasts until high adolescence (Hota & McGuiggan, 2007). In addition to the peers, the daycare facilities, the education system, neighbourhoods and the community are essential for children's socialisation (Vandell, 2000). The peer group is not only an immediate factor in socialisation but also an "environ-mental factor responsible for personality and socialisation into culture in gen-eral" (Vandell, 2000, p. 699). This means that the peer group, as an ecological factor, transmits the experiences of the entire community with tourists and the tourism industry through common cultural patterns. Shared experiences are not only the experiences of the generation with whom the children have direct contact, but they are also an accumulation of the experiences of previous gen-erations gathered and conveyed through collective memory.

In short, macro-systems can be differently "arranged" in different social sys-tems, but as a whole, they play their socialisation function (Bronfenbrenner, 1979). The division into the three levels of the socialisation process is only an academic, didactic division, aiming to show all the elements of the social environment that act in the socialisation process of children. In reality, it is a dialectical connection of all aspects of the social structure, which work simul-taneously, unitedly and in an uninterrupted flow. Social institutions are just one of many elements that fulfil their role in the socialisation of children, but also of other people who live and (co-)act in the development of an area. The fol-lowing example is likely to reflect this observation.

BOX 4.1 CASE STUDY: POSTCARDS FROM BANARAS/ VARANASI

Banaras, better known as Varanasi, is located on the left bank of the Ganges River and is one of the seven sacred cities of Hinduism in India. Some host children have been recorded selling postcards to tourists and bringing tourists to some shops whose owners then receive commissions. Hence, they have been labelled small "tourist workers" by Jenny Huberman, who studied their socialisation. Huberman (2005) noticed that "tourists stop loving them when they grow up" (p. 142). The latter results from children's self-reflection, which Huberman attached to tourism-induced socialisation. Huberman explains that belonging to a lower social class is very prominent because children can access tourists, build relationships and participate in the environment. However, the feeling that "tourists do not like them anymore" because they are "too old" for this type of work strengthens their status in a subordinate social group (Huberman, 2005, p. 142). This is nothing more than a socialisation circle of foreign tourists who observe the social environment from their domestic (probably European) perspective and children forced to offer their own identity to participate in the economic exchange of tourism.

Belonging to a community, or identifying and having a sense of place, is one of the most widespread topics in sociology and many other social disciplines, such as anthropology and economics. Some tourism scholars treat belonging to a local community, with its specificities and characteristics, as being branded, or so they say, living in "brand communities", sharing a system of values, consciousness, rituals and traditions, and a sense of "us" versus "them" (Bellezza & Keinan, 2014, p. 398). At the same time, the label *us* certainly means identifying the community's original members. On the other hand, the label *them* refers to those who immigrate to the area for various reasons. Many researchers say *them* represents a danger – a threat to a community's symbolic value, uniqueness and cultural unity (Bellezza & Keinan, 2014, p. 399). On the other hand, tourism is somewhat different because the local population does not feel threatened by tourists – the term brand means that the local population is proud to live in a place that provides many tourist opportunities (Huh & Vogt, 2007).

We should definitely mention the approaches to the concept of belonging to a community which has experienced explosive development in a very short time, in the context of using modern means of communication. Did these modern means of communication contribute to the cohesiveness of the community? Some research indicates a positive connection between the use of modern communication and the feeling of belonging to the community, that is, "the increase and distribution of social capital in local communities" (Damásio et al., 2012, p. 141). As young people and children are intensive users of social networks, it can be assumed that entire local communities will be able to access such networks with assistance from young people and children. Information communication technology (ICT) has significantly changed the organisation and activities of tourism and hospitality. With the introduction of ICT, potential tourists as service seekers can much better adapt their wishes and visitation plans to what is offered on the market. Consequently, children growing up in tourist-intensive areas have more access to information about their community, including various opinions about that destination. Hence, tourists' experiences are also available, often transmitted in a direct and not even slightly embellished form.

Without realising how impactful a critique of one's place of living might be, visitors unmercifully keep expressing their dissatisfaction online.

On the other hand, ICT also profoundly alienated the local population from tourists because the tourists seek less advice and guidance at the destination. For example, tourists can get to know the place by using route planning without having any contact with residents (Karagiannis et al., 2014). This creates an ever widening and deepening alienation gap in which the local population in the equation of vacation and tourist satisfaction represents only one of the functions that tourists predict in advance and map onto their vacation plan. Likewise, host children become invisible, missing out on essential socialisation benefits through tourism.

References

Bellezza, S., & Keinan, A. (2014). Brand tourists: How non-core users enhance the brand image by eliciting pride. *Journal of Consumer Research*, 41 (2), 397–417. doi:10.1086/676679.

Bond, M.H. (2013). Refining Lewin's formula: A general model for explaining situational influence on individual social behavior. *Asian Journal of Social Psychology*, 16 (1), 1–15. doi:10.1111/ajsp.12012.

Bourdieu, P. (1986). Forms of capital. In Richardson, J.G. *Handbook of Theory and Research for the Sociology of Education*. Bloomsbury, 241–258.

Bourdieu, P., & Passeron, J.-C. (1990). *Reproduction in Education, Society and Culture*. Sage Publications.

Bronfenbrenner, U. (1979). *The Ecology of Human Development: Experiments by nature and design*. Harvard University Press.

Brulliard, K. (2022). The Rainbow Family comes to Colorado, bringing peace, love and anxiety. *The Washington Post*. https://www.washingtonpost.com/nation/2022/07/03/rainbow-family-colorado/.

Canosa, A., Graham, A. & Wilson, E. (2019). My overloved town: The challenges of growing up in a small coastal tourist destination (Byron Bay, Australia). In Milano, C., Cheer, J. & Novelli, M. *Overtourism: Excesses, discontents and measures in travel and tourism*. CABI, 190–204.

Chan, S.M., Kwok, C.Y. & Siu, J.N. (2015). The Macau family-in-transition: The perceived impact of casino. *The Open Family Studies Journal*, 7 (1), 86–95. doi:10.2174/1874922401507010086.

Chen, C.-C., Zou, S. & Chen, M.-H. (2022). The fear of being infected and fired: Examining the dual job stressors of hospitality employees during Covid-19. *International Journal of Hospitality Management*, 102, 1–12. doi:10.1016/j.ijhm.2021.103131.

Conder, E.B., & Lane, J.D. (2021). Overhearing brief negative messages has lasting effects on children's attitudes toward novel social groups. *Child Development*, 92 (4), e674–e690. doi:10.1111/cdev.13547.

Crespi, F. (2006). *Sociologija kulture (Sociology of Culture)*. Politička kultura.

Damásio, M.J., Henrique, S. & Costa, C. (2012). Belonging to a community: The mediation of belonging. *Observatorio*, 127–146. https://recil.ensinolusofona.pt/bitstream/10437/2924/1/604-2447-1-PB.pdf.

Hota, M., & McGuiggan, R. (2007). The relative influence of consumer socialization agents on children and adolescents: Examining the past and modeling the future.

European Advances in Consumer Research, 7, 119–124. http://www.acrwebsite.org/volumes/13831/eacr/vol7/E-07.

Huberman, J. (2005). "Consuming children": Reading the impacts of tourism in the city of Banaras. *Childhood*, 12 (2), 161–176. doi:10.1177/0907568205051902.

Huh, C., & Vogt, C.A. (2007). Changes in residents' attitudes toward tourism over time: A cohort analytical approach. *Journal of Travel Research*, 46 (4), 446–455. doi:10.1177/0047287507308327.

Jordan, E.J., Lesar, L. & Spencer, D.M. (2021). Clarifying the interrelations of residents' perceived tourism-related stress, stressors, and impacts. *Journal of Travel Research*, 60 (1), 208–219. doi:10.1177/0047287519888287.

Jordan, E.J., Moran, C. & Godwyll, J.M. (2019). Does tourism really cause stress? A natural experiment utilising ArcGIS Survey123. *Current Issues in Tourism* 24, 1–15. doi:10.1080/13683500.2019.1702001.

Kalil, A., & Ryan, R. (2020). Parenting Practices and Socio-economic Gaps in Childhood Outcomes. *The Future of Children*, 30 (1), 29–54.

Karagiannis, S., Anthopoulos, L., Aspridis G.G., Sdrolias, L. & Polykarpidis, A. (2014). Green urban space utilisation for mild ICT-based touristic activities: the case of Pafsilipo Park in Greece. *Journal of Environmental and Tourism Analyses*, 2 (1), 83–96.

Kogazon, R. (2021). *Liberal States, Authoritarian Families – Childhood and education in early modern thought*. Oxford University Press.

Kompier, M.A. (2006). The "Hawthorne effect" is a myth, but what keeps the story going? *Scandinavian Journal of Work, Environment & Health*, 32 (5), 402–412. https://www.jstor.org/stable/40967593.

Kornrich, S., & Furstenberg, F. (2013). Investing in children: Changes in parental spending on children, 1972–2007. *Demography*, 50 (1), 1–23. doi:10.1007/s13524-012-0146-4.

Korstanje, M.E. (2018). Exegesis and myths as methodologies of research in tourism. *Mossoró/RN*, 7 (1), 7–21. doi:10.1080/13032917.2013.823877.

Koščak, M., Knežević, M., Binder, D., Pelaez-Verdet, A., Işik, C., Mićić, V., Borisavljević, K. & Šegota, T. (2023). Exploring the neglected voices of children in sustainable tourism development: A comparative study in six European tourist destinations. *Journal of Sustainable Tourism*, 31 (2), 561–580.

Kusluvan, S., Kusluvan, Z., Ilhan, I. & Buyruk, L. (2010). The human dimension: A review of human resources management issues in the tourism and hospitality industry. *Cornell Hospitality Quarterly*, 51 (2), 171–214. doi:10.1177/1938965510036287.

Prantner, K., Ding, Y., Luger, M., Yan, Z. & Herzog, C. (2007). Tourism ontology and semantic management system: State-of-the-arts analysis. In Isaías, P., Nunes, M.B. & Barr, J. *Proceedings of the IADIS International Conference WWW/Internet 2007 (WWW/Internet2007)*. International Association for the Development of the Information Society, 111–115. https://www.researchgate.net/publication/268424060.

Rasmussen, K., & Smidt, S. (2003). Children in the neighbourhood. In Christensen, P., & O'Brien, M. *Children in the City*. Routledge, 82–101.

Schänzel, H.A., & Yeoman, I. (2015). Trends in family tourism. *Journal of Tourism Futures*, 1 (2), 141–147. doi:10.1108/JTF-12-2014-0006.

Séraphin, H., & Vanessa, G. (2020). *Children in Hospitality and Tourism – Marketing and managing experiences*. Walter de Gruyter GmbH.

Shelton, L.G. (2019). *The Bronfenbrenner Primer*. Routledge.

Šegota, T., Mihalič, T. & Perdue, R. (2022). Resident perceptions and responses to tourism: Individual vs community level impacts. *Journal of Sustainable Tourism*. https://doi.org/10.1080/09669582.2022.2149759.

Vandell, D.L. (2000). Parents, peer groups, and other socializing influences. *Developmental Psychology*, 36 (6), 699–710. doi:10.1037//0012-1649.36.6.699.

van Schalkwyk, G.J., Tran, E. & Chang, K. (2006). The impact of Macao's gaming industry on family life. An exploratory study. *China Perspectives*, 64 (March–April). doi:10.4000/chinaperspectives.603.

Yang, M.J., Yang, E.C. & Khoo-Lattimore, C. (2019). Host-children of tourism destinations: Systematic quantitative literature review. *Tourism Recreation Research*, 1–16. doi:10.1080/02508281.2019.1662213.

5

QUALITY OF LIFE AND TOURISM IMPACTS

Introduction

Tourism activity is "a major socioeconomic force in both developing and developed markets" (Uysal et al., 2015). The most common advantages of the tourism industry in national economies are:

1. Economic contribution, with a significant role played by the increase in tax revenue.
2. Infrastructure development.
3. Diversification of the national and local economy.
4. Positive socio-cultural impacts.
5. Improvement in the standard of living of the local population.
6. Promotion of sustainable development.

The characteristics of tourism as an economic activity, as described here, lead to tourism being portrayed as a critical economic sector in many countries. In addition, many tourism researchers found that tourism activity directly impacts social, cultural and environmental well-being (Kim et al., 2013). This includes the feelings and attitudes of people who live in tourism communities, create and raise their families, care for their children and relatives, and care about a particular area's overall development.

One of the most significant characteristics of neo-liberal economic thinking is the emphasis on growth as the primary driver of economic progress. Of course, this approach could not bypass the tourism industry. The tourism-led growth hypothesis (TLGH) is introduced, which suggests that economic growth in the tourism industry can be achieved through increased labour and capital and a significant increase in exports (Brida et al., 2016). This economic thesis would

DOI: 10.4324/9781003374299-9

dominate tourism literature (Perles-Ribes et al., 2017), thus ushering neoliberal economics into the scientific and professional tourism literature of the 21st century. Consequently, the world's poorest countries increasingly rely on tourism revenues to enhance their foreign exchange earnings. Thus, for the 40 poorest countries in the world, tourism becomes the most crucial factor in foreign exchange inflows (Mastny, 2001).

Children in an environment of intense tourism activity

Socialisation is generally a process in people's lives in which they learn about the way of life in their social community and about essential values and norms that ensure the implementation of these values. It is probably one of the most important social processes and one of the most important sociological concepts. "The fact is that everyone is born within an already formed social context and within a specific culture" (Crespi, 2006, p. 18). Crespi speaks both about the participants and the results of that process. In this process, the participants are, on the one hand, those who accept the norms and values of a social environment, but at the same time, they participate in shaping these norms and values, changing and redefining them.

Taken as a whole, the socialisation model is described very simply but at the same time convincingly in the work of Kurt Levin and his famous formula $B = f(PE)$. It says that "behaviour evolves as a function of the interplay between person and environment" (Bronfenbrenner, 1979, p. 16); however, it also tells us that behaviour, as a result of the socialisation process, is a function of the environment in which that process took place (while, of course, we define the environment in a broader sense).

To emphasise the importance of the personal assessment of the situation by the participants in a social process, Michael Harris Bond revised Levin's formula to $B = f[P, S, P(S)]$, where $P(S)$ appears as a representative of a situation, but with the point of view of the person whose behaviour is being observed (Bond, 2013). Thus, the personal characteristics of the child's behaviour in a specific situation are emphasised in socialisation. In this way, the meaning of the socialisation process is extended beyond the social circle itself, and it also includes the characteristics of the child's personality, which are the result of long-term factors such as adapting to people in their surroundings.

This concept of adapting to people in the world around them is what Bourdieu will call "cultural capital" (Bourdieu, 2005). According to Bourdieu, the fundamental characteristic of cultural capital is the fact that in its "basic state, it is connected to the body and presupposes embodiment" (Bourdieu, 1986, p. 17). Cultural capital is the physical result and consequence of socialisation in and through the family circle and in connection with the environment. The importance of this concept for tourist areas lies precisely in the fact that it is understood how children born in areas of intensive tourist activity, with their entire psychophysical structure, immerse themselves in the environment in which they were born and in which they develop. And there is no such "ecological approach" that can protect these children from harmful effects of the environment because they are that environment. Of course, that environment is at their disposal in their growth and development and will be an essential factor in that development throughout their lives. It will give them the best it has, but it will also provide them with everything it has, and that does not always have to be the best.

The acquisition of cultural capital in the earliest developmental age means the acquisition of social knowledge and skills and the simultaneous internalisation of norms, social values and the development of social attitudes and behaviour in the socialisation process. All these socialisation elements occur at the beginning of the child's life in the family, in the usual dyad with the parents. However, raising children in areas of intensive tourist activity should be understood through the notion that tourism is a source of labour-intensive activities, with parents spending most of their time away from their families, especially during the peak of the tourist season. They carry with them all the frustrations and difficulties of doing highly intensive and tourist-facing jobs, coupled with additional frustrations originating from unexpected changes in raising a family. As much as socialisation is a universal process, especially when we talk about the earliest development phase, the conditions in which it takes place for children are not universal.

The environment of intensive tourist activity mandates the reality in which children and parents live and establishes a framework for their social reality. Within this framework, children seek answers to why some processes occur in a particular way and try to understand the meaning of the reality in which they live. The framework also helps children observe the relationships of their parents and other important people of their childhood with tourists. They also evaluate and assess these relationships and transfer them onto their attitudes and conduct towards tourists. It is often shown that the evaluations of tourists made by children are milder than those of parents – while very young, they do not have a direct relationship with tourists and can only hear or see the results of that relationship between parents and tourists. Children will likely have positive attitudes towards tourism if the latter is positive. If it is negative, they are likely to have negative attitudes towards tourism (Koščak et al., 2023).

Tourism and its impacts on children

One's success in the economic or social sense is never only the result of one's abilities and preferences but also the characteristics of the social group to which one belongs (Bowles & Gintis, 2002). Success is not only the result of socialisation in a social group but also a consequence of that socialisation on a personal and a group level. In other words, it is one of the components of the creation of social capital, whereby the term social capital is far broader than the term capital in the economic sense. The growth and development of young people in a specific environment are the results of several factors: that of a biological nature, genetic transfer of information from generation to generation, and development factors related to the transfer of cognitive potentials, but also non-cognitive personality characteristics that are transmitted intergenerationally and they remain recorded as an environmental factor. Regardless of a child's gender, members of a social group in an area with a highly developed tourism industry have high emotional intelligence, which is a characteristic that is almost as important for development as academic intelligence.

Raising children is, at the level of society, a political and economic function that develops through the social and economic development of the relationship between parents, children and the economic conditions of an area (Doepke & Zilibotti, 2017). The literature on tourism development almost certainly neglects children. It presents them very poorly in understanding the impacts of tourism on their upbringing and quality of life because children are viewed as passive objects of the socialisation process carried out over them by adults. Describing children as those whose growth and development are subordinated to the action of social institutions and their complete dependence on these institutions is a simplification that prevents the development of tourism activity as a transformative social practice ensuring children's active participation in the development of their communities.

The evolution of sustainability discourse positioned tourism and host communities alongside and within one another. With the prevalence of the sustainability paradigm, tourism impacts extend to a plethora of economic, socio-cultural and environmental impacts (see Table 5.1).

Tourism impacts shown in Table 5.1 can be either classified as (i) economic, socio-cultural and environmental impacts (e.g. Bestard & Nadal, 2007; Carmichael, 2000; Chen, 2015; Gursoy & Rutherford, 2004; Jurowski et al., 1997); or as (ii) positive economic, socio-cultural and environmental impacts, and negative economic, socio-cultural and environmental impacts (e.g. Andereck et al., 2007; Dyer et al., 2007; Kuvan & Akan, 2005; Šegota et al., 2017). The latter enables destination managers and policy-makers to understand better how the sustainability-influenced tripartite classification of impacts can be boiled down to those that are perceived as positive or negative.

Studies on resident attitudes that emerged over the recent decade presumed that "there is a reciprocal interaction between perceived living conditions and perceived tourism impacts" (Uysal et al., 2016, p. 246) once a community becomes a tourist destination. This new stream of research proposes that for tourism to thrive and obtain resident support, its purpose should not be limited to utilising and developing tourism resources and infrastructure, but it should expand to enhancing residents' quality of life. Quality of life should be understood at two levels:

- At an individual level, the quality of life represents one's satisfaction with various life domains (Cottrell et al., 2013; Kim et al., 2013; Nunkoo & So, 2015; Woo et al., 2015). It includes one's overall life satisfaction, how one spends one's life and satisfaction in various life dimensions (e.g. emotions, health, finances, personal relationships, etc.).

TABLE 5.1 Overview of tourism impacts

Economic impacts	Socio-cultural impacts	Environmental tourism impacts
• employment opportunities	• availability of recreational areas	• reduction of natural environment
• investments	• increase in crime rate	• crowding
• increase in standard of living	• variety of cultural activities	• pollution
• tax revenue	• quality of life (QoL)	• traffic congestion
• increase in prices of goods and services	• preservation of local culture	• litter problems
• increase of property prices	• quality of local services	• noise
• income for local businesses	• prostitution	• water pollution
• benefits to a small group of people	• entertainment	• conservation of natural resources
• more spending in community	• quality of public utilities	• negative impact on natural environment
• leakage of revenue	• greater understanding of other cultures	• poor architectural design
• infrastructure	• crowding	• preservation of environment and appearance of an area
• local income	• alcohol and drugs	• destroying local ecosystem
• more jobs for foreigners	• I suffer from living in a tourism destination	• air pollution
• cost of living	• vandalism	• destruction of natural environment
• increase in tax base	• enhancement of cultural exchange	• restoration of historical buildings and conservation of natural resources
• quality of public services	• meeting tourist is valuable experience	• preservation of natural beauty
• retail and restaurant opportunities	• high-spending tourists have a negative effect on the way of life in a region	• traffic congestion, noise and pollution
	• shopping opportunities	• roads and other public facilities are kept at higher standard
	• community spirit	• conservation of wildlife
	• noise and pollution	
	• restoration of historic buildings	
	• positive cultural identity	
	• negative effect on local culture	

Source: Authors (2023)

- At a community level, the quality of life reflects one's satisfaction with various community conditions, such as recreation opportunities, environment, public services, neighbourhood conditions, standard of living, politics, etc. (Andereck et al., 2007; Ko & Stewart, 2002; Roehl, 1999; Vargas-Sanchez et al., 2009). These very much resemble the tourism impacts presented in Table 5.1.

The following is a discussion on a few economic impacts that we deem essential for understanding the complexities of children's quality of life in tourism destinations.

Dialectic discussions of the economic tourism impacts

In economic terms, tourism is an enabler of many things, most notably for the community to gain financial means and develop. However, research has shown that tourism maintains precarious employment, deepening economic inequalities and contributing to deep social divisions (Robinson et al., 2018). This happens despite the expansionists' claim that tourism is an industry with a massive number of employees that continues to increase, and its contributing share of GDP continues to grow. Simply put, greater circulation of capital in the tourism industry does not mean greater well-being of employees in the industry; it seems that the opposite is true in the modern neoliberal industry. For this reason, greater circulation of a greater mass of capital does not mean greater well-being for children living in intensive tourist areas; it is probably the opposite.

Tourism is also one of those industries that employ many children, whether that is visible or hidden labour. Child labour is one of the most frequently mentioned topics by authors who deal with host children (Yang et al., 2019). One estimate of child labour in the tourism industry from two decades ago suggests that between 13 and 15 million children worked worldwide, probably about 15% of the total number of people employed in world tourism that year (International Labour Office, 2002). Given that we have seen a prolific expansion of tourism in the last two decades, it is unimaginable to think of the statistics linked to child labour in tourism. However, we will expand on this in one of the chapters that follows.

This short and superficial account of child labour is another contribution to the claims about the exploitation of children, primarily in the territories of intensive tourist development. The exploitation is exercised by the locals themselves, i.e. owners of certain businesses. However, we must understand that children's parents are often exploited as well, falling victim to capital, and encourage their children to work to help support their family.

Parents can influence their children's career preferences. They do that intentionally or unintentionally when communicating about a job's advantages or disadvantages. Another form of influencing children's careers is parents imposing restrictions on the professional preferences of their children, which is carried out, for example, by choosing or limiting their education. But probably one of the most common approaches to influencing the career preferences of children is achieving their life goals through work. In other words, children observe their parents' difficulties in doing their work and the good and bad sides of their parents' profession. Children very quickly notice the extent to which parents must be absent from the family during the peak tourist season, how late at night they return tired from work –when they do not have the strength to devote themselves to, for example, their children's school problems.

Intensive tourism affects almost all dimensions of the personal and professional lives of people from tourism communities. This is evident in the employment in tourism and hospitality across different European countries. For example, the largest share of employees in tourism and hospitality is recorded in southern, less developed European countries, such as Greece (9.4%), Cyprus (8.3%), Spain (6.6%), Italy (5.4%) and Portugal (5.3%). On the other hand, the lowest percentages of employment in tourism and hospitality are in the more developed European countries, namely Denmark (1.6%), Norway (1.9%), Sweden (2.0%) and Finland (2.6%).

Moreover, the tourism industry has opened its doors widely to those in the workforce from socially deprived groups, such as women, immigrants or less educated people (Ariza-Montes et al., 2019). The reason for such an opening towards deprived groups is certainly not the democratisation of the societies in which this happens (i.e. their liberalisation) but the fact that in these communities, for a long time, there has been high unemployment in the industry. It should be said that these employees *move* from the world of unemployed marginal people into the world of the marginalised labour force, i.e. precarious workers. The precarious nature of work in this industry is well illustrated through the Spanish example, where in 2017, over 4 million hospitality work contracts were signed, with almost half lasting barely a week (Ariza-Montes et al., 2019). The true paradox of this situation is that this happens in an industry where *employees' smiles are a proxy for the company's success*. The quality of work–life balance and economic safety, essential for employees to feel good, safe and protected, enable them to perform their work joyfully and enthusiastically. However, this has been significantly disturbed in the industry recently (Deery & Jago, 2009) without a proper long-term solution in sight.

The Covid-19 pandemic only exacerbated the difficulties of employees in the service industry. It illustrated their subordinate position and their health problems due to the conditions in which they work. Finch and Finch (2020) point out that at the beginning of the pandemic, the highest percentage of infected people was recorded in areas of extreme poverty and low wages. The latter includes workers serving and maintaining urban functions such as city cleaning, public transport and food selling. All these employees either have direct contact with people or/are more frequently exposed to infected material, and at the same time, they are paid far less and are unable to work from home. Moreover, many of these workers do not have adequately regulated health insurance and very often go to work sick to avoid losing their jobs (Finch & Finch, 2020).

Using the social justice lenses, those who barely escaped the category of poverty exposed themselves to the danger of infection with the Covid-19 virus to serve the higher social strata. This is similar to the structure of service workers employed in tourism. Dramatic developments related to the pandemic led to the loss of almost half of the jobs in the United States between April and May 2020 (Chen et al., 2022). At the same time, the majority of tourism and hospitality employees lived under stress, on the one hand, from the danger of infection and its consequences, and on the other hand, from the dramatic suspension of economic activities and job loss (Chen et al., 2022). This resulted in the dramatic impoverishment of families whose economic well-being depended exclusively on economic activity in tourism. Government assistance in those economic sectors most exposed to losses due to the pandemic was directed at owners and operators of tourism and hospitality businesses rather than employees (Chen et al., 2022). Such situations are a source of personal and economic stress for employees and entire families. Chen and coauthors also showed that the stress from the risk of infection was far less intense than the stress from job loss or the necessity of changing jobs. Younger employees were under greater stress during the pandemic, because they faced issues linked to inadequate accommodation, limitations in the functioning of many public services such as kindergartens and schools, and the closing of hotels and hospitality establishments (Chen et al., 2022).

References

Andereck, K.L., Valentine, K.M., Vogt, C.A. & Knopf, R.C. (2007). A Cross-cultural analysis of tourism and quality of life perceptions. *Journal of Sustainable Tourism*, 15 (5), 483–502.

Ariza-Montes, A., Hernández-Perlines, F., Han, H. & Law, R. (2019). Human dimension of the hospitality industry: Working conditions and psychological well-being among European servers. *Journal of Hospitality and Tourism Management*, 41, 138–147.

Baldigara, T., & Duvnjak, K. (2021). The relationships between tourism and hotel industry labour market determinants and the number of graduates. *Hospitality Management*, 27 (1), 43–61.

Bestard, A.B., & Nadal, J.R. (2007). Modelling environmental attitudes toward tourism. *Tourism Management*, 28 (3), 688–695.

Bond, M.H. (2013). Refining Lewin's formula: A general model for explaining situational influence on individual social behavior. *Asian Journal of Social Psychology*, 16 (1), 1–15.

Bourdieu, P. (1986). Forms of capital. In Richardson, J.G. *Handbook of Theory and Research for the Sociology of Education*. Bloomsbury, 241–258.

Bourdieu, P. (2000). *Pascalian Meditations*. Stanford University Press.

Bourdieu, P. (2005). *The Social Structures of the Economy*. Polity Press.

Bourdieu, P., & Passeron, J.-C. (1990). *Reproduction in Education, Society and Culture*. Sage Publications.

Bowles, S., & Gintis, H. (2002). The inheritance of inequality. *The Journal of Economic Perspectives*, 16 (3), 3–30.

Brida, J., Cortés-Jiménez, I. & Pulina, M. (2016). Has the tourism-led growth hypothesis been validated? A literature review. *Current Issues in Tourism*, 19 (5), 394–430.

Bronfenbrenner, U. (1979). *The Ecology of Human Development: Experiments by nature and design.* Harvard University Press.

Carmichael, B.A. (2000). A matrix model for resident attitudes and behaviours in a rapidly changing tourist area. *Tourism Management*, 21 (6), 601–611.

Chen, C., Haupert, S.R., Zimmermann, L., Shi, X., Fritsche, L. & Mukherjee, B. (2022). Global prevalence of post-coronavirus disease 2019 (Covid-19) condition or long Covid: A meta-analysis and systematic review. *The Journal of Infectious Diseases*, 226 (9), 1593–1607.

Chen, J.S. (2015). Tourism stakeholders' attitudes toward sustainable development: A case in the Arctic. *Journal of Retailing and Consumer Services*, 22 (3), 225–230.

Cottrell, S.P., Vaske, J.J. & Roemer, J.M. (2013). Resident satisfaction with sustainable tourism: The case of Frankenwald Nature Park, Germany. *Tourism Management Perspectives*, 8, 42–48.

Crespi, F. (2006). *Sociologija kulture (Sociology of Culture).* Politička kultura.

Deery, M., & Jago, L. (2009). A framework for work-life balance practices: Addressing the needs of the tourism industry. *Tourism and Hospitality Research*, 9, 97–108.

Doepke, M., & Zilibotti, F. (2017). Parenting with style: Altruism and paternalism in intergenerational preference transmission. *Econometrica*, 85 (5), 1331–1371.

Dyer, P., Gursoy, D., Sharma, B. & Carter, J. (2007). Structural modeling of resident perceptions of tourism and associated development on the Sunshine Coast, Australia. *Tourism Management*, 28 (2), 409–422.

Fang, J., Gozgor, G., Paramati, S.R. & Wu, W. (2020). The impact of tourism growth on income inequality: Evidence from developing and developed economies. *Tourism Economics*, 20 (10), 1–23.

Finch, W.H., & Finch, H.M. (2020). Poverty and Covid-19: Rates of incidence and deaths in the United States during the first 10 weeks of the pandemic. *Frontiers in Sociology*, 5, 1–19.

Gursoy, D., & Rutherford, D.G. (2004). Host attitudes toward tourism: An improved structural model. *Annals of Tourism Research*, 31 (3), 495–516.

Hagedoorn, E. (2013). *Child Labour and Tourism.* The International Centre for Responsible Tourism.

International Labour Office (2002). *A Future Without Child Labour.* International Labour Organization.

International Labour Organization (2017). *Global Estimates of Child Labour: Results and trends, 2012–2016.* International Labour Organization.

Janta, H., & Christoub, A. (2019). Hosting as social practice: Gendered insights into contemporary tourism mobilities. *Annals of Tourism Research* 74, 167–176.

Jurowski, C., Uysal, M. & Williams, D.R. (1997). A theoretical analysis of host community resident reactions to tourism. *Journal of Travel Research*, Fall, 3–11.

Kim, K., Uysal, M. & Sirgy, M.J. (2013). How does tourism in a community impact the quality of life of community residents? *Tourism Management*, 36, 527–540.

Ko, D.W., & Stewart, W.P. (2002). A structural equation model of residents' attitudes for tourism development. *Tourism Management*, 23 (5), 521–530.

Koščak, M., Colarič-Jakše, L.-M., Fabjan, D., Kukulj, S., Založnik, S., Knežević, M., ... Prevolšek, B. (2018). No one asks the children, right? *Tourism*, 66 (4), 396–410.

Koščak, M., Knežević, M., Binder, D., Pelaez-Verdet, A., Işik, C., Mićić, V., Borisavljević, K. & Šegota, T. (2023). Exploring the neglected voices of children in sustainable tourism development: A comparative study in six European tourist destinations. *Journal of Sustainable Tourism*, 31 (2), 561–580.

Kukulj, S. (2021). Body image, sexuality and relationship quality in different phases of transition to parenthood. Doctoral thesis. Zagreb: University of Zagreb, Faculty of Humanities and Social Sciences.

Kuvan, Y., & Akan, P. (2005). Residents' attitudes toward general and forest-related impacts of tourism: The case of Belek, Antalya. *Tourism Management*, 26 (5), 691–706.

Mastny, L. (2001) Treading lightly: New paths for international tourism. In Peterson, J. A. *World Watch Paper 159*. World Watch Institute.

Nunkoo, R., & So, K.K.F. (2015). Residents' support for tourism: Testing alternative structural models. *Journal of Travel Research*, 1–15.

Perles-Ribes, J.F., Ramon-Rodríguez, A.B., Rubia, A. & Moreno-Izquierdo, L. (2017). Is the tourism-led growth hypothesis valid after the global economic and financial crisis? The case of Spain 1957–2014. *Tourism Management*, 61 (C), 96–109.

Rafky, D.M. (1971). Phenomenology and socialisation: Some comments on the assumptions underlying socialization theory. *Sociological Analysis*, 32 (1), 7–20.

Robinson, R.N., Martins, A., Solnet, D. & Baum, T. (2018). Sustaining precarity: Critically examining tourism and employment. *Journal of Sustainable Tourism*, 27 (7), 1008–1025.

Roehl, W. (1999). Quality of life issues in a casino destination. *Journal of Business Research*, 44 (3), 223–229.

Šegota, T., Mihalič, T. & Kuščer, K. (2017). The impact of residents' informedness and involvement on their perceptions of tourism impacts: The case of Bled. *Journal of Destination Marketing & Management*, 6 (3), 196–206.

Uysal, M., Sirgy, M., Woo, E. & Kim, H. (2016). Quality of life (QoL) and well-being research in tourism. *Tourism Management*, 53 (4), 244–261.

Vargas-Sanchez, A., Plaza-Mejia, M.D.L.Á. & Porras-Bueno, N. (2009). Understanding residents' attitudes toward the development of industrial tourism in a former mining community. *Journal of Travel Research*, 47 (3), 373–387.

Woo, E., Kim, H. & Uysal, M. (2015). Life satisfaction and support for tourism development. *Annals of Tourism Research*, 50, 84–97.

Yang, M.J., Yang, E.C. & Khoo-Lattimore, C. (2019). Host-children of tourism destinations: Systematic quantitative literature review. *Tourism Recreation Research*, 45 (2), 231–246.

6

REFLECTIONS ON PART II

The Key Concepts

This chapter discusses and examines the Key Concepts from each preceding chapter in Part II.

Chapter 4

The Key Concepts may be categorised as follows:

- *Understanding that the economic-centric paradigm is prevalent in discussions on tourism.* The research and practice discuss different aspects of the economic dimension of tourism, which is sometimes related to the well-being and progress of the community. Many discussions are overwhelmed with data on the share of tourism activity in the GDP of a country, region or the world, the contribution of tourism to employment, migration, education and empowerment of specific groups. This relationship between facts (recurring and precisely measured) and deep trust in these facts is *the myth of scientific value*. Such focus diminishes the importance of content about children in tourism because a large part of this role is unmeasured or challenging to measure.
- *Family tourism and child exploitation and abuse dominate the child in tourism discourse.* Whenever the issues related to children in tourism are discussed, the two mutually distant themes appear: one on exploring the influence of children on family decisions regarding tourism, and one related to child exploitation and child abuse. The first category views children as initiators of tourism activities in the family, while the second discusses social and personal pathology associated with tourism.

DOI: 10.4324/9781003374299-10

- *Tourism is omnipresent in the socialisation of children living in tourist destinations.* The dyad is the initial communication element in relationships between people from the beginning of the socialisation process. Both children and parents who are participants in a dyad exchange experiences with each other, which means children's early socialisation practices differ significantly depending on the parents' social status. Moreover, several vital factors define different educational models in different socio-economic strata: financial restrictions, time constraints, information, values and preferences about parenting and child development, family and environmental stress, and prejudices when making decisions. In tourism destinations, these are different from the areas with less intensive tourism activity.

- *Children's attitudes towards tourism are influenced by their parents, teachers, peers and the community.* Children closely follow the developments in their families and are aware of the quality and dynamics of family life linked to tourism.

Chapter 5

The Key Concepts may be categorised as follows:

- *The tourism-led growth hypothesis.* The hypothesis suggests that economic growth in the industry can be achieved through increased labour and capital and a significant increase in exports. Consequently, the world's poorest countries increasingly rely on tourism revenues to enhance their foreign exchange earnings. Thus, for the 40 poorest countries in the world, tourism becomes the most crucial factor in foreign exchange inflow. Such a neo-liberal lens on the industry stirs away from the social justice questions related to tourism communities, families and children.

- *Children in an environment of intense tourist activity.* Raising children in areas of intensive tourist activity should be understood through the notion that tourism is a source of labour-intensive activities, with parents spending most of their time away from their families, especially during the peak of the tourist season. They carry with them all the frustrations and difficulties of doing highly intensive and tourist-facing jobs, coupled with additional frustrations originating from unexpected changes in raising a family. As much as socialisation is a universal process, especially when we talk about the earliest development phase, the conditions in which it takes place for children are not universal.

- *There is no knowledge of how children perceive tourism impacts.* Children are viewed as passive objects of the socialisation process carried out by adults. Hence, we do not understand the effects of tourism on children's upbringing and quality of life. Describing children as those whose growth and development are subordinated to the action of social institutions and their complete dependence on these institutions is a simplification that prevents the development of tourism activity as a transformative social practice ensuring children's active participation in the development of their communities.

- *Economic, environmental and socio-cultural impacts of tourism.* A plethora of tourism impacts are subject to various classifications. For example, the sustainability paradigm classifies tourism impacts into three categories, i.e. economic, socio-cultural and economic impacts, that can be further classified into positive and negative sub-categories. Once a community becomes a tourism destination, a reciprocal interaction exists between perceived living conditions and perceived tourism impacts. However, we know little about how children perceive the impacts and their sense of living conditions.

- *Dialectic discussions of the economic tourism impacts.* In economic terms, tourism is an enabler of many things, most notably for the community to gain financial means and develop. However, research has shown that tourism maintains precarious employment, deepening economic inequalities and contributing to deep social divisions. This happens despite the expansionists' claim that tourism is an industry with a very large number of employees that continues to increase and contributes a growing share to GDP. Simply put, greater circulation of capital in the tourism industry does not mean greater employee well-being.

The Critical Factors

Challenges to family life

Embracing tourism as a means of community economic development has its benefits and costs. One of the costs rarely discussed is how high-intensity tourism affects children's socialisation. Its challenges affect family life, where parents employed in tourism and hospitality work long hours, change shifts, earn less and are tired, contributing to spending less quality time with children. Moreover, working in the tourism industry did not contribute to family bonding or increase the harmony and functionality of family life, although it increased material security. All these challenges need better understanding to be efficiently addressed and mitigated, and thus, for tourism to stay on the path of being praised for its positive transformative power.

Tourism is stress

Once a community becomes a tourism destination, it shares its resources with residents and tourists. This causes stress – positive and negative. Residents in tourism communities experience stress regardless of how many people visit the area. Each tourist causes stress in philosophical terms. Parents who raise their children in stressful circumstances pass on to them their stress and the stress experienced by people in their immediate and distant environment. Perhaps this is one of the reasons for children's relatively low interest in tourism professions, which is observed in many tourist areas.

Us vs them

Belonging to a community, or identifying and having a sense of place, is one of the most widespread topics in sociology and many other social disciplines, such as anthropology and economics. Some tourism scholars treat belonging to a local community as being branded by sharing values, consciousness, rituals and traditions, and a sense of *us* versus *them*. This represents a danger to a community's symbolic value, uniqueness and cultural unity.

Avoiding delineation caused by ICT

A critical issue is understanding how information communication technology (ICT) affects children's sense of place and alienates tourists from locals. ICT allows tourists quick and rich information searches, but also allows them to voice their satisfaction or dissatisfaction using electronic word of mouth. Consequently, children growing up in tourist-intensive areas also have access to information about their community, including various opinions about that destination, often transmitted in a direct and not even slightly embellished form. The critique can be very impactful and distressing for locals, which is worth addressing by destination managers. On the other hand, ICT can alienate locals from tourists because the tourists seek less advice and guidance at the destination. This creates an ever-widening and deepening alienation gap between guests and hosts, making host children invisible and causing them to miss out on essential socialisation benefits through tourism.

Quality of life of host children – the great unknown

"Too young to know" is often used to justify why children are not included in tourism planning and development. A big mistake! Children are drivers of innovation and development, and as they strive to grow, learn and improve, they are aware of their role in taking concrete actions for a sustainable future. Instead of unjustifiable silencing of children, policymakers, researchers, and industry professionals should make young people an integral part of the decision-making process. Their ideas are fresh, imaginative and innovative and can help advance strategies for improving the quality of life in tourism destinations. Children and young people might not know what they want, but they are confident in knowing what they do not want, and that is for tourism to affect their life negatively. However, we are yet to uncover what children believe the quality of life is, how it changes with their development and how tourism affects it, both positively and negatively.

Connections

In this section, we suggest some elements based on the issues raised in Part II. We uncovered and discussed some critical "incidents" where tourism should exaggerate and promote socially just transformations instead of focusing on economic achievements. The relationship between communities and tourism is complex, and we need to deviate from a unidimensional perspective. By understanding how tourism affects life in a community, from its youngest members to those employed in the industry, we should also ensure that the momentum to create *just* tourism is the prerequisite of the future. Furthermore, we must embrace our ignorance or disinterest in knowing about tourism's influence on family life and the socialisation of children and actively work on assessing the impacts, refreshing the perspectives and improving strategies to address tourism impacts holistically. Following these underlying discussions, we have sought to develop some connections for readers as follows:

- For students, we pose some questions which may assist the connections between teaching and learning.
- For researchers (graduate or professional), we suggest some guidelines for further research.
- For practitioners, we raise matters of concern for their progress in balancing economic gain with the socially just transformational power of tourism.

Teaching and learning

Students should discuss the following points:

a   Tourism's contribution to community development is usually inundated with numbers that expose direct and indirect financial gains and job creation. However, growth is not exclusively an economic term. What are other perspectives on tourism's effects on the community?

b   Socialisation is one of the most important processes in one's life. Children are exposed to the opinions, experiences and conduct of adults (i.e. parents, teachers, community members). In that sense, what are tourism's less explicit effects on children?

c   We are presenting with two theses: 1) tourism is an industry of high-intensity labour, and 2) tourism brings stress to communities. How do these two theses manifest in tourist communities with links to family life and social upbringing?

d   Once a community becomes a tourism destination, tourism impacts are omnipresent. How do children experience these impacts, and which are most relevant for their socialisation?

Guidelines for researchers

Researchers may wish to consider the following:

a   Little is known about children's attitudes towards tourism and how tourism affects their quality of life. What paradigm shifts are needed to move away from the tourism-led growth hypothesis and embrace fresh and innovative perceptions of one of the most marginalised groups in tourism communities?

b   *Let's bring back tourismology.* The attempt to establish the discipline of *tourismology* did not achieve a broader consensus. Thus, tourism academics rely on concepts from other disciplines, making tourism multidisciplinary in nature that does little to avoid being trapped in self-limitation in a specific discipline. Perhaps researching the tourism–children relationships represents an opportunity to revive the creation of a unique discipline, i.e. tourismology, which would cover tourism in all its depth and breadth.

c   The transformation and disruption of tourist communities make tourism a powerful social force. Its economic benefits and costs are widely known and explicitly measured, while other impacts are scarcely operationalised through measurements. Since children are not perceived as direct financial beneficiaries of tourism development until adulthood, how can research on children help improve our understanding of other-than-financial tourism relationships?

Keynotes for practitioners

Practitioners may wish to review the following points:

a   How do we radically reconsider the juxtaposition of high labour intensity and low wages for a socially just transformation of tourism?

b   How do we fundamentally redesign the growth of the tourism and hospitality industry by balancing financial gains and social effects delicately?

c   How do we create strategies to improve the position of employees in the industry to mitigate the effects on one's well-being and family life?

PART III

What are children doing for tourism?

INTRODUCTION TO PART III

Historically, children have been "contributing" to tourism in many ways. The literature recognises child labour and strongly condemns it. However, many (unintentionally) turn a blind eye to the so-called invisible sacrifice, which is often witnessed in highly seasonal destinations. This includes children giving away their private space (i.e. rooms) in the summer so parents can use the space as rent-for-tourism accommodation. Similarly, many underaged children are employed as high school students, interns or apprentices in hospitality and tourism to help their parents during the season or to "make a buck" for the winter. Willing or unwilling children's contributions to tourism will be discussed through two chapters represented by the following topics: witnessed vs invisible child labour, tourism seasonality and co-sharing space with tourists, and children's perceptions of current and future employment tourism opportunities.

In Chapter 7 we posit that child labour is condemnable! Childhood should essentially be about discovery, play, enjoyment and learning. Thus we wish to expose the hidden practices many academics fail to see – the invisible child labour masked under tourism and hospitality apprenticeship or family-owned tourism businesses. We will also discuss the issues of seasonality and co-sharing space with tourists, which makes many children unwilling and unknowingly become "victims" of tourism activity that simultaneously contributes to and depletes their quality of life. For example, many highly seasonal tourism destinations are focused on huge demand for accommodation facilities. As a result of this demand, many families offer their living space to tourists or invite them to co-share the place. Naturally, such activity will benefit the family financially, but it is currently a non-researched area as to how children feel about sharing their living space with strangers. In this chapter, we wish to raise awareness of similar cases that we know exist and are frequent in highly seasonal destinations.

DOI: 10.4324/9781003374299-12

In Chapter 8 we review the tourism industry through the lens of its employment opportunities and weaknesses and how that may influence children's attitudes towards tourism. Many tourism destinations have suffered from staff shortages in hospitality and tourism in the recent decade. This worsened during the Covid-19 pandemic as many employees took up new opportunities outside of tourism and hospitality or migrated to their homeland. Children recognise that the industry creates employment opportunities. However, they also realise that work demands an all-day commitment and negatively affects family life. These perceptions may have created a sense of indecision or indeed opposition towards the concept of potential employment in tourism and hospitality. Such perceptions undoubtedly do little to change the view of tourism becoming a desired life orientation and a force for social change.

In Chapter 9 we summarise the Key Concepts and Critical Factors in the two preceding chapters, as well as examine the most appropriate Connections for students, researchers and practitioners.

7

CHILD LABOUR, TOURISM AND SEASONALITY

Introduction

When it comes to children, tourism is one of those world industries that employ a considerable number of children, despite the long-term efforts of many organisations to try to ban child labour. Child labour is one of the most frequently mentioned topics by authors who deal with the area of children hosts (Yang et al., 2019). One estimate of child labour dating back to 2002 suggests that between 13 and 15 million children worked in the industry worldwide, probably about 15% of the total number of people employed in world tourism that year. They worked in primarily lower-paid jobs such as porters and maids, dishwashers, beach guards, shopkeepers and golf caddies (International Labour Organization, 2021). The International Labour Organization (ILO) estimated that only 5% of employed children worked in the formal economy, while the rest were abused by local entrepreneurs, especially in child sex jobs. Of course, the users of child sexual services are foreign tourists, but those who benefit materially from this work are people from local communities (International Labour Organization, 2021). Most of the jobs in the tourism industry where children work are jobs where working hours are long, jobs are insecure, wages are low and labour laws are often violated (Hagedoorn, 2013).

Of course, most jobs where children are employed are not jobs the public can generally observe. We often talk about jobs hidden from the public eye and mostly dangerous for children's health. This does not mean only jobs in sex tourism, for example, but also many jobs outside of that heinous activity, which can represent a significant health hazard for the children who have to do them. For example, travel companies and travellers do not often ask who cleaned the room, washed the vegetables or made a craft product (Hagedoorn, 2013). This short and superficial account of child labour is another contribution

DOI: 10.4324/9781003374299-13

to the claims about the exploitation of children, primarily in the territories of intensive tourist development. It happens primarily at that hands of the local population, i.e. owners of certain businesses and trades who exploit child labour. In this exploitation of children, often in the roughest and most complex ways, their parents are often forced to participate as well. They also fall victim to the owners of businesses and trade and succumb to engaging their children to financially support, often very large, families.

Child labour in numbers

According to the International Labour Organization (2021), child labour globally remains at high levels, particularly child labour that is hazardous or exploitative. Across the world, there are 160 million children aged 5–17 who are engaging in child labour, predominantly in family-based economic activities, of which most are in agriculture. In Europe, the USA and Canada, the level of employment in the 15–17 age group is around 3.8 million (2% of the global level). In these northern hemisphere advanced economies, exploitative child labour appears in marginalised socio-economic situations, more particularly among deprived immigrant populations and ethnic groups such as Roma. Employment of young people makes them disadvantaged in the workplace; those aged 15–24 have an unemployment rate three times greater than those aged 25 and over. A significant issue is that around 24% of young people globally (i.e. from compulsory school leaving age to 24 years old) are not in education, employment or training. Over five years, between 2012 and 2016, as many as 152 million children in the world were forced to work, and 73 million worked in jobs that can be considered dangerous for their health and their lives (International Labour Organization, 2017).

As we mentioned earlier, it is rare for travel companies and travellers to question who cleaned the room, washed the vegetables or made the craft. However, the ILO numbers show that the likelihood of travellers unknowingly benefiting from child labour is alarmingly high. The estimates for children working in tourism range from 13 to 19 million children under the age of 18, which accounts for around 10–15% of the formal tourism labour market (Hagedoorn, 2013). We would suggest that numbers are probably much higher, considering that the informal/unofficial/hidden work was not included in the estimates. Sexual exploitation of 12- to 18-year-olds is also apparent in poor-to-middle-income countries where tourists are highly present (e.g., the Caribbeans, Thailand and the Philippines).

The most common stereotype is that the problem of child labour is limited to less developed countries in Africa, Asia and Central and South America, or the so-called Global South. However, we also find child labour in European countries, such as Portugal, Spain and Italy. For example, in Spain, around 200,000 children under the age of 14 were employed in small production facilities, mainly for footwear production (International Labour Organization, 2017).

BOX 7.1 CASE STUDY: CHILD LABOUR IN SERBIA

The West Balkan countries outside the EU and without advanced EU candidate status have a poor economic situation (e.g. Albania, Bosnia and Hercegovina, Montenegro, North Macedonia and Serbia). Furthermore, they also have high levels of *informal* child employment. A recent report by the International Labour Organization (2023) indicates that 19.7% of Serbian children aged 15–17 were casually employed household heads, and 13.3% were children with formally employed household heads. Among children in households where both parents are employed, the child labour rate is 11.2%, while the rate is 8.2% if only one parent works and drops to 4.5% if both parents do not work. This appears to reflect the concentration of child labour in the Serbian agriculture sector, where children are often engaged in agriculture with their parents as unpaid family workers. The percentage of children in agriculture is 60% in the age group 15–17, where 70% say they partake in jobs to supplement the family income.

In Serbia, children aged 15–17 work 23 hours per week, although this rises to 30 hours in urban areas (International Labour Organization, 2023). The Serbian youth unemployment rate stands at 26.4%, underperforming the EU average of 16.6%. Informal employment for 15–17-year-olds (i.e. unregistered with tax or labour services) stands at 16.4%, whilst unpaid family workers represent 4.6%, which means that 21% of youths are operating in the *grey economy*. Furthermore, whilst 84% of the 15–17 population attend secondary school, a further 10% attend school and hold part-time jobs.

Tourism seasonality

The consensus in the literature is that tourism is subject to natural and institutional seasonality (Butler, 2001), which are often complementary rather than unrelated events. A destination's climatic conditions, such as day length, insolation, the temperature of the air and sea (or rivers and lakes), relative humidity, rainfall, etc., are considered determinants of *natural seasonality* (Mihalič & Kaspar, 1996). However, *institutional seasonality* results from human decisions concerning the time to take a vacation, which is influenced by religion, culture, ethnicity, fashion and socio-political factors (BarOn, 1975; Butler, 2001; Hartman, 1986). Therefore, natural and institutional seasonalities predetermine the availability of natural, social and cultural attractions and related activities. In other words, seasonality, the tendency of tourist flows to become concentrated in short periods of the year, causes a temporal imbalance related to the peaking and overuse of community resources (Butler, 2001).

According to Koenig-Lewis and Bischoff (2005), these determinants trigger *in the same place, at the same time* an influx of tourists, regarding which Butler and Mao (1997) identified three basic patterns – non-peak, one-peak and two-peak. Non-peak seasonality means tourism activities occur throughout the year

(Karamustafa & Ulama, 2010). One-peak seasonality is represented by tourism activities occurring in specific months, with no or little activity during the rest of the year. Such examples are sun and beach tourism destinations, for which it has been shown that most tourist visitation occurs during the warm summer months (Andriotis, 2005; Fernández-Morales, 2003; Kožić, 2013; Nadal et al., 2004; Šegota & Mihalič, 2018; Volo, 2010). Two-peak seasonality refers to tourism activities in two seasons (Karamustafa & Ulama, 2010). And it is the latter two patterns (i.e. one-peak and two-peak) that make up the essence of the seasonality problem: "an uneven distribution of use over time (peaking) [that is] causing inefficient resource use, loss of profit potential, the strain on social and ecological carrying capacities, and administrative scheduling difficulties" (Manning & Powers, 1984, p. 25). Moreover, Trajkov et al. (2016) expressed that these peaks or short intervals of tourist concentration are repeated yearly, making them difficult to change or mitigate.

Negative and positive outcomes of seasonality

Seasonality outcomes have been researched from both the supply side (i.e. employees, locals, tourism operators) and the demand side (i.e. tourists). Studying the supply-side effects, seasonality was seen as having largely negative impact in economic environment of the destination, emphasising mainly different types of costs (e.g. the increase in prices, income instability, recruiting costs) (Ball, 1989; Krakover, 2000; Commons & Page, 2001; Jang, 2004), resource utilisation (Van der Werff, 1980; Jeffrey & Hubbard, 1988; Commons & Page, 2001; Jang, 2004) and employment (Clarke, 1981; Ball, 1989; Witt & Moutinho, 1994; Krakover, 2000; Commons & Page, 2001; Goulding et al., 2005). Additionally, there is an increase in research focusing on the natural environment (Mathieson & Wall, 1982; Murphy, 1985; Pearce, 1989; Muir & Chester, 1993; Witt & Moutinho, 1994; Butler, 2001), and socio-cultural environment (Murphy, 1985; Cuccia & Rizzo, 2011).

Focusing on the demand side, seasonality was seen as harming visitors' satisfaction because of crowding (Jang, 2004). Moreover, crowding is often connected to increasing vulnerability to safety and threats (Jang, 2004), reduction of available accommodation (Krakover, 2000), putting pressure on the transport system and infrastructure (Commons & Page, 2001) and resulting in low-quality holidays for tourists (Jang, 2004).

However, Grant et al. (1997) suggest that the off-season is usually a time when maintenance work on buildings and attractions is scheduled, whilst Murphy (1985) noted that many communities relieve the stress accumulated during the peak season, which helps to *normalise* the traditional social patterns that have been disrupted. Moreover, Butler (2001) and Hartman (1986) suggested that the off-season allows fragile environments in highly seasonal destinations to rejuvenate and recuperate so that visitors can again admire their delicate nature once the visitations re-start.

Responses to seasonality

Several approaches to managing seasonality exist (Butler, 2001; Jang, 2004; Koenig-Lewis & Bischoff, 2005). The first is to develop appropriate tourism products that include all-weather activities and facilities (Andriotis, 2005). The second approach relates to different pricing incentives (i.e. discounts and special offers) during the off-season (Andriotis, 2005; Butler, 2001). Baum and Hagen (1999) believe that this approach might damage the business in the long run since aggressive pricing might do more to damage a destination's overall reputation. The third approach refers to attracting new market segments in the off-season periods, with researchers proposing to focus on attracting tourists whose activities would not be too weather-sensitive. For example, in the case of Andalusia, Cisneros-Martínez and Fernández-Morales (2015) suggest focusing on domestic tourists interested in cultural attractions and activities. Similarly, Fernández-Morales and Mayorga-Toledano (2008) propose attracting British and Nordic tourists to Costa del Sol in Spain in the winter months.

Finally, another approach is to develop so-called seasonality coping mechanisms (Andriotis, 2005; Nunkoo & Ramkissoon, 2011), which have been considered economically unattractive. The ultimate rigorous measures of the tourism industry would be to either close some facilities to save costs "when it is not possible to increase the demand outside the peak season substantially" (Koenig-Lewis & Bischoff, 2005, p. 213) or to carry out some renovation works in the off-season aiming to improve tourism infrastructure and services (Mathieson & Wall, 1982; Weaver & Oppermann, 2000).

Tourism seasonality and its impact on children

Living in a tourism destination means that adults need to bear the positives and negatives of tourism. As do children. However, when researchers, practitioners and policy-makers discuss strategies to mitigate tourism seasonality, they look at the community as a whole, not as a synthesis of different groups. However, some groups may be more affected by seasonality than others.

Housing problems of families and children

Housing for residents and tourists alike has been at the centre of academic debate for over a decade. Issues were raised over second-home ownership (Hao et al., 2011; Litvin et al., 2013; Mantecón & Huete, 2011) and peer-to-peer accommodation (Garau-Vadell et al., 2019; Paulauskaite et al., 2017; Stergiou & Farmaki, 2020) decreasing opportunities for the resident to find appropriate and affordable housing. European destinations like Croatia, Slovenia, Montenegro and Albania have seen a decline in housing buildings and expansion in the uncontrolled development of houses exclusively used for tourism. Such growth is taking its toll on residential housing (Bertocchi & Visentin, 2019;

Pavlić et al., 2019; Seraphin et al., 2018). Moreover, this also makes these communities vulnerable to house price hikes due to tourism (Vizek et al., 2022). In addition, communities also partake in privatising socially owned housing stock and denationalisation (Bejaković & Mrnjavac, 2019). The latter might have helped many buy apartments to rent to tourists.

Several issues with seasonality and children's lives in tourism communities are linked to housing. For example, single-peek tourism seasonality enabled the following accommodation malpractice: property owners would offer their apartments or houses to residents from late autumn to early spring (i.e. October to March), whilst they would expect a tenant to vacate the property to make space for tourists in summer. Such malpractice affects children tremendously. Firstly, children need stability in terms of housing, without having to move from one place to another during the school year. They need to have a safe and secure space where they can learn and grow. Also, in many countries, only in exceptional circumstances will a child change several schools of the same level during their education. An exceptional case is not moving houses within the community. Hence, if a child is forced to move homes within a community area, they will likely face other seasonal issues linked to traffic congestion and limited transport.

Single-peek tourism seasonality also sees many families renting their whole homes or inviting tourists to share the space during summer. As much as this gives the tourists a special flavour of local life and an authentic peek into family life, this could have severe consequences for children. If the family moves briefly in summer and rents their home for direct financial benefits, children might develop a special sentiment that we coin as *not in my bed (NIMB)*. This is very similar to NIMBY, the shortened form of "not in my backyard", which signifies one's opposition to the locating of something considered undesirable in one's neighbourhood (Britannica, n.d.). Conversely, NIMB, or not in my bed, means children's opposition to their beds being used for accommodating tourists.

However, some families open their doors to tourists. Such practice has significantly increased with the popularisation of peer-to-peer accommodation, which sees families renting parts of their homes to tourists. The smallest room may be the first to be rented, meaning children's room. Moreover, "do not talk to strangers" is usually a prevalent phrase in parenting, while we see the opposite in co-sharing homes with tourists. This gives mixed signals to children and plays a role in their socialisation that we know very little about.

BOX 7.2 CASE STUDY: PRIVATE ACCOMMODATION IN CROATIA

Croatia is one of the countries that attracts visitors with its natural and cultural heritage, while the quality and variety of newly opened tourist attractions are lagging in the offering. The most important natural attraction is the sea, an indented coast with many islands and preserved beaches. The country is rich in national and nature parks, with numerous cultural and historical attractions protected by UNESCO. Numerous city centres are also protected by UNESCO, making them hotspots for tourists, which has encouraged the emergence of small hotels and private accommodation facilities (i.e. apartments and rooms). Some examples are the historical Old Town of Dubrovnik, Diocletian's Palace in Split, the historical city of Trogir and the city of Hvar (Matešić, 2008; Puljić et al., 2019).

Current figures show that over 106,000 households are engaged in renting, with more than 600,000 beds registered, accounting for about 60% of the total accommodation in Croatian tourism (Croatian Tourist Office, 2023). Household facilities had 44 million overnight stays in Croatia in 2022, slightly less than half of all overnight stays. At the same time, this is the accommodation segment with the shortest season, with 15% annual occupancy (Croatian Ministry of Tourism and Sport, 2023).

Crowding and children

Overtourism might be a new buzzword for the negative impacts associated with crowing, yet the issue of "in the same place, at the same time" tourism and its consequences remain a constant (Mihalič, 2020). As previously discussed, tourism seasonality is one of the characteristics of coastal destinations. It might represent a "way of life" (Andriotis, 2005) because residents developed different coping mechanisms to deal with tourism-related stress (Jordan et al., 2015; Jordan, Lesar et al., 2019). Children and young people form opinions about tourism based on where they live in a tourism destination (closer to spots of tourist activity), if their family is economically dependent on tourism (i.e. family members or distant relatives employed in tourism, family business with direct links to tourism) and what type of tourism activity is dominant. Research has shown that children living in rural tourism destinations will have different perspectives from those living in urban destinations (Knežević et al., 2020).

Tourism creates employment and economic opportunities but also damages natural and cultural environments (Koščak & O'Rourke, 2023). This has been exacerbated by overtourism, where there are some scenarios linked to children that researchers and practitioners need to take into consideration:

a   Large numbers of tourists may create traffic jams and overuse public transport. Thus, children travelling from home to school and back face significant traffic congestion and inability to use public transport, which delays and impedes their journeys.

b   Overtourism may result in the physical degradation of the natural environment, such as destroying paths, forest walks or city streets by the sheer impact of their footfall. Unjustifiably, children are deprived of enjoying the natural resources in their community.

c   Large-scale tourism affects children by promoting knowledge of languages used by the top visiting markets (for example, in Europe, these are English,

German, Italian, French, Russian and Chinese). The results are to the detriment of local languages, including regional dialects.

d Gentrification of local culture demotes local culture and heritage to a theme-park level; it converts the history, culture and landscape into a "Disney World" spectacle for the sole purpose of satisfying tourists' desire for authentic experiences.

e Tourism creates large numbers of low-paid, exploitative jobs with harsh working hours. If the local population is unhappy to accept these jobs at the pay and conditions offered, this may lead to an influx of foreign workers, which then aggravates the potential for racial conflicts in tourism areas.

In the years leading up to the pandemic, residents in many tourism destinations started mobilising against tourism, demanding immediate actions against the negative impacts of tourism. Hence, we have witnessed residents and groups in Barcelona, Mallorca, Venice and Dubrovnik marching across the cities, expressing their dissatisfaction with tourism (Coldwell, 2017; Puljić et al., 2019). The marches or the mobilisation against tourism known as the anti-tourist movements (Bertocchi et al., 2020; Seraphin et al., 2018) are a result of the rapid increase in visitor numbers in destinations and place changes that residents perceived to be negative, despite various direct or indirect economic benefits felt by individuals and communities. On the other hand, the Covid-19 pandemic shocked tourism to unimaginable proportions, and its dramatic economic and social effects were experienced by travel, hotel, food, entertainment and other related businesses (Schmöcker, 2021). At the same time, some residents whose income was not dependent on tourism appeared relieved and took back control of the streets and their cities to enjoy them without large crowds. For example, during the pandemic, Kyoto residents enjoyed cherry blossoms at major sights instead of travelling out of the city to avoid crowds (Schmöcker, 2021). However, the post-pandemic period is not looking bright. The once mass tourism destinations are again inviting tourists despite their residents experiencing the negative impacts of tourism.

The pre- and post-pandemic situations described above relate to the values and trade-offs between economic, social, cultural and environmental factors of social exchange in tourism. The pre-pandemic situation might have looked like people were "biting the hand that feeds them", while the post-pandemic situation could result in people "biting their tongues" when tourists return to the community. The hand–tongue biting idioms here related to how people place values on community resources being shared with tourists and how they perceive tourism impacts and respond to them. Hence, limiting the number of one-day visitors, tourists and private accommodations may have been a low priority in some destinations. Also, studies suggested that during the pandemic, the mobility of people was not entirely restricted, and many destinations might have experienced an influx of domestic tourists (Cvelbar et al., 2021; Schmöcker, 2021). The latter could have helped residents develop emotional solidarity with tourists (Woosnam & Norman, 2010), which was reported to influence support for tourism positively (Joo et al., 2021; Maruyama et al., 2017; Woosnam & Norman, 2010).

Regarding children, studies on how children perceive tourism pre- and post-pandemic are relatively non-existent. Some studies were done before the pandemic but have not been repeated post-Covid-19. A survey of notable mentions was done by a research team from Croatia that used cognitive neuroscience to reflect on exposure and behavioural consequences of Covid-19 in the Croatian city of Dubrovnik (Mandić et al., 2023). Delving into the nuanced experiences of the youngest residents of Dubrovnik, the research unveiled several significant insights into how overtourism shapes their daily lives, aspirations and perceptions of the place they call home. Interestingly, they exhibited sadness when exposed to pictures containing fewer visitors than the *new normal* of the record-breaking period in Dubrovnik's tourism between 2015 and 2020. This means that children's perceptions of crowing are different from adults'. As much as the study in Dubrovnik is a breakthrough in research on children, more such studies are needed to get a better overview of the influence of tourism seasonality on children's lives.

References

Andriotis, K. (2005). Seasonality in Crete: Problem or a way of life? *Tourism Economics*, 11 (2), 207–224. https://doi.org/10.5367/0000000054183478.

Ball, R.M. (1989). Some aspects of tourism, seasonality and local labour markets. *Area*, 2(1), 35–45.

BarOn, R.R.V. (1975). *Seasonality in Tourism – A guide to the analysis of seasonality and trends for policy making*. Technical Series No. 2, The Economist Intelligence Unit.

Baum, T., & Hagen, L. (1999). Responses to seasonality: The experiences of peripheral destinations. *International Journal of Tourism Research*, 1 (Sept/Oct), 299–312.

Bejaković, P., & Mrnjavac, Ž. (2019). Housing policy and labour market in Croatia. In Gladoić Håkansson, P. & Bohman, H. *Investigating Spatial Inequalities*. Emerald Publishing, 159–173. https://doi.org/10.1108/978-1-78973-941-120191010.

Bertocchi, D., Camatti, N., Giove, S., & van der Borg, J. (2020). Venice and overtourism: Simulating sustainable development scenarios through a tourism carrying capacity model. *Sustainability (Switzerland)*, 12 (2). https://doi.org/10.3390/su12020512.

Britannica (n.d.). NIMBY (online). https://www.britannica.com/topic/NIMBY.

Butler, R.W. (2001). Seasonality in tourism: Issues and implications. In Baum, T. & Lundtorp, S. *Seasonality in Tourism*. Elsevier, 5–22.

Butler, R.W., & Mao, B. (1997). Seasonality in tourism: Problems and measurement. In Murphy, P.E. *Quality Management in Urban Tourism*. Wiley, 9–23.

Cisneros-Martínez, J.D., & Fernández-Morales, A. (2015). Cultural tourism as tourist segment for reducing seasonality in a coastal area: The case study of Andalusia. *Current Issues in Tourism*, 18 (8), 765–784. https://doi.org/10.1080/13683500.2013.861810.

Clarke, A. (1981). Coastal development in France. *Annals of Tourism Research*, 8 (3), 447–461. https://doi.org/10.1016/0160-7383(81)90008–90006.

Coldwell, W. (2017). First Venice and Barcelona: Now anti-tourism marches spread across Europe. *The Guardian*. https://www.theguardian.com/travel/2017/aug/10/anti-tourism-marches-spread-across-europe-venice-barcelona.

Commons, J., & Page, S. (2001). Managing seasonality in peripheral tourism regions: The case of Northland, New Zealand. In Baum, T. & Lundtorp, S. *Seasonality in Tourism.* Pergamon, 153–172.

Croatian Ministry of Tourism and Sport (2023). *Turizam u brojkama 2022.* https://www.htz.hr/sites/default/files/2023-07/HTZ%20TUB%20HR_%202022.pdf.

Croatian Tourist Office (2023). *Smještajni kapaciteti Hrvatskog turizma s analizom popunjenosti i sezonalnosti prometa prema vrstama smještajnih kapaciteta – izdanje 2022.* https://www.htz.hr/sites/default/files/2023-01/Smje%C5%A1tajni%20kapaciteti%20Hrvatske%20-%20analiza%20popunjenosti%20-%20izdanje%202022_0.pdf.

Cuccia, T., & Rizzo, I. (2011). Tourism seasonality in cultural destinations: Empirical evidence from Sicily. *Tourism Management,* 32 (3), 589–595. https://doi.org/10.1016/j.tourman.2010.05.008.

Cvelbar, L.K., Farčnik, D. & Ogorevc, M. (2021). Holidays for all: Staycation vouchers during Covid-19. *Annals of Tourism Research Empirical Insights,* 2 (2), 100019.

Fernández-Morales, A. (2003). Decomposing seasonal concentration. *Annals of Tourism Research,* 30 (4), 942–956. https://doi.org/10.1016/S0160-7383(03)00090–00092.

Fernández-Morales, A., & Mayorga-Toledano, M.C. (2008). Seasonal concentration of the hotel demand in Costa del Sol: A decomposition by nationalities. *Tourism Management,* 29 (5), 940–949. https://doi.org/10.1016/j.tourman.2007.11.003.

Garau-Vadell, J.B., Gutiérrez-Taño, D. & Díaz-Armas, R. (2019). Residents' support for P2P accommodation in mass tourism destinations. *Journal of Travel Research,* 58 (4), 549–565. https://doi.org/10.1177/0047287518767067.

Goulding, P.J., Baum, T.G. & Morrison, A.J. (2005). Seasonal trading and lifestyle motivation. *Journal of Quality Assurance in Hospitality & Tourism,* 5 (2–4), 209–238. https://doi.org/10.1300/J162v05n02_11.

Grant, M., Human, B. & Le Pelley, B. (1997). Seasonality. *Insights,* 9 (1), 5–9.

Hagedoorn, E. (2013). Child labour and tourism. How travel companies can reduce child labour in tourism destinations. Occasional Paper 25 for the ICRT, Durham, United Kingdom. https://respect.international/wp-content/uploads/2017/10/Child-Labour-and-Tourism.pdf.

Hao, H., Long, P. & Kleckley, J. (2011). Factors predicting homeowners' attitudes toward tourism: A case of a coastal resort community. *Journal of Travel Research,* 50 (6), 627–640. https://doi.org/10.1177/0047287510385463.

Hartman, R. (1986). Tourism, seasonality and social change. *Leisure Studies,* 5 (1), 25–33. https://doi.org/10.1080/02614368600390021.

International Labour Organization (2017). *Global Estimates of Child Labour: Results and trends, 2012–2016.* https://www.ilo.org/wcmsp5/groups/public/—dgreports/—dcomm/documents/publication/wcms_575499.pdf.

International Labour Organization (2021). *Child Labour: Global estimates 2020, trends and the road forward.* https://www.ilo.org/ipec/Informationresources/WCMS_797515/lang–en/index.htm.

International Labour Organization (2023). *ILO Report on Child Labour in Serbia.* https://www.ilo.org/wcmsp5/groups/public/—ed_norm/—ipec/documents/publication/wcms_888666.pdf.

Jang, S.C. (2004). Mitigating tourism seasonality – A quantitative approach. *Annals of Tourism Research,* 31 (4), 819–836. https://doi.org/10.1016/j.annals.2004.02.007.

Jeffrey, D., & Hubbard, N.J. (1988). Temporal dimensions and regional patterns of hotel occupancy performance in England: A time series analysis of midweek and weekend occupancy rates in 266 hotels, in 1984 and 1985. *International Journal of Hospitality Management,* 7 (1), 63–80. https://doi.org/10.1016/0278-4319(88)90010–90012.

Joo, D., Xu, W., Lee, J., Lee, C.K. & Woosnam, K.M. (2021). Residents' perceived risk, emotional solidarity, and support for tourism amidst the Covid-19 pandemic. *Journal of Destination Marketing and Management*, 19 (January), 100553.

Jordan, E. J., Lesar, L. & Spencer, D. M. (2019). Clarifying the Interrelations of Residents' Perceived Tourism-Related Stress, Stressors, and Impacts. *Journal of Travel Research*. https://doi.org/10.1177/0047287519888287.

Jordan, E. J., Vogt, C. A. & DeShon, R. P. (2015). A stress and coping framework for understanding resident responses to tourism development. *Tourism Management*, 48 (June), 500–512. https://doi.org/10.1016/j.tourman.2015.01.002.

Karamustafa, K., & Ulama, S. (2010). Measuring the seasonality in tourism with the comparison of different methods. *EuroMed Journal of Business*, 5 (2), 191–214. https://doi.org/10.1108/14502191011065509.

Knežević, M., Koščak, M., O'Rourke, T. & Šegota, T. (2020). Inter-generational concepts of sustainability and the role of children in local tourism destinations. In Koščak, M., & O'Rourke, T. *Ethical and Responsible Tourism – Managing sustainability in local tourism*, 1st edition. Routledge, 129–141.

Koenig-Lewis, N., & Bischoff, E.E. (2005). Seasonality research: The state of the art. *International Journal of Tourism Research*, 7 (4–5), 201–219.

Koščak, M., & O'Rourke, T. (2023). *Ethical and Responsible Tourism – Managing sustainability in local tourism*, 2nd edition. Routledge.

Kožić, I. (2013). Kolika je sezonalnost turizma u Hrvatskoj? *Ekonomski Vjesnik*, 26 (2), 470–480.

Krakover, S. (2000). Partitioning seasonal employment in the hospitality industry. *Tourism Management*, 21 (5), 461–471. https://doi.org/10.1016/S0261-5177(99)00101–00106.

Litvin, S.W., Xu, G., Ferguson, A.C. & Smith, W.W. (2013). Too attractive for its own good? South of broad, second/vacation-homes and resident attitudes. *Tourism Management Perspectives*, 7, 89–98. https://doi.org/10.1016/j.tmp.2013.04.003.

Mandić, A., Pavlić, I., Puh, B. & Séraphin, H. (2023). Children and overtourism: A cognitive neuroscience experiment to reflect on exposure and behavioural consequences. *Journal of Sustainable Tourism*, 1–28. https://doi.org/10.1080/09669582.2023.2278023.

Manning, R. E., & Powers, L. A. (1984). Peak and off-peak use: Redistributing the outdoor recreation/tourism load. *Journal of Travel Research*, 23 (2), 25–31. https://doi.org/10.1177/004728758402300204.

Mantecón, A., & Huete, R. (2011). Sociological insights on residential tourism: Host society attitudes in a mature destination. *European Journal of Tourism Research*, 4 (2), 109–122.

Maruyama, N.U., Woosnam, K.M. & Boley, B.B. (2017). Residents' attitudes toward ethnic neighborhood tourism (ENT): Perspectives of ethnicity and empowerment. *Tourism Geographies*, 19 (2), 265–286.

Matešić, M. (2008). *Strategija održivog razvoja: Krovni razvojni dokument RH*. https://hrcak.srce.hr/file/57548.

Mathieson, A., & Wall, G. (1982). *Tourism: Economic, physical and social impacts*. Longman.

Mihalič, T. (2020). Concpetualising overtourism: A sustainability approach. *Annals of Tourism Research*, 84 (July). https://doi.org/10.1016/j.annals.2020.103025.

Mihalič, T., & Kaspar, C. (1996). *Umweltökonomie im Tourismus (St. Galler Beiträge zum Tourismus und zur Verkehrswirtschaft, 27)*. Paul Haupt.

Muir, F., & Chester, G. (1993). Managing tourism to a seabird nesting island. *Tourism Management*, 14 (2), 99–105. https://doi.org/10.1016/0261-5177(93)90042-J.

Murphy, P. E. (1985). *Tourism: A Community Approach*. Methuen.

Nadal, J.R., Font, A.R. & Rossello, A.S. (2004). The economic determinants of seasonal patterns. *Annals of Tourism Research*, 31 (3), 697–711. https://doi.org/10.1016/j.anna ls.2004.02.001.

Nunkoo, R., & Ramkissoon, H. (2011). Developing a community support model for tourism. *Annals of Tourism Research*, 38 (3), 964–988.

Paulauskaite, D., Powell, R., Coca-Stefaniak, J.A. & Morrison, A.M. (2017). Living like a local: Authentic tourism experiences and the sharing economy. *International Journal of Tourism Research*, 19 (6), 619–628. https://doi.org/10.1002/jtr.2134.

Pavlić, I., Portolan, A. & Puh, B. (2019). Segmenting local residents by perceptions of tourism impacts in an urban World Heritage Site: The case of Dubrovnik. *Journal of Heritage Tourism*. https://doi.org/10.1080/1743873X.2019.1656218.

Pearce, D.G. (1989). *Tourist Development*. Longman Scientific and Technical.

Puljić, I., Knežević, M. & Šegota, T. (2019). Case study 8: Dubrovnik, Croatia. In World Tourism Organization (UNWTO), Centre of Expertise Leisure, Tourism & Hospitality, NHTV Breda University of Applied Sciences & NHL Stenden University of Applied Sciences "*Overtourism*"? *Understanding and managing urban tourism growth beyond perceptions*, Volume 2: Case Studies. UNWTO, 40–43.

Schmöcker, J.-D. (2021). Estimation of city tourism flows: Challenges, new data and Covid. *Transport Reviews*, 41 (2), 137–140.

Seraphin, H., Sheeran, P. & Pilato, M. (2018). Over-tourism and the fall of Venice as a destination. *Journal of Destination Marketing and Management*, January, 1–3.

Stergiou, D.P., & Farmaki, A. (2020). Resident perceptions of the impacts of P2P accommodation: Implications for neighbourhoods. *International Journal of Hospitality Management*, 91, 102411. https://doi.org/10.1016/j.ijhm.2019.102411.

Šegota, T., & Mihalič, T. (2018). Elicitation of tourist accommodation demand for counter-seasonal responses: Evidence from the Slovenian Coast. *Journal of Destination Marketing & Management*, 9, 258–266.

Trajkov, A., Biljan, J. & Andreeski, C. (2016). Overview and characteristics of tourism seasonality in Ohrid. *Economic Themes*, 54 (4), 485–498. https://doi.org/10.1515/ethemes-2016-0024.

Van der Werff, P. E. (1980). Polarising implications of the Pescaia tourist industry. *Annals of Tourism Research*, 7 (2), 197–223. https://doi.org/10.1016/0160-7383(80)90004-90003.

Vizek, M., Stojčić, N. & Mikulić, J. (2022). Spatial spillovers of tourism activity on housing prices: The case of Croatia. *Tourism Economics*, 135481662211064. https://doi.org/10.1177/13548166221106442.

Volo, S. (2010). Research note: Seasonality in Sicilian tourism demand – An exploratory study. *Tourism Economics*, 16 (4), 1073–1080. https://doi.org/10.5367/te.2010.0010.

Weaver, D.B., & Oppermann, M. (2000). *Tourism Management*. John Wiley and Sons Australia.

Witt, S.F., & Moutinho, L. (Eds.). (1994). *Tourism Marketing and Management Handbook*. Prentice Hall.

Woosnam, K.M., & Norman, W.C. (2010). Measuring residents' emotional solidarity with tourists: Scale development of Durkheim's theoretical constructs. *Journal of Travel Research*, 49 (3), 365–380.

Yang, M.J., Yang, E.C. & Khoo-Lattimore, C. (2019). Host-children of tourism destinations: Systematic quantitative literature review. *Tourism Recreation Research*, 45 (2), 231–246.

8

EMPLOYMENT IN TOURISM

Introduction

The previous chapter considered child labour and highlighted its visible and hidden manifestations. Hence, children can be viewed as *employees* in tourism (part-time or full-time, legally or informally employed), *participants* in households where tourism is the primary income source and *members* of communities in which tourism has substantial impacts.

Many tourism destinations have suffered from staff shortages in hospitality and tourism in the recent decade. Apart from the dramatic effects of the Covid-19 pandemic, its post-recovery period saw many employees taking up new opportunities outside of tourism and hospitality. The latter may have offered more convenient working hours, been less affected by tourism seasonality and sometimes provided better pay. This left gaping holes in all levels of tourism activity due to the absence of experienced workers. Children in tourism communities would see this course of events highlighting the more negative features of working in tourism and hospitality. Thus, attracting youth into the sector – as employees, trainees or students – is also a major problem despite high levels of youth unemployment in the advanced economies.

Tourism and the economy – initial observations

Due to the disruption created by the Covid-19 pandemic and data collection problems, most of the information is Eurocentric; thus, we will focus on EU countries. However, according to the European Commission (2023a), although the EU covers only 5.6% of the global population, it is the destination for 45.8% of all international tourist arrivals. Furthermore, the importance of tourism in the EU is underscored by our estimate that by 2025 it will represent

DOI: 10.4324/9781003374299-14

6% of all gross value added. In comparison, we estimate gross value added for Canada at 3%, Costa Rica at 5% and New Zealand at 6%.

However, looking at tourism as a share of non-financial business services (Eurostat, 2022), the share of the economy for tourism is 9.6% across the entire EU. By observing the individual Union member states in 2022, Greece scored the highest (27.8%) number of non-financial business services, followed by Cyprus (20.0%), Malta (14.6%), Croatia (13.3%) and Austria (13.1%). It may be argued that devoting over a quarter of a national economy to an economic sector that has displayed alarming sensitivities linked to the pandemic, terrorism and climate change might be dangerous. Undoubtedly, Covid-19 affected labour markets, with the entire EU labour market shrinking by 1.3% between 2019 and 2020 (OECD, 2023) and rising by a similar amount in 2021.

Yet a further Covid-19 effect was nominal wage growth. In 2019, the estimate was that nominal wages would grow 1% year-on-year (hereinafter y-o-y). However, by 2023, the nominal wage growth rose to 5.0% y-o-y (OECD, 2023). More recent data from Eurostat (2023a) indicates that this trend has continued; across the EU economy, nominal hourly labour costs to enterprises rose by 5.0% in the second quarter of 2023 compared to the same period in 2022. Actual wage costs rose by 6.6%, whilst non-wage costs (e.g. social and pension contributions and other charges) increased by 10.1%. If we specifically look at accommodation and food services, which include hotel and catering, the nominal hourly labour costs rose by 14.5% in Croatia (second highest after Hungary), 6.6% in Cyprus, 4.5% in Greece and 2.2% in Malta (the lowest).

BOX 8.1 CASE STUDY: MALTA

Looking specifically at Malta, unemployment across the Maltese economy stood at 2.8% in May 2023. Almost 15% of its working population is aged 15–24 and is a native Malti speaker, but also speak English (96%), Italian (55%), French (30%) and German (30%). Of the total population, 20% have culinary skills, of which 25% are females (National Statistical Office, Malta, 2022). Thus, in the face of a rapid rise in tourism activity and low unemployment, nominal labour costs in tourism and hospitality currently remain below the other 26 EU countries. The many job vacancies in Maltese tourism and hospitality represent employment opportunities for skilled workers from the UK, Central Europe, Australia, the Middle East, the Philippines and North Africa. Yet, there would not appear to be an absence of young people with language skills who may be available for the domestic tourism workforce.

Passion, flexibility and the desire to develop a long-term career are some of the main drivers of employees in the industry. On the other hand, a recent Irish labour market report indicated that the sector suffers low job security, low pay, unsocial hours and variable working practices (Fáilte Éireann, 2022). Yet interestingly, 36% of Irish tourism and hospitality employers are now being recruited directly from local schools and colleges, channelling the industry's perception of young people as an answer to recruitment problems and minimising the economic and wage costs (Fáilte Éireann, 2022).

European young workforce map

Looking specifically at the EU27 countries, 16.2% of employees in tourism and hospitality are aged between 15–29. However, by individual countries, this ranges from 20.2% of the national population (Cyprus) to 14.9% (Italy). These statistics indicate that in the EU27, there is no significant spread of young people employed in the industry (see Tables 8.1 and 8.2), which can be linked to the ageing European population.

An important element to clarify is that labour age will be primarily determined by the age at which compulsory education ends. The latter frequently determines the conditions at which children and young people may legally enter the workforce. In 37 European countries, there are 16 of them with a compulsory education leaving age of 16 (European Education & Culture Agency, 2022). In ten countries, the compulsory age is 15, but in two countries, children and

TABLE 8.1 15–29-year-olds as % of total population: Top 5 (*highest share*)

Country	% of those 15–29 years
Cyprus	20.2
Denmark	19.2
Luxembourg	18.7
Netherlands	18.7
Ireland	18.6
EU27	*16.2*

Source: Eurostat (Population statistics, May 2022)

TABLE 8.2 15–29-year-olds as % of total population: Bottom 5 (*lowest share*)

Country	% of those 15–29 years
Bulgaria	14.1
Latvia	14.5
Slovenia	14.6
Czechia	14.8
Italy	14.9
EU27	*16.2*

Source: Eurostat (Population statistics, May 2022)

youth between 15–18 must attend further education/training in schools, colleges or workplaces after the compulsory leaving age. In five countries, age 18 is the mandatory leaving age; in two countries, it is 17. However, in Germany, the leaving age varies between the federal states; in 11 states, it is 19 and in five states, it is 18 (European Education & Culture Agency, 2022). Furthermore, there is usually a restriction on children working during school hours and on the total number of hours they can work. Usually, the number of hours that can be worked increases once children are above school leaving age and until 18 unless specific local regulations prohibit this. Work experience organised for educational purposes is treated differently.

Unemployment among children and young people

In the middle of 2023, the youth unemployment rate was 14.1% in the EU27, down from 14.5% in July 2022. Table 8.3 indicates youth unemployment in ten European tourism destinations and EU27 data.

The general unemployment rate in the EU27 was 5.9% in July 2023 compared to 6.1% in July 2022. This indicates that youth unemployment remains consistently higher than unemployment levels in the general working population (aged 30–65).

Looking from a broader economic perspective, data from the advanced economies indicates that in OECD countries in 2022, the 15–19 age group represented 3.0% of all employees – the same as in 2019. Over the three years, all employees grew by 2.1%, while the 15–19 segment grew by 2.6%. In 2022, unemployed 15–19-year-olds represented 8.4% of the workforce, a decline of

TABLE 8.3 Youth unemployment in ten European tourism destinations

Destination	As at July 2023
Austria	9.6%
Croatia	19.0%
Cyprus	10.8%
EU27	14.1%
France	16.9%
Greece	23.6%
Ireland	7.4%
Malta	8.7%
Portugal	17.2%
Slovenia	5.6%
Spain	27.4%

Source: Eurostat (Youth unemployment statistics, August 2023)

Note: there is no comparative data for the UK, as the latest was issued in 2020 and only covers ages 16–19

9.3% on the 2019 level (OECD, 2023). In the 15–24 age group, unemployment rose from 12.5% in 2008 to an annualised average of 17.4% during 2009–2010 as the global recession began to bite. The situation improved to an annualised average of around 12% between 2010 and 2019 (OECD, 2023).

If we examine the employment of children and young people in tourism, we have to recognise the wider situation about those who do not appear in any statistical information, i.e. their records are not held in the workforce or unemployment records. An initial issue is the compulsory school leaving age variation in many advanced economies (see Table 8.3). We describe those not in employment, education or training as NEETs. The existence of this category of young people who are NEETs and do not appear on workforce records poses a clear policy challenge. "High and persistent youth unemployment in the aftermath of the global financial crisis showed that once young people have lost touch with the labour market, re-connecting them can be very hard" (OECD, 2020).

Evidence from the global financial crisis shows that early intervention is crucial for a successful labour market integration of young people and resulted in the European Union's Youth Guarantee, a commitment made by all EU member states in 2020 to ensure that all young people under the age of 30 receive a good-quality employment, apprenticeship or training offer within four months of leaving school or becoming unemployed (European Council, 2020). A policy paper prepared by OECD in 2020 very clearly identified policy challenges in supporting youth in the specific instance of Slovenia (OECD, 2020) given Slovene evidence reveals that many young people do not reach out to the public employment service for support and their share is higher than might be expected. Therefore, the Youth Employment Guarantee is essential in pulling youth from the NEETs situation.

BOX 8.2 CASE STUDY: NEETS – SLOVENIA

A widely identified problem is not simply the level of youth unemployment but rather the size of the larger 15–29 cohort who are classified as NEETs and not registered in the labour market. The data between 2011 and 2018 showed that 46% of those classified as NEETs failed to contact Slovenia's employment services. Of those unregistered NEETs, only 10% are in the 15–19 category, 30% in the 19–24 category and the remaining 60% in the 25–29 category. Of the total unregistered NEETs across the 15–29 age range, 30% had low educational attainment, and 90% had no work experience. Furthermore, the regions with the highest number of unregistered NEETs are Central Slovenia at 59% and Coastal-Karst at 58%. Interestingly, these two regions host two of the most visited Slovenian destinations (the capital of Ljubljana in Central Slovenia and the Slovenian coast in the Coast-Karst region). The lowest level of unregistered NEETs is the Carinthia region (46%), an Alpine region with intensive family-run tourism businesses (OECD, 2020).

The rights of children and young people in employment

The general legal requirements for employment of children under the compulsory school leaving age have been established by the UN under Article 32 – supported by Article 24 – of the UN Convention on the Rights of the Child (UN General Assembly, 1989). The UN Convention states:

> **Article 32.1–** *The right of the child to be protected from economic exploitation and from performing any work that is likely to be hazardous or to interfere with the child's education, or to be harmful to the child's health or physical, mental, spiritual, moral or social development.*
>
> **Article 24.1–** *The right of the child to the enjoyment of the highest attainable standard of health and to facilities for the treatment of illness and rehabilitation of health and right of access to such health care services.*

Under EU/EEA law, there are specific age limits on the employment of children younger than 15, albeit higher in some countries where compulsory full-time schooling continues after age 15. Children may be employed between 14 and 15 years old as part of a work/training or work experience scheme. Many countries allow employers to hire young workers if the jobs are required for their vocational training. This is particularly relevant in the hotel, catering and tourism industry, where many young people begin vocational training and work after age 15 or 16.

Influencing children's attitudes towards responsible and sustainable tourism

Many unknowns need to be uncovered from children's attitudes towards tourism. Some of the issues surveyed, though they just scratch the surface, are linked to the following attitudes:

- On local issues concerning transport and travel, such as travel for school or work, leisure and family activities.
- On responsible and sustainable tourism from a consumption perspective.
- As participants in families and local communities in tourism destinations.
- In destinations where overtourism creates employment and economic opportunities but damages natural and cultural environments.

The governments are eager to reduce car travel and increase more sustainable travel options, all in line with achieving Net Zero by 2045. Hence, some governments made proposals to tackle sustainable travel behaviour in children, young people and families. Although the focus is on such issues as diminishing car use for travel by children and young people, governments also acknowledge that it is not always achievable. For example, the Scottish government accepted that children and young people living in deprived areas and Scotland's rural and island communities may experience particular barriers to sustainable travel. The travel options in Scotland may thus impact children's wider opportunities. Hence, instead of reducing the car travel agenda, they focus on promoting and supporting changes in children's attitudes from around the age of 12 towards more sustainable transportation and leisure experiences (Colley et al., 2022). Also, as of January 2022, all children and young people in Scotland under 22 were provided with free access to bus transport at a national level. This covers travel to school and educational institutions and leisure and vacation travel.

Regarding consumer roles, children are influencers and users. According to Eurobarometer (2022), they are much more likely to find the activities available in the destination an important factor when choosing where to travel. Also, they are more flexible in changing and adapting their travel habits, with only 11% of younger respondents being less flexible. They will base their transport options on the ecological impacts, with 41% of those aged 15–25 making more sustainable decisions. They can comprehend trustworthy information on the carbon emissions of transportation options (39%).

We should also be aware that with the dynamic linkage to climate change, children and young people face an uncertain future as they grow into adulthood over the next three decades. They will have greater exposure to global warming. In Europe alone, this will lead to desertification of the northern Mediterranean and far warmer temperatures in northern and northwestern Europe. As a result, mass tourism in southern Spain, southern Italy, Malta and Greece, for example, may only become tolerable in the October–March period, which is likely to dramatically affect the operation of tourism in those regions during the April–September period.

Long-term trends

A very important trend that will impact the future of child and youth engagement in tourism in the advanced economies is the decline in the 15–29 population compared to the growth of the 55+ population. The EU population is projected to be lower in 2100 than it was in 2022, and its structure will be increasingly old, with a considerable reduction in the number and share of working-age people (Eurostat, 2023c). Demographic trends do not affect every country and every region in the same way; although the European population is ageing as a whole, demographic developments are far from uniform, with considerable variations between and within individual EU member states. Population decline has been particularly acute in some eastern EU member states, which have experienced high levels of emigration and people moving within their home countries from rural regions to predominantly urban areas in search of better opportunities for work education and training possibilities. The resulting demographic differences can exacerbate existing economic, social and territorial inequalities and provoke political divides (European Commission, 2023b). One immediate impact is that the so-called silver tourism market will expand as a balance shifts in advanced economies towards an ageing population (fewer younger people, and an increase in older people). Given longer life expectancy and earlier retirement, this market may shift towards active and culturally rich experiences rather than cruises and sun–sea–sand tourism.

In the long run, the increase in the number of days with unusually high temperatures and heat waves may have long-lasting consequences on mortality. Research suggests that around 70,000 deaths could be attributed to the extreme temperatures of the July and August 2003 heat waves, which affected many parts of Europe. About 3,000 deaths in France were attributed to the heat waves in 2015. In addition, analysis of weekly death counts by age across the EU for 2015–2022 shows that the increases in mortality during summer months since 2018 are starting to become significant. These increases in mortality during summer represent an additional systematic seasonal component of elderly mortality at the same significance level as the winter peaks associated with influenza (European Commission, 2023b). Also, several EU member states are projected to experience a decline in their population over the period 2024–2030 (European Commission, 2023b). Population decline may affect tourism activity for countries that are significant recipients of global tourist visitors, i.e. Bulgaria, Greece, Croatia and Italy. At the same time, Ireland, Cyprus and Malta will grow in population. Nonetheless, it should be noted that all these countries will likely be affected by climate change from 2030 to 2050. Except for Ireland, which is likely to suffer far more storms and flooding at low levels, the rest will suffer from excessive heat, lack of water and heightened potential for forest fires. Such climate change-related events will have a profound effect on children. For example, they may significantly reduce the suitable outdoor play time and available activities.

As the population in rural Europe tends to be older than in urban/suburban areas, this potentially makes employment for young people more challenging. This challenge is frequently exacerbated by the natural movement of youth towards cities with better educational opportunities or training. The effect of the rural–urban drift trends is that urban dwellers take vacant properties for second homes, pushing up real estate prices and effectively pricing young people or families out of the housing market. This then compounds the employment problems in rural areas, facing a lack of workforce or constant population (Aurambout et al., 2021). The European Commission has the view that in Europe, these demographic trends are "coupled with a lack of connectivity, poor infrastructure, productivity challenges, and low access to public services including education and care, and indicative of the lower attractiveness of rural areas as places to live and work" (European Commission, 2023b).

An ageing and shrinking working age population, connected to a potential slowdown in economic development, has the potential to lead to a decrease in motivation for highly skilled and younger workers. This socio-economic challenge can result in economic diversification potentials, over-reliance on declining sectors and low innovation capacity. This creates underperforming labour markets, poor adult learning rates and depressed social outcomes. Across Europe, particularly in poorer and disadvantaged regions, there is a specific "talent development trap" regarding early leavers from education and training. Clearly, a greater number of young people in these regions do not complete further education and have poor employment prospects. Infrequent and insufficient mobility is part of the problem, an issue in many developed economies, where poor transport infrastructure outside key capital or tourism destinations creates difficulty in access to jobs and learning (European Commission COM, 2023).

References

Aurambout, J.P., Batista E.S.F., Bosco, C., Conte, A., Ghio, D., Kalantaryan, S., Kompil, M., Perpiñá Castillo, C., Proietti, P., Scipioni, M., Sulis, P. & Tintori, G. (2021). *The Demographic Landscape of EU Territories.* Publications Office of the European Union. doi:10.2760/49621.

Colley, K., Brown, C., Nicholson, H., Hinder, B. & Conniff, A. (2022). *Encouraging Sustainable Travel Behaviour in Children, Young People and Their Families* (Climate Exchange report for the Scottish Government). https://www.climatexchange.org.uk/m edia/5570/cxc-encouraging-sustainable-travel-behaviour-in-children-young-people-and-their-families-september-2022.pdf.

Corbanese, V., & Rosas, G. (2017). *ILO Guide for Developing National Outreach Strategies for Inactive Young People.* https://www.ilo.org/wcmsp5/groups/public/—ed_emp/documents/publication/wcms_613351.pdf.

European Commission COM (2023). *Harnessing Talent.* https://ec.europa.eu/regional_p olicy/sources/communication/harnessing-talents/harnessing-talents-regions_en.pdf.

European Commission (2023a). *News Release of 27.09.2023.* https://ec.europa.eu/eurosta t/en/web/products-eurostat-news/w/edn-20230927-1.

European Commission (2023b). *The Impact of Demographic Change in a Changing Environment.* https://commission.europa.eu/system/files/2023-01/Demography_report_2022_0.pdf.

European Council (1994). *Council Directive 94/33/EC of 22 June 1994 on the Protection of Young People at Work.* https://eur-lex.europa.eu/legal-content/EN/ALL/?uri=CELEX: 31994L0033.

European Council (2020). *Council Recommendation of 30 October 2020 on A Bridge to Jobs – Reinforcing the Youth Guarantee and replacing the Council Recommendation of 22 April 2013 on establishing a Youth Guarantee (2020/C 372/01).* https://ec.europa. eu/social/main.jsp?catId=1079.

European Education & Culture Agency (2022). *Compulsory Education in Europe 2022/ 2023.* https://eurydice.eacea.ec.europa.eu/media/2837/download.

Eurostat (2022). *Key Figures on European Business.* https://ec.europa.eu/eurostat/docum ents/15216629/15230677/KS-06-22-075-EN-N.pdf/930f2188-48cb-ef84-678e-e6f96682b072? t=1672841155329.

Eurostat (2023a). *Eurostat Indicators* (104/2023–2015.09.23).

Eurostat (2023b). *Youth Unemployment Statistics.* https://ec.europa.eu/eurostat/data browser/view/UNE_RT_M__custom_7373874/default/table?lang=en.

Eurostat (2023c). *Population Projections.* https://ec.europa.eu/eurostat/statistics-expla ined/index.php?title=Population_projections_in_the_EU#Population_projections.

Eurobarometer (2022). *Attitudes of Europeans towards Tourism.* https://data.europa.eu/ data/datasets/s2283_499_eng?locale=en.

Fáilte Éireann (2022). *Tourism Careers – Labour market report.* www.failte.ie.

Knežević, M., Koščak, M., O'Rourke, T. & Šegota, T. (2020). Inter-generational con cepts of sustainability and the role of children in local tourism destinations. In Koščak, M., & O'Rourke, T. *Ethical and Responsible Tourism – Managing sustain ability in local tourism,* 1st edition. Routledge, 129–141.

Koščak, M., & O'Rourke, T. (2023). *Ethical and Responsible Tourism – Managing sustainability in local tourism,* 2nd edition. Routledge.

National Statistical Office, Malta (2022). *NSO Skills Survey 2022.*

National Statistical Office, Malta (2023). *NSO Tourism Statistics Release 123/2023.*

OECD (2020). *Policy Challenges in Supporting Youth: The hidden NEETs in Slovenia.* https://www.oecd.org/employment/youth/OECD-2020-Hidden-NEETs-Slovenia.pdf.

OECD (2023). *Authors' Analysis and Projections from OECD data from the OECD Database.* https://www.oecd.org/employment/onlineoecdemploymentdatabase.htm.

UN General Assembly (1989). *UN Convention on the Rights of the Child.* General Assembly Resolution 44/25 of 20.11.89 (entry into force 02.09.90, in accordance with Article 49). https://www.unicef.org.uk/wp-content/uploads/2016/08/uni cef-convention-rights-child-uncrc.pdf.

9
REFLECTIONS ON PART III

The Key Concepts

This chapter discusses and examines the Key Concepts from each preceding chapter in Part III.

Chapter 7

The Key Concepts may be categorised as follows:

- *Child labour numbers are alarming.* Across the world, there are 160 million children aged 5–17 who are engaging in child labour, predominantly in family-based economic activities. The estimates for underaged children working in tourism are from 13 to 19 million, representing around 10–15% of the formal tourism labour market. Children work in primarily lower-paid jobs such as porters and maids, dishwashers, beach guards, shop-keepers and golf caddies.
- *Child labour is geographically omnipresent.* The most common stereotype is that the problem of child labour is limited to less developed countries in Africa, Asia, Central and South America, or the so-called Global South. However, we also find child labour in European countries, such as Portugal, Spain and Italy. For example, around 200,000 children under 14 in Spain were employed in small production facilities, mainly for footwear production.
- *Natural and institutional seasonality are inter-related.* Tourism seasonality represents the tendency of tourist flows to become concentrated in short periods, causing a temporal imbalance related to the peaking and overuse of community resources. It is subject to natural and institutional conditions, often complementary. Determinants of natural seasonality are the

DOI: 10.4324/9781003374299-15

destination's climatic conditions, while institutional seasonality results from human decisions concerning the time to take a vacation.

• *Tourism seasonality has positive and negative outcomes.* Largely negative impacts are linked to economic costs (e.g. the increase in prices, income instability, recruiting costs), resource utilisation and employment, but also severely affect the natural environment and socio-cultural aspects of community life. Seasonality also harms visitors' satisfaction because of crowding, increased vulnerability to safety and threats and reduced available accommodation, while it puts pressure on the transport system and infrastructure, and results in low-quality holidays for tourists. On the other hand, the positives of tourism seasonality are the ability to perform maintenance work on critical tourism and hospitality infrastructure, relieving the community of the stress accumulated during the peak season, which helps to normalise the traditional social patterns. Even more so, the off-season allows fragile environments to rejuvenate and recuperate.

• *Not in my bed (NIMB).* This is the term we wish to coin to express children's negative sentiments towards their beds being used for accommodating tourists. This specifically proliferated with the popularisation of peer-to-peer accommodation, with an increasing number of families renting their homes to tourists while they move briefly for the urgency of acquiring financial benefits.

Chapter 8

The Key Concepts may be categorised as follows:

• *Tourism is a sector of employment opportunities.* The share of the economy for tourism is 9.6% across the entire EU. However, the industry is experiencing labour shortages, with smaller countries already finding opportunities for importing workers from developing countries. For example, the many job vacancies in Maltese tourism and hospitality represent employment opportunities for skilled workers from the UK, Central Europe, Australia, the Middle East, the Philippines and North Africa, despite the high availability of a qualified domestic workforce that is undecided nor motivated to take those jobs.

• *European young workforce map.* Looking specifically at the EU27 countries, 16.2% of employees in tourism and hospitality are aged between 15 and 29 years. However, by individual countries, this ranges from 20.2% of the national population (Cyprus) to 14.9% (Italy). These statistics indicate that in the EU27, there is no significant spread of young people employed in the industry, which can be linked to the ageing of the European population.

• *Children's rights are important.* Under EU/EEA law, specific age limits exist on the employment of children younger than 15. Children may be employed between 14 and 15 years old as part of a work/training or work experience scheme. Many countries allow employers to hire young workers if the jobs are required for their vocational training. This is particularly relevant in the hotel, catering and tourism industry, where many young people begin vocational training and work after age 15 or 16. However, one cannot forget about UN Article 32, which states that *"the right of the child to be protected from economic exploitation and from performing any work that is likely to be hazardous or to interfere with the child's education, or to be harmful to the child's health or physical, mental, spiritual, moral or social development"*.

The Critical Factors

Housing issues in tourism communities

Second-home ownership and peer-to-peer accommodation are decreasing opportunities for the residents to find appropriate and affordable housing. Many European destinations like Croatia, Slovenia, Montenegro and Albania have seen a decline in housing buildings and expansion of the uncontrolled development of houses exclusively used for tourism. Such growth is taking its toll on residential housing, but these communities are also vulnerable to house price hikes.

Living with strangers

Some families open their doors to tourists. Such practice has significantly increased with the popularisation of peer-to-peer accommodation, which sees families renting parts of their homes. As much as it is financially beneficial and supports the family, such practice is socially controversial. Moreover, "do not talk to strangers" is usually a prevalent phrase in parenting, while we see the opposite in co-sharing homes with tourists. This gives mixed signals to children and plays a role in their socialisation that we know very little about.

Back to pre-Covid-19 statistics

In the years leading to the pandemic, we witnessed residents mobilising against tourism, demanding immediate action against the negative impacts of tourism. The marches or the mobilisation against tourism result from the rapid increase of visitor numbers and place changes that residents perceived as negative. On the other hand, the Covid-19 pandemic shocked tourism to unimaginable proportions, while some residents found it a relief to live without large crowds. However, the once mass tourism destinations are again inviting tourists despite their residents experiencing the negative impacts of tourism. Hence, the overall feeling is that the pre-pandemic struggles will also remain post-pandemic.

The long-term perspective on the future of children

Unpromising demographic trends (i.e. ageing and shrinking of the working population) and severe climate change issues (i.e. scoring temperatures, heatwaves and natural crises), connected to a potential slowdown in economic development, have the potential to lead to a decrease in motivation for highly skilled and younger workers to seek employment in tourism. This socio-economic challenge can result in economic diversification potentials, over-reliance on declining sectors and low innovation capacity. This creates underperforming labour markets, poor adult learning rates and depressed social outcomes. Across Europe, particularly in poorer and disadvantaged regions, there is a specific "talent development trap" regarding early leavers from education and training.

Connections

In this section, we suggest some elements based on the issues raised in Part III. We uncovered and discussed some critical "incidents" linked to child labour, tourism seasonality and employment. Tourism is hailed as the generator of jobs, but its dark side must be revealed. Tourism is home to child labour and questionable social practices hidden from the eyes of the industry and travellers. By uncovering and digging deeper into the malpractices of the sector, we can strive to create *just* tourism. The long-term trends are not stimulating. Yet, we do not wish to be negative and unstimulating. With our discussions, we aim to shed light on practices that need global awareness so that they are addressed early and strategies for their mitigation are put in place. Following these underlying discussions, we have sought to develop some connections for readers as follows:

- For students, we pose some questions which may assist the connections between teaching and learning.
- For researchers (graduate or professional), we suggest some guidelines for further research.
- For practitioners, we raise matters of concern for their progress in creating jobs while considering children's rights.

Teaching and learning

Students should discuss the following points:

a   Child labour manifests in many different forms. What are the hidden and visible manifestations of child labour linked to family life and tourism?
b   Employment opportunities are vast in tourism. In the case of Malta, there seems to be a sufficient number of skilled workers among Maltese youth. How can Malta address its talent development trap and migration of foreign workers?

c We are coining a new term – *NIMB*. How should families address NIMB, and what alternatives to it exist?

d Tourism seasonality appears to have negative and positive impacts. What possible responses to these impacts can be observed in communities inundated with summer tourism?

Guidelines for researchers

Researchers may wish to consider the following:

a Child labour is taking unimaginable proportions across industries, especially in tourism. Policies to protect children from being exploited often go unnoticed or obscured by the local population or even children's families. What is the level of awareness among family members of children's rights, and what other communication is needed for the family to protect, instead of exploit, their youngest members?

b *Not in my bed.* In an attempt to describe the negative sentiment of children forced to resign their beds to tourists, we coined the term *NIMB*. However, the term needs further exploration, understanding and empirical evidence.

c There are a handful of studies on resident attitudes and seasonality. Greater emphasis should be given to tourism seasonality, as the long-term natural and social trends are not projecting a brighter future for the next generation of children.

Keynotes for practitioners

Practitioners may wish to review the following points:

a How do we radically reduce the visible employment of children in tourism and expose and reduce those hidden?

b How do we find solutions to tourism seasonality and help reduce the extensive numbers of private accommodations over-popularised by the sharing economy?

c How do we mitigate the doomsday projections of demographic trends and climate change effects to sustain the industry and, more importantly, to sustain the quality of life in communities?

PART IV

What can children do for tourism?

INTRODUCTION TO PART IV

Planning and developing tourism for children without asking children is absurd. This has been supported by valuable academic studies, which have showed that children are an important, vocal, yet marginalised stakeholder group in tourism. The theoretical underpinnings of the two chapters will include participatory planning, i.e. Arnstein's ladder of citizen participation and empowerment. These theoretical frameworks will be discussed within the broader setting of children's contribution to tourism development and improving the quality of life within families and communities. The latter will be represented by empowering children to embrace tourism as a lifestyle and future employment opportunity and empowering them to have their say in future tourism development.

In Chapter 10 we discuss the concept of empowerment in its lexical sense and the sense of tourism as a scientific discipline. The idea of empowerment is described through the Foucauldian lens, discussing the omnipresence of power and tourism, power in tourism networks, the tourist gaze and, less talked about, repressive and productive power over tourists. The multidimensionality of empowerment is also presented through psychological, social and political empowerment. Psychological empowerment helps communities re-evaluate their culture, natural resources and traditional knowledge – all three significant elements of tourism activity. Social empowerment is represented by the community's cohesion and its members working together for a common goal. Political empowerment emphasises the need for residents to have control over tourism development. Children are often neglected in having a voice, let alone influencing decisions related to tourism in the community. Children are not alone. Women, who have regained some power with tourism, are still under-represented in the power the tourism industry should (ideologically) balance.

Chapter 11 relates to how in the contemporary environment successful destination performance requires a new and practical tourism paradigm that

DOI: 10.4324/9781003374299-17

combines excellence, co-creation, cooperation and high-quality services. Co-creation and cooperation rest on participatory planning that is encouraged by destination management. In the first instance, participatory planning forms an integral part of future place-making processes and planning by capturing the importance of the public perspective in the process. Secondly, it stresses the importance of creative participatory processes to attract stakeholders and enhance their willingness to partake in the process. Finally, it identifies innovative participatory planning tools that may improve participatory planning within the process. Unfortunately, academic research has shown that children often are not part of this process or at least not at an adequate level. Therefore, through the theoretical underpinning of Arnstein's ladder of citizen participation, we discuss possibilities for including children in the tourism planning process. Furthermore, we also review child-centric participatory planning, including adequate representation of interests, shared vision, goal accomplishment, good working relationships, open communication between stakeholders, and strong leaders and administrative support.

In Chapter 12 we summarise the Key Concepts and Critical Factors in the two preceding chapters, as well as examine the most appropriate Connections for students, researchers and practitioners.

10

EMPOWERMENT THROUGH TOURISM

Introduction

Empowerment is a prerequisite for sustainable tourism development (Cole, 2006). This thought makes tourism conceptually centred on the people and their environment rather than production and profits (Friedmann, 1992). In contemporary academic literature, empowerment seems to be a new buzz-word, which modern dictionaries define as the strengthening of someone to do something or the right of someone to do something (Merriam-Webster. com, 2023).

In social psychology, empowerment is described as a process of building rela-tionships among individual members of a social group in ways that they learn from each other and create a greater sense of community (Aghazamani & Hunt, 2017). In medicine and healthcare, empowerment describes overcoming health-related problems by focusing on the collective action of groups of individuals (Aghaza-mani & Hunt, 2017). Of course, the use of this term is primarily conditioned by the social circumstances in which it appears.

However, one of the broadest definitions of the concept can be found in the activity of the Cornell Empowerment Group, which defines the concept as: "an intentional, ongoing process centred in the local community, involving mutual respect, critical reflection, caring, and group participation, through which people lacking an equal share of valued resources gain greater access to and control over those resources" (Cornell Empowerment Group, 1989 in Zimmer-man, 2000, 43). By raising the individual's ability to participate in community activities, the collective interdependence of the community is increased, as it gives a greater voice to its members, both individually and collectively (Good-kind & Foster-Fishman, 2002).

DOI: 10.4324/9781003374299-18

Empowerment in tourism

A notable debate in resident attitude research revolves around how an individual's power to influence tourism development affects their perceptions and responses to tourism. Researchers have suggested that residents who feel powerful enough to influence tourism development are likely to perceive tourism positively, whilst more powerless residents perceive tourism negatively (for example, Boley et al., 2014; Choi & Murray, 2010; Lee, 2013; Nunkoo & Smith, 2013). However, these studies did not consistently confirm the significance of the relationships whenever the broader construct of "power" was used as an antecedent to perceptions and reactions to tourism (Boley et al., 2014; Šegota et al., 2017). Commenting on the resident empowerment construct being too broadly defined and thus open to various interpretations, Boley et al. (2014) suggest distinguishing between its social, psychological, and political dimensions. All three empowerment dimensions were shown to have "had direct and significant relationships with resident perceptions of tourism's impacts" (Boley et al., 2014, p. 46). More importantly, throughout different studies, Boley and co-authors (e.g. Palardy et al., 2018; Strzelecka et al., 2017; Maruyama et al., 2017) show that empowerment dimensions differently influence the formation of resident perceptions of tourism impacts. For example, social and psychological empowerment were better predictors of resident support for tourism than political empowerment (Strzelecka et al., 2017).

Social empowerment

Social empowerment in tourism occurs when tourism helps increase a community's cohesion (Scheyvens, 1999). It is represented by the community's cohesion and its members working together for a common goal. Skills, knowledge and community relationships form social power that the community can use to build blocks for political and psychological empowerment (Friedmann, 1992). A tourist destination that strives for excellence and enhances the quality of visit can bring the community together and make all its members feel that they are contributing, that they belong and that they are partaking in an important role to achieve the community's goal. For Boley et al. (2014), social empowerment is related explicitly to tourism in local communities:

- Making residents feel more connected to their community.
- Fostering a sense of *community spirit* within residents.
- Providing ways for residents to get involved in their community.

Psychological empowerment

An individual's self-esteem and their sense of potency represent the essence of psychological empowerment (Friedmann, 1992). Potency stands for magnitude, strength, force, social power and expansiveness (Heise, 2010). Psychological studies have shown that psychological empowerment predicts participation (Cattaneo & Chapman, 2010). Psychological empowerment in tourism represents the latter's ability to renew residents' sense of pride in the "universal value of their culture and environment" (Di Castri, 2004, p. 52). One's self-esteem or sense of pride originates from an individual's awareness that others outside their community recognise the uniqueness and value of natural and cultural resources of their community. Hence, psychological empowerment helps communities re-evaluate their culture, natural resources and traditional knowledge – all three significant elements of tourism activity. Moreover, psychological empowerment rests on pride and self-esteem, and the more residents feel psychologically empowered, the more they will support tourism and see it as beneficial for the community. Hence, Boley et al. (2014) suggest that psychological empowerment in tourism encapsulates how tourism:

- Makes residents proud to be a member of the community.
- Makes residents feel special because people travel to see their community's unique features.
- Makes residents want to tell others about what they have to offer in the community.
- Reminds residents that they have a unique culture to share with visitors.
- Makes residents want to work to keep the community special.

Political empowerment

Political empowerment represents inclusion in the democratic decision-making process (Miller, 1994) and for community residents to gain their voice in the community's government. Gaining a voice and being included in decision-making extends beyond the mere ability to vote. Friedmann (1992, p. 33) describes political empowerment as a function of "power of voice and collective action". In the context of tourism, political empowerment shall be understood as providing all community groups with a forum to equally and fairly raise concerns and questions about tourism development (Scheyvens, 1999). Political empowerment entices the feeling of everyone being equally represented in tourism development and planning. It emphasises the need for residents to have control over tourism development. Hence, Boley et al. (2014) suggest that political empowerment in tourism:

- Helps residents have a voice in the community's tourism development decisions.
- Enables residents to access the decision-making process when it comes to tourism.
- Gives residents an equal opportunity to make a difference in how tourism is developed.
- Creates an outlet for residents to share their concerns about tourism development.

Foulcault's lenses for empowerment in tourism

At the core of the term empowerment, power is universal, permeating all levels of human activity, as pointed out by Foucault (Colin, 1980). Colin (1980) conveys Foucault's words that "between every point of a social body, between a man and a woman, between the members of a family, between a master and his pupil, between everyone who knows and everyone who does not, there exist relations of power" (p. 187). This universality of power is an important feature both in the academic relationships to the phenomenon, i.e. descriptions, research or in the practical, everyday relationships between individuals and social groups. This means that we can expect power as a constituent in all situations and all forms of relations between people. Social institutions also represent a form of human activity based on power. Understanding this, we also need to remember that social institutions are thus not the exclusive area of power's action but one of many areas.

By taking Foucault's perspective of power in tourism, we cannot avoid discussing different manifestations of power in tourism, visible or hidden. By highlighting the work of Cheong and Miller (2000), Foucault's four features of power in tourism are as follows.

The omnipresence of power and tourism

If power is a constituent of all kinds of relations between people, it is undoubtedly also a constituent of relations between people in a tourist area. According to Foucauldian analysts, power relations are evident in many dimensions of tourism, even those that look like equal relations. One of those seemingly equal relationships is present in the assertion that residents are hosts and tourists are guests in a destination. Hosts and guests should bond and create positive qualities of the visit and life from their interaction. However, given that the vast majority of resident attitudes towards tourism literature discusses tourism impacts, both positive and negative, that might not always be true.

When it comes to children, research indicates that children perceive tourists as powerful enough to affect their lives through their activity. The study was done mainly in geographical areas where tourism is either the only or the most important economic activity (Koščak et al., 2023). Potency is mainly in first place among the significant characteristics children associate with tourists. The fact that children perceive tourists as of high magnitude, great strength, impactful force, great social power and very expansive (Koščak et al., 2023) probably confirms Foucault's assertion about the omnipresence of power and its attachment to tourist activity.

In a similar study, Koščak et al. (2018) investigated the differences between how children assess the potency of tourists and how children see their parents' assessment of the potency of tourists. The latter represented the result of children's observation of the parents' attitudes. Understanding how parents perceive tourists conveyed by children is precisely how one can have a window into a socialisation process in which children take on some social concepts they encounter in their parents' home. Even more so, the research by Koščak et al. (2018) found that children rated the potency of tourists significantly higher than their parents, signalling that not only internalised by socialisation but also their observation of tourist activity makes tourists powerful and omnipresent in a destination.

Power in tourism networks

This power is based on the generalisation of those participating in the tourism system, i.e. the residents of a tourist destination, who at the same time depend on that activity in an economic sense, as well as tourists who visit a destination. As previously mentioned, the host–guest relationship is usually accompanied by a saying that "in successful tourist destinations, the natives are always friendly" (Selwyn, 1996, p. 21). This myth should mean an equal division of power between tourists and hosts; however, this is entirely incorrect because the roles are fundamentally different, with tourists dominating in many dimensions and hosts subordinated. This power relationship leads to "residents of the periphery coming to perceive their own culture as inferior and dependent on the center" (Půtová, 2018, p. 79). Especially in the era of modern tourism, in "conjunction with the increasing global mobility and its impact on destinations, tourism space appears an assertion of the privilege and power imbalance" (Tomassini & Cavagnaro, 2020, p. 3). This uneven distribution of power is already sensed relatively early in childhood. Children very clearly see the difference in power relations between tourists and hosts (Koščak et al., 2023): "residents are perceived as being more passive, evaluated worse than tourists, and seen as weak, whereas tourists are evaluated more positively" (Koščak et al., 2023, p. 14). Of course, power relations in a highly tourist-intensive area are dynamic and change as the destination develops.

However, tourists can also be overpowered by residents. We need to understand that tourists are also a vulnerable group, deprived of many things in a destination, although not in the same way as hosts. Tourists are often in politically and culturally unfamiliar territory and communicate in a language unknown to the hosts (Cheong & Miller, 2000). Moreover, Cheong and Miller say that "they are stripped of many of their cultural and family ties and protective institutions and are exposed to new norms and expectations" (Cheong & Miller, 2000, p. 380). In this way, the position of power that tourists *grab* is often the result of their vulnerability in staying outside the safety of their cultural and normative environment.

The tourist gaze

The tourist gaze (Urry & Larsen, 2011) is a fascinating phenomenon. Using the Foucauldian lens, the tourist gaze refers to how tourists see their environment, and this ability to observe the environment under the conditions of the use of power creates the concept of the tourist (Cheong & Miller, 2000). Thus, power relations are at the very basis of the existence of tourists as a social phenomenon. Urry and Larsen (2011) find that power is part of all systems and is located in all social networks in the tourist area. In this social network, power relations create conditions for ethnocentric pressure on tourists; however, it helps to prevent the host's prejudices against tourists. This balance of power is disturbed in some situations. For example, overtourism represents a prevalence of the influence of tourists and, consequently, the efforts of the local population to limit tourist activities. These restrictions refer to "what tourists can and cannot do, where they can and cannot go, and what they should choose and what they should reject" (Cheong & Miller, 2000, p. 383). In this way, the tourist gaze is actually defined by non-tourist dimensions in social power relations. To explain, an important factor in tourist activity is tour guides. It is about staging the tourist gaze, terms used in tourism research, i.e. "ability to talk to tourists in their language, knowledge of popular trails and interesting flora and fauna, narrating cultural and architectural histories, knowledge of local customs and so on" (Cheong & Miller, 2000, p. 384). The power of tour guides manifests in the fact that sometimes tourists change their usual patterns of behaviour and incorporate into them the principles introduced by the tour guides with their power.

Repressive and productive power over tourists

The repressive but productive nature of power in tourism stems primarily from its swift and dynamic expansion in all dimensions of development as an industry. It is the direct and indirect contribution of tourism to the economy and development. From this understanding, we need yet again to place tourists in a subordinate position, being targeted by both tourism businesses and residents. In this environment, tourists are subjected to the processes of referral, education and reformation, but, on the other hand, to the processes of inspection, monitoring and general management as well (Cheong & Miller, 2000).

The perspective of tourists being a vulnerable group, to the extent exploited by tourism businesses and locals, is a perspective that is often overlooked in science. This is because tourism academic activity was developed within frameworks of history, geography, business sciences, cultural anthropology, sociology, public affairs, political science, psychology, marketing, etc. There is no "tourismology", a unique discipline that discusses the phenomenon of tourism independently. Limited lenses stem from the fact that specific academic disciplines in their dealings with tourism are unilaterally connected with various economic and political factors, extracting their share of the social pie of tourism, funnelling down the division of power and effects.

Using empowerment in tourism as a transfer of power

Tourism impacts individuals' quality of life and communities' well-being (Moscardo, 2012; Uysal et al., 2016). Therefore, governments favour it as a development tool because of its economic, social, and cultural benefits. Even more so, three key agendas accelerating sustainable consumption and production worldwide (i.e. the Sustainable Tourism Programme, the 2030 Agenda for Sustainable Development and the Sustainable Development Goals) highlight tourism as a force for change that can be used to improve quality of life, promote inclusivity and advance knowledge (WTO & UNDP, 2017). For tourism to exercise its role in fostering its regenerative role and encouraging sustainable development, it must include all voices (Šegota et al., 2017), even those hidden under the prevailing seabed of disciplinary lenses and limits. Taking a Foucauldian perspective on tourism can overcome the lenses and limitations and uncover fresh perspectives.

At first glance, empowerment is a very simple construct, which means the transfer of power from someone (or something) with more power to someone with less power. Scientists distinguish between two basic categories of empowerment, each different according to the participants in the process. Structural empowerment refers to strengthening social structures, while psychological empowerment refers to individuals (Amor et al., 2021). Structural empowerment is a crucial component of tourism organisational effectiveness: if power can be defined as the "ability to get things done, to mobilise resources" (Kanter, 1997, p. 260), then structural empowerment is the strengthening of a social structure that enables it to mobilise resources, necessary for the adequate performance of their social functions. These resources usually mean "financing, materials, time, and support necessary to do the job" (Jáimez Román & Bretones, 2013, p. 1). The empowerment of tourism social structure "will result in greater employee satisfaction, commitment and productivity" (Jáimez Román & Bretones, 2013). Behind this, i.e. employees' satisfaction, commitment and higher productivity, are professional opportunities for learning and development (Amor et al., 2020).

Both structural and psychological empowerment should look at the transfer of power between genders. Even today, the traditional role of men is to provide materially for their families, and women to maintain the household and take care of the development of children. In a large portion of today's tourist environments, the situation is still very similar, with the fact that women are given, in addition to their traditional role, the duty of working in the tourism and hospitality industry, where they do tough jobs, mainly at the bottom of the work hierarchy. Admittedly, in some areas, tourism has enabled forms of education for women that were not even remotely available to them before, strengthening their social position. It was also observed that women have access to jobs that require higher levels of education, thus allowing them access to higher levels in the industrial sector and, thus far, greater development opportunities (Nunkoo & Ramkissoon, 2013). However, this should not be seen as a general process responsible for developing the tourism industry. A more likely reason is the lack of qualified labour, which has forced the activity organisers to invite women into the work process, although this does not mean that it equates them with men. Despite the hundred-year feminist search for equality, according to UN data:

> women perform 66% of the world's work, produce half its food, but earn 10% of its income and own 1% of its property. Three-quarters of the world's poor are female. ... The hospitality industry is an important employer for women, with an average female participation rate of 55% globally and up to 70% in some regions.
>
> *(Morgan & Pritchard, 2019, p. 40).*

Given this observation, empowering women is one of the priorities in tourism.

As mentioned earlier, in tourism-intensive areas, employment in tourism often means social subjugation because it is a labour-intensive industry, which does not take into account the free time of the people who work in it or the circumstances of family life. For children living in tourism destinations, tourism represents a force that shapes their quality of life or/and an imminent future as an employment opportunity once they reach adulthood (Koščak et al., 2023). Therefore, from the perspective of academic science and professional practice, tourism must embrace its role as an enabling environment to empower children's voices and for their needs, priorities and rights to become an integral part of public policies, programmes and economic decisions.

References

Aghazamani, Y., & Hunt, C.A. (2017). Empowerment in tourism: A review of peer-reviewed literature. *Tourism Review International*, 21 (4), 333–346.

Amor, A., Vazquez, J.P. & Faína, J.A. (2020). Transformational leadership and work engagement: Exploring the mediating role of structural empowerment. *European Management Journal*, 38 (1), 169–178.

Amor, A., Xanthopoulou, D., Calvo, N. & Vazquez, J. (2021). Structural empowerment, psychological empowerment, and work engagement: A cross-country study. *European Management Journal*, 39 (6), 779–789.

Barlitz, L. (1960). *The Servants of Power: A history of the use of social science in American industry*. Wesleyan University Press.

Boley, B. Bynum, McGehee, N.G., Perdue, R.R. & Long, P. (2014). Empowerment and resident attitudes toward tourism: Strengthening the theoretical foundation through a Weberian lens. *Annals of Tourism Research*, 49, 33–50.

Calvès, A.-E. (2009). Empowerment – The history of a key concept in contemporary development discourse. *Revue Tiers Monde*, 200 (4), 735–749.

Castillo, D.P. (2019). *An Ecological Theology of Liberation*. Orbis Books.

Cattaneo, L.B., & Chapman, A.R. (2010). The process of empowerment: A model for use in research and practice. *American Psychologist*, 65 (7), 646.

Cheong, S.-M., & Miller, M.L. (2000). Power and tourism: A Foucauldian observation. *Annals of Tourism Research*, 27 (2), 371–390.

Choi, H.-S.C., & Murray, I. (2010). Resident attitudes toward sustainable community tourism. *Journal of Sustainable Tourism*, 18 (4), 575–594.

Cole, S. (2006). Information and empowerment: The keys to achieving sustainable tourism. *Journal of Sustainable Tourism*, 14 (6), 629–644.

Colin, G. (1980). *Michel Foucault: Power/Knowledge: Selected Interviews and Other Writings*. Pantheon Books.

Di Castri, F. (2004). Sustainable tourism in small islands: Local empowerment as the key factor. *INSULA-PARIS*, 13 (1/2), 49.

Feldbauer, I., & Jeffrey, H. (2021). Disempowered hosts? A literature review of Muslim women and tourism. In Slak Valek, N., & Almuhrzi, H. *Women in Tourism in Asian Muslim Countries*. Springer, 13–23.

Friedmann, J. (1992). *Empowerment: The politics of alternative development*. Blackwell.

Gadotti, M., & Torres, C. (2009). Paulo Freire: Education for development. *Development and Change*, 40 (6), 1255–1267.

Gilliam, D.A., & Voss, K. (2013). A proposed procedure for construct definition in marketing. *European Journal of Marketing*, 47 (1/2), 5–26.

Goodkind, J.R. & Foster-Fishman, P.G. (2002). Integrating diversity and fostering interdependence: Ecological lessons learned about refugee participation in multiethnic communities. *Journal of Community Psychology*, 30 (4), 389–409.

Habermas, J. (1986). The genealogical writing of history: On some aporias in Foucault's theory of power. *Canadian Journal of Political and Social Theory*, 10 (1–2), 1–9.

Hale, G.A. (2002). *Kierkegaard and the Ends of Language*. University of Minnesota Press.

Heise, D.R. (2010). *Surveying Cultures*. John Wiley & Sons.

Jáimez Román, M.J., & Bretones, F.D. (2013). Spanish adaptation of the structural empowerment scale. *Spanish Journal of Psychology*, 16, 1–7.

Kanter, R. (1997). *Man and Woman of the Corporation*. Basic Books.

Koščak, M., Colarič-Jakše, L.-M., Fabjan, D., Kukulj, S., Založnik, S., Knežević, M., … Prevolšek, B. (2018). No one asks the children, right? *TOURISM*, 66 (4), 396–410.

Koščak, M., Knežević, M., Binder, D., Pelaez-Verdet, A., Cem, I., Mićić, V., … Šegota, T. (2023). Exploring the neglected voices of children in sustainable tourism development: A comparative study in six European tourist destinations. *Journal of Sustainable Tourism*, 31 (2), 561–580.

Kroger, J. (1985). Prophetic-critical and practical-strategic tasks of theology: Habermas and liberation theology. *Theological Studies*, 46 (1), 3–20.

Lee, T.H. (2013). Influence analysis of community resident support for sustainable tourism development. *Tourism Management*, 34, 37–46.

Maruyama, N.U., Woosnam, K.M. & Boley, B.B. (2017). Residents' attitudes toward ethnic neighborhood tourism (ENT): Perspectives of ethnicity and empowerment. *Tourism Geographies*, 19 (2), 265–286.

Merriam-webster.com (2023). *Empowerment*. https://www.merriam-webster.com/dictionary/empowerment#h1.

Miller, B. (1994). Political empowerment, local-central state relations, and geographically shifting political opportunity structures: Strategies of the Cambridge, Massachusetts, Peace Movement. *Political Geography*, 13 (5), 393–406.

Morgan, N., & Pritchard, A. (2019). Gender matters in hospitality. *International Journal of Hospitality Management*, 76 (B), 38–44.

Moscardo, G. (2012). Building social capital to enhance the quality-of-life of destination residents. In Uysal, M., Perdue, R.R. & Sirgy, M.J. *Handbook of Tourism and*

Quality-of-Life Research: Enhancing the lives of tourists and residents of host communities. Springer, 403–422.

Norwood Evans, E. (1992). Liberation theology, empowerment theory and social work practice with the oppressed. *International Social Work*, 35 (2), 135–147.

Nunkoo, R., & Ramkissoon, H. (2013). Stakeholders' views of enclave tourism: A grounded theory approach. *Journal of Hospitality & Tourism Research*, 40 (5), 557–558.

Nunkoo, R., & Smith, S.L.J. (2013). Political economy of tourism: Trust in government actors, political support, and their determinants. *Tourism Management*, 36, 120–132.

Palardy, N.P., Boley, B.B. & Johnson Gaither, C. (2018). Residents and urban greenways: Modeling support for the Atlanta BeltLine. *Landscape and Urban Planning*, 169 (May), 250–259.

Pratto, F. (2016). On power and empowerment. *British Journal of Social Psychology*, 55 (1), 1–20.

Půtová, B. (2018). Anthropology of tourism: Researching interactions between hosts and guests. *Czech Journal of Tourism*, 7 (1), 71–92.

Rappaport, J. (1981). In praise of paradox: A social policy of empowerment over prevention. *American Journal of Community Psychology*, 9 (1), 1–25.

Scheyvens, R. (1999). Ecotourism and the empowerment of local communities. *Tourism Management*, 20 (2), 245–249.

Šegota, T., Mihalič, T. & Kuščer, K. (2017). The impact of residents' informedness and involvement on their perceptions of tourism impacts: The case of Bled. *Journal of Destination Marketing & Management*, 6 (3), 196–206.

Selwyn, T. (1996). *The Tourist Image: Myths and myth making in tourism*. John Wiley & Sons.

Strzelecka, M., Boley, B.B. & Strzelecka, C. (2017). Empowerment and resident support for tourism in rural Central and Eastern Europe (CEE): The case of Pomerania, Poland. *Journal of Sustainable Tourism*, 25 (4), 554–572.

Tomassini, L., & Cavagnaro, E. (2020). The novel spaces and power-geometries in tourism and hospitality after 2020 will belong to the "local". *Tourism Geographies*, 22 (2), 1–7.

Urry, J., & Larsen, J. (2011). *The Tourist Gaze 3.0*. Sage.

Uysal, M., Sirgy, M.J., Woo, E. & Kim, H.L. (2016). Quality of life (QOL) and well-being research in tourism. *Tourism Management*, 53, 244–261.

Wise, J.B. (2005). *Empowerment Practice with Families in Distress*. Columbia University Press.

WTO, & UNDP (2017). *Tourism and the Sustainable Development Goals – Journey to 2030*. https://www.e-unwto.org/doi/book/10.18111/9789284419401 (accessed 15 January 2021).

Zimmerman, M.A. (2000). Empowerment theory – Psychological, organizational and community levels of analysis. In Julian, R., & Seidman, E. *Handbook of Community Psychology*. Kluwer Academic/Plenum Publishers, 43–63.

11

PARTICIPATION AND INVOLVEMENT

Introduction

Many terms in tourism literature and practice infer inclusivity or participation, including alliances, coalitions, forums and task forces. Over recent years, the notion of *partnership* has become particularly prevalent. It is a term used mainly by governments and practitioners to describe regular, sometimes cross-sectoral, interactions between groups who aim to achieve a set goal or policy objective. The partnership is seen as a long-term relationship with the potential to promote discussion, negotiation and building mutually acceptable proposals about how tourism should be developed.

There are several reasons why cooperative approaches appear to sit well with the principles of sustainable development (Koščak & O'Rourke, 2023):

- Collaboration among various stakeholders, including non-economic interests, might promote more significant consideration of the natural, built and human resources that must be sustained.
- By involving stakeholders' diverse interests, there may be greater potential for integrative and holistic approaches to policy development, which may advance sustainability.
- If multiple stakeholders affected by tourism development were involved in the policy-making process, this might lead to a more equitable distribution of the resulting benefits and costs. The idea is that participation would raise awareness of tourism's impacts on all stakeholders, and this heightened awareness should lead to fairer policies.
- Broad participation in policy-making could help democratise decision-making, empower participants and lead to capacity building and skill acquisition amongst participants.

DOI: 10.4324/9781003374299-19

The OECD suggests the following strategies to engage the public (Mossey & Manohran, 2020):

1. Information sharing: one-way communication; government produces and delivers information for use by citizens.
2. Consultation: two-way communication; citizens provide feedback to the government, for example, citizen surveys and opinion polls.
3. Active participation: partnership between the public and government; citizens are involved in decision- and policy-making processes.

The various democratic theories advance the notion that governments that make efforts to increase citizen participation benefit from having a greater engagement of citizens in their decision-making process.

The UNEP (2020) suggests eight key areas for local engagement of policy-makers:

1. Planning: land use and sectoral planning present opportunities to combine agriculture and forest management with other land uses. Planning can also balance productive industry with maintaining a landscape attractive for tourism.
2. Management: local governments can identify ways to integrate the economic benefits of ecosystem services into management practices.
3. Regulation and protection: local governments play a crucial role in interpreting and implementing regulations encouraging best practices and ecosystem protection.
4. Coordination and collective action: negotiation and coordination between different interest groups inevitably occurs locally. Local governments can support the formation of resource management committees and integrate formal and informal institutions to ensure effective participation and outcomes.
5. Investment: local governments can invest in ecosystem services through supporting locally oriented purchasing policy. They can buy local timber for government buildings, or support by buying locally produced food, for example, through local labels for local products, etc.
6. Incentives: local governments can create positive incentives for improved ecosystem services management, for example, funds to help promote green business projects or investments that aim to secure the long-term viability of ecosystem services.
7. Extension services and capacity building: many environmental problems occur because people do not understand the full implications of their actions or the available alternatives. Farmers may not be aware of other options that allow for more sustainable land use while at the same time being financially affordable and yielding profits.

8. Research and promotion: local agencies often conduct research to assess the role of local ecosystem services. The success of monitoring and other measures often depend on collaborating with well-informed local stakeholders. Once benefits are assessed, this information can be used to promote local products or services.

The main objective of the participatory planning process is to establish a consulting body involving the main stakeholders in the destination's decision-making processes and action plan development and implementation (CEETO, 2018). The crucial scenes of the participation are the "local forums". A forum involves stakeholders that are interested in the development of tourism in the area. These are local communities, local authorities, institutes, ministries, tourism service providers, tourist associations and external experts, SMEs, local guides, etc.

The forums and similar tourism planning and development meetings are usually conducted by specialists in communication and group collaboration (facilitators), who use several consolidated collaboration techniques, as depicted in Figure 11.1.

Despite the selected meeting technique, to design an effective and time-saving participatory planning process, each manager should respond to the following questions:

1. Is the goal of the process clear and understandable to everyone?
2. What are the interests affected by the results of the process?
3. Who is representing those interests?
4. What kind of conflicts/alliances can/should the process bring forth?

Answers to these questions require each manager to clearly understand the stakeholders' level of involvement and commitment and what type of participatory planning process should be implemented to reach the stated goal.

Brainstorming	Matalón	Nominal Group
World Cafe	Focus Group	Ideas Factory
Photo voice	Goal-oriented project planning	Critical accident

FIGURE 11.1 Consolidated collaboration techniques
Source: CEETO (2018)

Also, destination managers should define the expected results before involving the local community in the participatory planning process. It is also important to outline an understandable message to potential stakeholders, considering that most of them are unfamiliar with technical or scientific terminology. The potential stakeholders might partake in the participatory planning process only when they understand that the goal is interesting for them. When the goal is clear, it is easier to avoid confusion and false expectations.

Managing a participatory planning process implies the creation of a favourable discussion. The result of the participatory planning process should be the integration of convergences between the tourist destination's mission and the local community's interests. Those managing the process should know that conflicts between stakeholders cannot be solved within the process itself. Too many conflicts might undermine the whole process, shifting the focus from the goal of the process to the reason for the conflict. Conversely, a participatory planning process may create or enhance positive alliances based on convergences of interests. Drawing a map of explicit or latent conflicts and alliances enables the anticipation of obstacles and threats and enlightening opportunities.

Arnstein's Ladder of Citizen Participation

The Ladder of Citizen Participation, proposed by Sherry Arnstein in 1969, is one of the most widely referenced and influential models in democratic public participation. Arnstein's seminal model is essential for local leaders, organisers and facilitators who want to understand foundational public engagement and participation theories and how empowered public institutions and officials deny power to citizens. The model also influenced many later models, including Elizabeth Rocha's Ladder of Empowerment and Roger Hart's Ladder of Children's Participation.

Arnstein's penetrating, no-nonsense, even pugnacious analysis advanced a central argument that remains as relevant today as it was in 1969: citizen participation in democratic processes if it is to be considered "participation" in any genuine or practical sense, requires the redistribution of power. In Arnstein's formulation, *citizen participation is citizen power*. Without an authentic reallocation of power, for example, in the form of money or decision-making authority, the participation merely "allows the power holders to claim that all sides were considered, but makes it possible for only some of those sides to benefit. It maintains the status quo" (Arnstein, 1969, p. 216).

Arnstein (1969) starts the discussion about participation with a straightforward observation, one that can be seen in many democratic contexts of today (p. 216):

> The idea of citizen participation is a little like eating spinach: no one is against it in principle because it is good for you. Participation of the governed in their government is, in theory, the cornerstone of democracy – a revered idea that is vigorously applauded by virtually everyone. The

applause is reduced to polite handclaps, however, when this principle is advocated by the have-not blacks, Mexican-Americans, Puerto Ricans, Indians, Eskimos, and whites. And when the have-nots define participation as redistribution of power, the American consensus on the fundamental principle explodes into many shades of outright racial, ethnic, ideological, and political opposition.

The main question is, "*What* is citizen participation, and what is its relationship to the social imperatives of our time?" Her detailed answer is as follows (Arnstein, 1969, p. 216, emphasis in original):

> My answer to the critical *what* question is simply that citizen participation is a categorical term for citizen power. It is the redistribution of power that enables the have-not citizens, presently excluded from the political and economic processes, to be deliberately included in the future. It is the strategy by which the have-nots join in determining how information is shared, goals and policies are set, tax resources are allocated, programs are operated, and benefits like contracts and patronage are parcelled out. In short, it is the means by which they can induce significant social reform which enables them to share in the benefits of the affluent society ... participation without redistribution of power is an empty and frustrating process for the powerless.

Despite her thoughts being screamed about for decades in political circles of research and practice, many of her views have not seen the light when it comes to participatory planning in tourism, especially linked to children and youth.

The Eight Rungs of the Ladder of Citizen Participation

Arnstein's typology of citizen participation is presented as a metaphorical ladder, with each ascending rung representing increasing levels of citizen agency, control and power. In addition to the eight rungs of participation, Arnstein includes a descriptive continuum of participatory power that moves from *non-participation* (no power) to *degrees of tokenism* (counterfeit power) to *degrees of citizen participation* (actual power). The original 1969 illustration of Sherry Arnstein's Ladder of Citizen Participation appeared in the *Journal of the American Planning Association*. The ladder features eight rungs that describe three general forms of citizen power in democratic decision-making: Non-participation (no power), Degrees of Tokenism (counterfeit power) and Degrees of Citizen Power (actual power).

The eight rungs of the Ladder of Citizen Participation are as follows.

1 Manipulation

Manipulation occurs when public institutions, officials or administrators mislead citizens into believing they are being given power in a process that has been intentionally manufactured to deny them power. Hence, it represents an illusory form of participation. According to Arnstein (1969, p. 218):

> in the name of citizen participation, people are placed on rubber stamp advisory committees or advisory boards for the express purpose of "educating" them or engineering their support. Instead of genuine citizen participation, the bottom rung of the ladder signifies the distortion of participation into a public relations vehicle by power holders.

2 Therapy

Participation as therapy occurs when public officials and administrators "assume that powerlessness is synonymous with mental illness" (Arnstein, 1969, p. 218), and they create pseudo-participatory programmes that attempt to convince citizens that *they are the problem* when, in fact, it's established institutions and policies that are creating the problems for citizens. In Arnstein's (1969, p. 218) words: "What makes this form of 'participation' so invidious is that citizens are engaged in extensive activity, but the focus of it is on curing them of their 'pathology' rather than changing the racism and victimisation that create their 'pathologies'".

3 Informing

While Arnstein (1969, p. 219) acknowledges that *informing* "citizens of their rights, responsibilities, and options can be the most important first step toward legitimate citizen participation", she also notes that:

> too frequently the emphasis is placed on a one-way flow of information – from officials to citizens – with no channel provided for feedback and no power for negotiation ... meetings can also be turned into vehicles for one-way communication by the simple device of providing superficial information, discouraging questions, or giving irrelevant answers.
>
> *(Arnstein, 1969, p. 219)*

Information flows from official levels may intimidate citizens through the perceived power of the sender. Hence, citizens accept the information provided as fact or endorse the proposals put forward by those in power.

4 Consultation

Consultation does not happen without inviting citizens to express their opinions. Just like the step of informing citizens, consultation is also a step toward their full participation. However, when *consultation* processes are not combined with other modes of participation, this ladder rung offers little assurance that citizen concerns and ideas will be considered. Consultation is usually done via attitude surveys, neighbourhood meetings and public hearings. However, when the citizens' ideas and opinions are solely restricted to this level, participation becomes just one of the window dressing rituals, leaning towards non-participation. Consultation should move beyond perceiving people as statistical abstractions, and participation should not be measured by how many come to meetings, take brochures home or answer a questionnaire. What citizens achieve in all these activities is that they have "participated in participation", giving power holders the evidence that they have gone through the required motions of participatory planning.

5 Placation

Participation as *placation* occurs when citizens are granted a limited degree of influence in a process, but their participation is largely or entirely tokenistic: citizens are merely involved in demonstrating that they were involved. In Arnstein's (1969, p. 220) words:

> An example of placation strategy is to place a few hand-picked "worthy" poor on boards of Community Action Agencies or on public bodies like the board of education, police commission, or housing authority. If they are not accountable to a constituency in the community and if the traditional power elite hold the majority of seats, the have-nots can be easily outvoted and outfoxed.

6 Partnership

Participation as *partnership* occurs when public institutions, officials or administrators allow citizens to negotiate better deals, veto decisions, share funding or put forward requests that are at least partially fulfilled. The power exhibited in this ladder rung is redistributed through negotiation between citizens and power holders. Planning and decision-making responsibilities should be shared through such structures as joint policy boards, planning committees and mechanisms for resolving impasses. This requires establishing ground engagement roles and should not be subjected to unilateral change. However, Arnstein (1969) notes that in many partnership situations, power is not voluntarily shared by public institutions, but *citizens take it* through actions such as protests, campaigns or community organising.

7 Delegated power

Participation as *delegated power* occurs when public institutions, officials or administrators give up at least some degree of control, management, decision-making authority or funding to citizens. For example, a citizen board or corporation tasked with managing a community programme rather than merely participating in a programme operated by a city would be an example of delegated power. Similar examples can be seen in the so-called participatory budget when local governments ask citizens to provide ideas for local planning and development based on a budget that is allocated for citizen initiatives. In Arnstein's (1969, p. 222) words:

> At this level, the ladder has been scaled to the point where citizens hold the significant cards to assure accountability of the program to them. To resolve differences, power holders need to start the bargaining process rather than respond to pressure from the other end.

8 Citizen control

Participation as *citizen control* occurs when "participants or residents can govern a program or an institution, be in full charge of policy and managerial aspects, and be able to negotiate the conditions under which 'outsiders' may change them" (Arnstein, 1969, p. 223). In citizen-controlled situations, for example, public funding would flow directly to a community organisation, which would have complete control over how that funding is allocated.

Limitations of the model

Like any model, framework, or simplifying metaphor, the Ladder of Citizen Participation can only explain so much. A standard criticism of two-dimensional models – particularly those that can be interpreted as graduated hierarchical scales that ascend from lower to higher – is:

1. They cannot adequately represent the layered complexity or fluctuating power dynamics that are typically in play in real-world participatory situations.
2. There is the tendency to interpret lower levels as universally negative (or worse than) and higher levels as universally positive (or better when).

For example, it may be perfectly appropriate to inform community members about already-made decisions in some situations (e.g. district administrative decisions about teacher and staff salaries) or to withhold control from citizens in others, such as when they may not have the specialised skills or expertise required for a given task (e.g. managing public funds on a large project). Yet, as Arnstein (1969, p. 217) notes, the model's simplicity makes it effective as a conceptual tool: "The ladder juxtaposes powerless citizens with the powerful to highlight the fundamental divisions between them".

Arnstein (1969, pp. 217–218) describes a few other limitations of the model:

- "The justification for using such simplistic abstractions is that in most cases, the have-nots really do perceive the powerful as a monolithic 'system,' and power holders actually do view the have-nots as a sea of 'those people,' with little comprehension of the class and caste differences among them." Yet, in reality, "neither the have-nots nor the power holders are homogeneous blocs. Each group encompasses a host of divergent points of view, significant cleavages, competing vested interests, and splintered subgroups."

- The ladder does not include an analysis of the "roadblocks" to authentic citizen participation and empowerment. "These roadblocks lie on both sides of the simplistic fence. On the power holders' side, they include racism, paternalism, and resistance to power redistribution. On the have-nots' side, they include inadequacies of the poor community's political, socioeconomic infrastructure and knowledge base, plus difficulties of organising a representative and accountable citizens' group in the face of futility, alienation, and distrust."
- Arnstein is also aware that in "the real world of people and programs, there might be 150 rungs with less sharp and 'pure' distinctions among them" and that "some of the characteristics used to illustrate each of the eight types might be applicable to other rungs. For example, employment of the have-nots in a program or on a planning staff could occur at any of the eight rungs and could represent either a legitimate or illegitimate characteristic of citizen participation. Depending on their motives, power holders can hire poor people to co-opt them, to placate them, or to utilise the have-nots' special skills and insights. Some mayors, in private, actually boast of their strategy in hiring militant black leaders to muzzle them while destroying their credibility in the black community."
- While *citizen control* appears at the apex of the ladder, and it offers many advantages as a model of citizen participation, Arnstein notes several potential disadvantages:

  - It supports separatism.
  - It creates balkanisation of public services.
  - It is more costly and less efficient; it enables minority group "hustlers" to be just as opportunistic and disdainful of the have-nots as their white predecessors.
  - It is incompatible with merit systems and professionalism.
  - Ironically enough, it can turn out to be a new Mickey Mouse game for the have-nots by not allowing them sufficient dollar resources to succeed.

The other seven ladder rungs present similar complexities and a host of potential advantages and disadvantages.

Importance of local community participation in tourism development

Unlike other sectors of the economy, tourism has the potential to uplift the economy in remote areas. With its increasing reach in every corner of the world, tourism can affect the local community in several ways. Tourism may be a dominant factor in some local communities' overall development. In other communities, it might cause negative impacts such as displacement of local people to make way for tourism facilities, depletion of local resources, increased cost of living and commercialisation of culture. So, it is important that the local community's active involvement in tourism activities increases tourism's benefits and minimises the negative impacts (Dolma Eco-tourism, 2018).

Local community participation is one of the core elements of tourism development because it is central to the sustainability of the tourism industry. Several sectors are involved in tourism development, such as government, the private sector, various non-governmental organisations and individuals. However, in that list of involvement, local communities are probably the only legitimate and moral stakeholders in tourism development.

Involvement of the local community has substantial value in tourism for the local population, their lifestyle and environmental, cultural and traditional factors, which are the main attractions in tourism. Thus, the needs and aspirations of locals must be maintained. Tourism development and the involvement of local community will result in sustainable development and bring economic, environmental and cultural benefits. Active participation of communities in tourism ensures the enrichment of the broader tourism experience as well.

A community's involvement in tourism development guarantees them a place as an active partner. It provides checks and balances since they have a particular stake in the region and a commitment to environmental quality. Tourism can work over the long term, although its feasibility is dependent on the support and engagement of the local community. There are several examples when high local involvement in tourism projects has been successful in community-led projects in France, Spain, the Scottish Highlands and rural Greece (agri-tourism) (Dolma Eco-tourism, 2018).

There has been an argument that tourism contributes to local development by providing destination countries with economic benefits, and the benefits from tourism may not be distributed to all levels of society. However, local community involvement assists in the proper distribution of economic benefits and, at the same time, improves the long-term prospect of tourism development. Local community involvement also confirms higher employment levels with reasonable pay and seasonal job opportunities. Local involvement can prevent leakage of foreign currency (and potentially depletion of national foreign currency reserves) by encouraging local ownership guiding services, transportation, accommodation, restaurants, handicrafts and the retailing of local products. However, there arises the same problem of irregular income distribution; ownership by local investors who dominate local economic activity and tourism outlets may not necessarily lead to an equitable distribution of benefits nor encourage environmental accountability.

Homestay (self-catering accommodation) or agri-tourism holidays are a further encouragement to local involvement as they provide the tourist with an enriching alternative to the mass market. Community-led projects and small-scale businesses at a local level can contribute to a significant degree in improving the lifestyle. However, commercial success and a need to meet demand make it hard to avoid small enterprises evolving into medium/large-scale enterprises. However, the infrastructure of mass tourism can, in turn, help to develop successful small projects involving local actors.

Tourism development gives local people the time to adjust to new environmental, social and economic conditions; it assists in preventing the negative results of rapid uncontrolled development. Involving local people in determining their development will prevent conflicts, which would inevitably affect the sustainability of tourism. Community-based tourism has a higher prospect in rural tourism development, given that its success depends on better community leadership, support and the participation of local administrative groups (Dolma Eco-tourism, 2018).

Local community participation in tourism development is vital in attaining sustainability goals and improving the local community's welfare. The involvement of that community ensures the conservation of the local environment and culture.

Constraining factors influencing local community participation in tourism development include the following.

Lack of financial support

Locals in developing countries face a hard time investing in tourism and starting a business. For example, in Nepal, there is a trend where men go to Gulf countries as labourers, and the rest of the family engages in subsistence farming. Although they wish to start their own business in their homeland, they are compelled because they lack financial support. Such a situation is experienced in many developing countries, from which we have seen many workers finding employment in tourism and hospitality in developed countries.

Lack of tourism knowledge

Although locals know the significance of local-level participation, the actual participation is less than expected. It is because of an inability and incapacity to understand the key objectives and concepts of tourism. Lack of understanding about community participation and the purpose of tourism development can be a major constraint.

Negative views of tourism

Local people usually view tourism as a seasonal and less income-generating business. They hesitate to invest in tourism because of the unpredictable number of visitors in different seasons.

Dominance by higher-class people

Local people are lacking knowledge and confidence. They see themselves as invisible compared to the elite, i.e. officials and professionals. As they may have little or no experience and expertise in tourism, they think they will be provided with equal opportunities compared to the officials and professionals.

Despite these constraints, the local community must be involved in the decision-making and policy-making process to uplift the trust and confidence of the local population concerning tourism development. Community involvement ensures improvement of planning and service delivery whilst promoting a sense of community belonging, pride and sharing of the common objectives. Local-level participation in tourism supports the upholding of local culture, traditions and the indigenous knowledge of local people. It confirms the achievement of sustainability goals, the welfare of the local community and the conservation of the environment. Thus, the community should actively participate through involved work, decision-making and representation in structured communities. Community participation aims for proper communication amongst locals to facilitate better decision-making and more sustainable growth and development.

BOX 11.1 OVERTOURISM – THE NEED FOR PARTICIPATORY PLANNING

When discussing the problems of overtourism, whether pre-Covid (i.e. up to 2019) or post-Covid (i.e. 2022 onwards), one should go beyond the mere concern with what may be perceived as a realistic number of tourists on some destinations and include the perception of the residents regarding the level of tourism input. In effect, overtourism occurs when there are too many visitors to a particular destination. *Too many* is a subjective term, but it may be defined in each destination and by each stakeholder. For example, when rent prices push out local tenants to make way for holiday rentals, that is overtourism. When narrow roads become jammed with tourist vehicles, that is overtourism. However, while the term itself was coined in 2012, it did not hit the headlines until the summer of 2017. This was not because of the increase in tourist numbers, which had not been particularly dramatic. What made the news in 2017 was the sudden backlash from residents, a phenomenon that had not previously occurred on any significant scale. There had been a slow drip feed of tourism into cities such as Barcelona, Venice and Dubrovnik, into places one thought of as remote, such as Iceland and Skye, and finally, as the balance tipped and this new concept was given a name, the protests spread. There were marches in the streets, graffiti saying "Tourist go home" (Coldwell, 2017) and, in some cases, local authorities responded by increasing fees, refusing to issue permits for more tourist-focused businesses in city centres, and even closing entire islands to visitors (McKinsey & Company & WTTC, 2017). It was these actions that made the news.

Problems of overtourism occur when there is no application of a correct process of participatory planning. Participatory approaches to research "with" and not merely "on" communities or peoples are ideologically grounded and underpinned by theoretical interests linked to social justice and democratic principles (Bergold & Thomas, 2012). Some have argued that the critical or transformative worldview is the only viable paradigmatic stance for researchers who make use of qualitative participatory approaches (Cammarota & Fine, 2008). Critical and participatory approaches in research should aim to deconstruct power and privilege so that "an emancipatory praxis can be co-developed with communities and peoples suffering oppression" and marginalisation (Higgins-Desbiolles & Whyte, 2013, p. 249). In participatory research, power is decentralised, and through collaboration, the *researched* becomes the *researcher* and is allowed to participate actively in the research process (McCartan et al., 2012). Because of its emancipatory values, participatory research is particularly suited to uncovering the voices and perspectives of marginalised members of the community and initiating some form of social action to change and positively enhance the conditions in which they find themselves (Creswell, 2014).

Primarily, an essential element to avoid the problem of overtourism is to study the impacts of tourism on host communities, as well as on host cultures. "Culture or civilisation, taken in its wide ethnographic sense, is that complex whole which includes knowledge beliefs, arts, morals, law, customs, and any other capabilities and habits acquired by man as a member of society" (Tylor, 1871). Malinowski (1931) gave a more universal and less anthropocentric definition, namely, "a culture is functioning, active, efficient, well-organised unity, which must be analysed into component institutions in relation to one another, and in relation to the environment, man-made as well as natural". In a report on Wales, Jones and Travis (1983) defined culture as "the system of values, beliefs, behaviours, morals, and other social phenomena shared by a group of people, based on their common experience of life, language and history". This testifies to tourism not simply being an economic sector, but also, amongst other things, a culture in the broader contextual sense. It is a culture that is transmitted inter-generationally, as, indeed, the broader concept of culture is transmitted. Efforts to address the complex linkages between culture and development require, on the one hand, promoting the inclusion of minorities and disadvantaged groups in social, political and cultural life; and, on the other hand, harnessing the potential of the creative sector for job creation, economic growth and poverty reduction efforts more broadly.

The inclusion of minorities and disadvantaged groups in social, political and cultural life remains an ongoing development priority. Tourism can play a significant role in achieving all of this due to its character as a horizontal sector with a value chain that goes across almost every existing economic, human or cultural activity in each place. Compared with other economic activities, the special relationship of tourism with the environment and society makes it an ideal tool for sustainable development. This is due to its unique dependency on quality environments, cultural distinctiveness, social interaction, security and well-being. On the one hand, if poorly planned or developed to excess, tourism may destroy those unique qualities which have such a central relationship to sustainable development. On the other, it may be a driving force for their con-servation and promotion – directly through the raising of awareness and income to support them and indirectly by providing an economic justification for the provision of such support by others.

To ensure sustainable tourism development and avoid problems of over-tourism, *all voices* need to be heard (Byrd, 2007; Šegota et al., 2017). In line, sustainable tourism development requires a carrying capacity study; that is, an estimate of "the maximum number of people who can use a site without an unacceptable alteration in the physical environment and without an unac-ceptable decline in the quality of the experience" (Mathieson & Wall, 1982) to both visitors and residents. The factors that need to be considered are:

1.   Physical impact of tourists.
2.   Ecological impact of tourists.
3.   Perceptions of overcrowding.
4.   Cultural and social impact on residents.

The carrying capacity study is central to meeting the objectives of sustainable tourism development (Koščak, 2002), which is to ensure that:

- The tourists and day visitors attracted to the particular destination will not have a deleterious impact on the cultural or natural sites.
- Overcrowding will not result in visitor dissatisfaction.
- Local people will not feel antagonistic towards their guests.

This is essential if tourism is to contribute to the conservation of cultural and natural heritage through the realisation of economic value and raising awareness of, and commitment to, the local patrimony.

Children and the participatory planning process

Children and young people have been an "under-researched" and "undervalued" field of enquiry in tourism studies (Thornton et al., 1997, p. 287). Almost 20 years after this initial statement, recent studies acknowledge the absence of chil-dren in tourism literature (Poria & Timothy, 2014; Small, 2008). Notable excep-tions include recent studies on the role of children and young people in family travel decision-making (e.g. Schänzel et al., 2012) and studies on children's and young people's experiences and memories of family holidays (e.g. Small, 2008).

The early perspectives were based on a dialectic approach to tourism and modernity and dichotomies such as tourists as guests and residents as hosts (Meethan, 2001). On the one hand, tourists wished to escape modernity in search of authenticity, and on the other hand, hosts would stage such cultural performances for economic benefits (Cohen & Cohen, 2012).

Although research on youth and tourism is beginning to gain traction among scholars, most of these studies do not rely on data generated directly from children (Poria & Timothy, 2014). In addition, previous studies have focused primarily on children and youth as guests (tourists) rather than hosts, meaning little attention has been given to children and young people as residents of host communities. The insights provided by Graburn (1983), although focused on tourists, can potentially be applied to understand how growing up in a host community affects children and young people at a critical stage.

Children and young people have often been defined as a "muted" or even "silent" social group compared to research with/about other social categories. This is evident in tourism studies where children and young people's experiences have been marginalised (Khoo-Lattimore, 2015; Poria & Timothy, 2014; Small, 2008). In particular, there is a lack of research informed by young people's experiences of growing up in a tourist destination and their perceptions and attitudes towards tourism (Canosa, Wilson et al., 2016).

The impact of participatory approaches to research with children is evident in pioneering methods such as Kellett's (2010) "child-led" research approach. According to Kellett (2010), children have a unique *insider* perspective that makes them experts in their own lives, and thus, they are uniquely placed to carry out research with the support and encouragement of adult researchers. Actively involving children in studies becomes an empowering process which leads to "a virtuous circle of increased confidence and raised self-esteem, resulting in more active participation by children in other aspects affecting their lives" (Kellett, 2010, p. 197).

In the current childhood studies paradigm, participatory methods have acquired substantial significance and popularity. These methods are often described as "democratised" as the power relations in the research process are challenged, and the academic researcher reinvents "definitions and practices of authority" (Dentith et al., 2012, p. 16). Hence, the shift to more participatory approaches has also been accompanied by a call for closer attention to key ethical considerations and the important nexus between method and ethics (Graham et al., 2013).

Clearly, children are influenced by and involved in tourism, often being the most significant influence in family tourism choices and major consumers of volunteer and adventure experiences during later teenage years. It makes sense, then, that interest in undertaking research with those under 18 is increasing within tourism studies. However, as flagged earlier, whilst children's participation in research is developing as a new area for tourism, it is now relatively a routine in other fields and disciplines. Not only does this offer tourism researchers the opportunity to build on existing knowledge about why and how to involve children in research, but it also potentially positions tourism researchers at the cutting edge of advancing ethically sound research in this space (Canosa, Moyle et al., 2016).

As Small (2008, p. 773) argues, involving children in tourism research should go "beyond the commercial incentive". This is to say that, along with the perceived methodological and ethical complexities, another possible reason why children's voices have been neglected is the view that they are not contributing stakeholders in the business/managerial milieu of tourism. Nevertheless, with the propagation of a critical scholarship, there is now an opportunity to end the silence of marginalised community members and place child-centred research on the agenda in tourism studies (Canosa, Moyle et al., 2016).

References

Arnstein, S. (1969). A Ladder of Citizen Participation. *Journal of the American Planning Association*, 35 (4), 216–224.

Bergold, J., & Thomas, S. (2012). Participatory research methods: A methodological approach in motion. *Forum Qualitative Sozialforschung/Forum: Qualitative Social Research*, 13 (1). http://www.qualitative-research.net/.

Byrd, E. T. (2007). Stakeholders in sustainable tourism development and their roles: Applying stakeholder theory to sustainable tourism development. *Tourism Review*, 62 (2), 6–13.

Cammarota, J., & Fine, M. (2008). Youth participatory action research: A pedagogy for transformational resistance. In Cammarota, J., & Fine, M. *Revolutionising Education: Youth participatory action research in motion*. Routledge, 1–11.

Canosa, A., Moyle, B. & Wray, M. (2016). Can anybody hear me? A critical analysis of young residents' voices in tourism studies. *Tourism Analysis: An Interdisciplinary Journal*, 21 (2), 325–337.

Canosa, A., Wilson, E. & Graham, A. (2016). Empowering young people through participatory film: A postmethodological approach. *Current Issues in Tourism*, 1–14. http://dx.doi.org/10.1080/13683500.2016.1179270.

CEETO (2018). *Capacity Building Workplan for Protected Areas*, May 2018. CEETO Project. www.ceeto-network.eu.

Cohen, E., & Cohen, S.A. (2012). Current sociological theories and issues in tourism. *Annals of Tourism Research* 39 (4): 2177–2202.

Coldwell, W. (2017). First Venice and Barcelona: Now anti-tourism marches spread across Europe. *The Guardian*. https://www.theguardian.com/travel/2017/aug/10/anti-tourism-marches-spread-across-europe-venice-barcelona (accessed 10 March 2018).

Creswell, J.W. (2014). *Research Design: Qualitative, quantitative and mixed methods approaches*, 4th edition. Sage Publications.

Dolma Eco-tourism (2018). https://www.linkedin.com/pulse/local-community-participation-tourism-development-dolma-eco-tourism/ (accessed 26 June 2023).

Dentith, A.M., Measor, L. & O'Malley, M.P. (2012). The research imagination amid dilemmas of engaging young people in critical participatory work. *Forum Qualitative Sozialforschung/Forum: Qualitative Social Research*, 13 (1), 22–44.

Graburn, N.H.H. (1983). Editorial comments. *Annals of Tourism Research*, 10 (1), 1–3.

Graham, A., Powell, M.A., Taylor, N., Anderson, D.L. & Fitzgerald, R.M. (2013). *Ethical Research Involving Children.* UNICEF Office of Research – Innocenti. www.childethics.com.

Higgins-Desbiolles, F., & Whyte, K.P. (2013). No high hopes for hopeful tourism: A critical comment. *Annals of Tourism Research*, 40, 428–433.

Jones, A., & Travis, A. (1983). *Cultural Tourism: Toward a European Charter: Report to WTB.* EW Tourism Consultancy.

Khoo-Lattimore, C. (2015). Kids on board: Methodological challenges, concerns and clarifications when including young children's voices in tourism research. *Current Issues in Tourism*, 18 (9), 845–858.

Kellett, M. (2010). Small shoes, big steps! Empowering children as active researchers. *American Journal of Community Psychology*, 46 (1–2), 195–203.

Koščak, M. (2002). Heritage trails: Rural regeneration through sustainable tourism in Dolenjska and Bela Krajina. *Rast, XIII*, 2 (80), 204–211.

Koščak, M., & O'Rourke, T. (Eds.). (2023). *Ethical and Responsible Tourism: Managing sustainability in local tourism destinations*, 2nd edition. Routledge. https://doi.org/10.4324/9781003358688.

Malinowski, B. (1931). Culture. In Andreson Seligman, E.R., & Saunders Johnson, A., *Encyclopedia of the Social Sciences.* Macmillan, 621–645.

Mathieson, A., & Wall. G. (1982). *Tourism: Economic, physical and social impacts.* Longman.

McCartan, C., Schubotz, D. & Murphy, J. (2012). The self-conscious researcher – postmodern perspectives of participatory research with young people. *Forum Qualitative Sozialforschung/Forum: Qualitative Social Research*, 13 (1). http://www.qualitative-research.net/.

McKinsey & Company, & WTTC (2017). *Coping with Success: Managing overcrowding in tourism destinations.* WTTC. https://www.wttc.org/priorities/sustainable-growth/destination-stewardship/.

Meethan, K. (2001). *Tourism in Global Society: Place, culture, and consumption.* Palgrave Macmillan.

Mossey, S., & Manohran, A. (2020). *Citizen Participation, E-Government and Information Technology Management: Concepts and best practices*, September 2020. https://www.researchgate.net/publication/344103086_CITIZEN_PARTICIPATION (accessed 26 June 2023).

Poria, Y., & Timothy, D.J. (2014). Where are the children in tourism research? *Annals of Tourism Research*, 47, 93–95.

Schänzel, H., Yeoman, I. & Backer, E. (2012). *Family Tourism: Multidisciplinary perspectives.* Channel View.

Šegota, T., Mihalič, T. & Kuščer, K. (2017). The impact of residents' informedness and involvement on perceptions of tourism impacts: The case of the destination Bled. *Journal of Destination Marketing and Management*, 6 (3), 196–206.

Small, J. (2008). The absence of childhood in tourism studies. *Annals of Tourism Research*, 35 (3), 772–789.

Thornton, P.R., Shaw, G. & Williams, A.M. (1997). Tourist group holiday decision-making and behaviour: The influence of children. *Tourism Management*, 18 (5), 287–297.

Tylor, E.B. (1871). *Primitive Culture: Researches into the development mythology.* Harper Collins.

UNEP (2010). *TEEB – The Economics of Ecosystems and Biodiversity for Local and Regional Policy Makers.* http://docs.niwa.co.nz/library/public/TEEBguide.pdf (accessed 26 June 2023).

UNEP (2020). *Handbook for Stakeholder Engagement at the United Nations Environment Programme (UNEP)*, Civil Society Unit Governance Affairs Office United Nations Environment Programme, Nairobi, Kenya. www.unenvironment.org/civil-society-engagement (accessed 26 June 2023).

12

REFLECTIONS ON PART IV

The Key Concepts

This chapter discusses and examines the Key Concepts from each preceding chapter in Part IV.

Chapter 10

The Key Concepts may be categorised as follows:

- *Empowerment is a prerequisite for sustainable tourism development.* This thought makes tourism conceptually centred on the people and their environment rather than production and profits. Empowerment should be understood as an intentional, ongoing process which places the local community at the centre of development, giving them greater access to and control over those resources whilst inundated with mutual respect, critical reflection, caring and group participation. By raising the individual's ability to participate in community activities, the collective interdependence of the community is increased, as it gives a greater voice to its members, both individually and collectively.
- *Empowerment is a multidimensional concept.* Residents who feel powerful enough to influence tourism development are likely to perceive tourism positively, whilst more powerless residents perceive tourism negatively. However, it was not until recently that empowerment was seen as a multidimensional construct extending to social, psychological and political dimensions, with each differently influencing the formation of resident perceptions of tourism impacts.

DOI: 10.4324/9781003374299-20

- *Social empowerment in tourism is about increasing community cohesion.* A tourist destination that strives for excellence and enhances the quality of visit can bring the community together and make all its members feel as contributing, belonging and partaking in an important role in achieving the community's goal. Social empowerment is all about making residents feel more connected to their community, fostering a sense of community spirit within residents and providing ways for residents to get involved in their community.
- *Psychological empowerment creates pride.* Tourism can renew residents' sense of pride and build their self-esteem by increasing an individual's awareness that others outside their community recognise the uniqueness and value of natural and cultural resources of their community. The more residents feel psychologically empowered, the more they will support tourism and see it as beneficial for the community.
- *Political empowerment represents residents' regained voice in the community's government.* Gaining a voice and being included in decision-making extends beyond the mere ability to vote. In tourism, political empowerment shall be understood as providing all community groups a forum to raise concerns and questions about tourism development equally and fairly. It entices the feeling of everyone being equally represented in tourism development and planning.
- *Unlocking hidden manifestations of power using Foulcault's lenses.* At the core of empowerment is the term power, which is universal, permeating all levels of human activity. By taking Foucault's perspective of power in tourism, we cannot avoid discussing visible or hidden manifestations. Scientists and professionals should be aware of the omnipresence of power and tourism, power in tourism networks, the tourist gaze and, less talked about, repressive and productive power over tourists.

Chapter 11

The Key Concepts may be categorised as follows:

- *Public engagement is a central component of sustainability.* When people help shape their city as a tourist destination, they have greater ownership and commitment to its care and preservation. To meet sustainability goals fully, development processes and outcomes need to be equitable and socially just, which entails participatory planning and the inclusion of all members of society, especially marginalised groups.
- *Include the children in participatory planning.* Planning should not be grounded in existing communities but rather include existing and new residents. By new we mean those who moved to the community but were born elsewhere. While half the world's children reside in urban environments, they are not typically included in planning processes, nor the academic literature promoting social justice in planning.

- *Managing a participatory planning process implies the creation of a favourable discussion.* The result of the participatory planning process should be the integration of convergences between the mission of the tourist destination and the interests of the local community. A participatory planning process should create or enhance positive alliances based on intersections of interests. The process is not meant to solve conflicts, but it can help draw a map of explicit or latent conflicts and alliances to anticipate obstacles and threats and enlighten opportunities.
- *Participatory processes identify the solution using different viewpoints.* Participatory processes improve implementation, as a decision or a policy will be more effective if a broad coalition of stakeholders support the proposal and work together to deliver it. They also increase public trust, as openness to conflicting claims and views increases the credibility of the final decision and stimulates active civil society involvement.
- *The Ladder of Citizen Participation.* This is a metaphorical ladder, with each ascending rung representing increasing levels of citizen agency, control and power. In addition to the eight rungs of participation, the ladder also includes a descriptive continuum of participatory power that moves from non-participation (no power) to degrees of tokenism (counterfeit power) to degrees of citizen participation (actual power).
- *Importance of local community participation in tourism development.* Local community participation is one of the core elements of tourism development because it is central to the sustainability of the tourism industry. Tourism may be a dominant factor in some local communities' overall development. In other communities, it might cause negative impacts such as displacement of local people to make way for tourism facilities, depletion of local resources, increased cost of living and commercialisation of culture. So, it is important that the local community's active involvement in tourism activities increases tourism's benefits and minimises the negative impacts.

The Critical Factors

Empowerment, tourism and children

The key factors that contribute to both strengthening the community and reinforcing the elements of structure within the community and certainly enable the empowerment of individuals are the factors that must empower children in environments with intensive tourist activity. Children are an inseparable element of every social structure due to their relationship with their parents, primarily if they work in tourism and hospitality, and all the aspects of the tourism sector that affect the children living there. Children are a continuously repeating factor in strengthening and weakening the position of people from lower social strata residing in these areas. Their parents have to care for their future, often equally complex and uncertain, as was their parents' past. On the other hand, children are often neglected in having a voice, let alone influencing decisions related to tourism in the community. Therefore, an inevitable part of any empowerment activity in a local tourism community should be placed on the relationship between children and tourism and how to empower children. Without empowering children, any existing local community is not strengthening or sustaining its development.

Structural and personal elements of strengthening the community

Social organisations within local communities are internally complex, while their connections with external and internal environments are carefully analysed. They represent structural elements of community empowerment, and their analysis enables the growth and development of children. On the other hand, the personal aspect of community empowerment is mainly psychosocial. It pertains to models of personal change that enable better integration into the society of adults and better integration of children into the local community. Structural and personal elements should be organised together, strengthening the population engaged in tourism activities in a specific geographical area. When analysing these elements, the following needs to be considered: (1) issues related to residents; (2) issues related to tourists; (3) issues related to gender; (4) issues related to disempowerment; and (5) issues related to tourism and hospitality employees.

No participatory planning; no sustainable development

Collaboration amongst various stakeholders, including non-economic interests, promotes greater consideration of the varied natural, built and human resources required to be sustained. By involving stakeholders from several fields and diverse interests, there may be greater potential for an integrative/holistic approach to policy development, which seeks to advance sustainability. If multiple stakeholders affected by tourism development are involved in the policy-making process, the resulting benefits and costs may lead to a more equitable distribution. The idea is that participation raises awareness of tourism impacts on all stakeholders, and this heightened awareness leads to fairer policies. Broad involvement in policy-making may help democratise decision-making, empowering participants and leading to capacity building and skills acquisition amongst participants.

Benefits of participatory planning

The beneficial nature of the participatory approach includes:

- *Coverage*: to reach and involve the stakeholders on a broader scale.
- *Efficiency*: to obtain a cost-efficient design and implementation of a project. The beneficiaries will contribute more actively to project planning and

performance by providing ideas, human resources and/or other (cost sharing), consequently using resources more efficiently.

- *Effectiveness*: people involved get a say in determining objectives and actions and assist in operations like project administration, monitoring and evaluation. They also receive more opportunities to contribute to the project and thus facilitate the diagnosis of environmental, social and institutional constraints and the search for viable solutions.
- *Adoption of innovations*: the stakeholders can develop greater responsiveness to new production methods, technologies and services offered.
- *Sustainability*: more and better outputs and impact are obtained in a project; thus there is longer-term viability and more solid sustainability. By stressing decentralisation, democratic decision-making processes and self-help, various key problems can be solved, including recurrent costs, cost-sharing with beneficiaries, and operation and maintenance.

Reasons for failure

Participation becomes a must, since complex organisation makes it necessary to mobilise stakeholders' experience and skills to deliver compelling long-term results. This is even more important if the purpose is to set up a new way of practising, interacting and organising, i.e. introducing innovative processes in a given local context. Sometimes innovative approaches or processes can fail for the following reasons:

- Difficulty in development or lack of common strategic visions.
- Goals not understood at the lower organisational levels.
- Objectives becoming *moving targets*.
- Plans encompassing too much in too little time.
- People not working toward the exact specifications.
- Lack of instruments and methods to expedite actual participation.
- Difficulty in communication.
- Lack of effective management and leadership.
- Competition and conflicts.
- Exclusion of key stakeholders.

These problems arise, on the one hand, from the complexity of the project scope and, on the other hand, from the lack of participation of the key stakeholders in the former design stages. Both aspects find participation a vehicle for increasing the project's effectiveness. When people have a genuine stake in development activity and are actively involved in decision-making, they are likely to provide more significant commitment, and shared objectives are more likely to be met.

Limitations for citizen participation in planning

Very often, citizens do not take part in decision processes due to the following:

- *The political conditions* or power structures of the country and project area influence citizens' participation, mainly those who do not trust the decision-makers.
- *Lack of funding*: there is a perception that heritage is a luxury compared to dealing with issues such as education, health, employment and defence.
- *Legislative obstacles*: national regulations that limit or deny the modification or construction of infrastructures (houses, bridges, roads, etc.) are perceived by citizens as a limit to growth.
- *Administrative obstacles*: complex, bureaucratic procedures impede genuine participation as well as one-way, top-down planning performed solely by professionals.
- *Socio-cultural impediments*: a serious obstacle is the widespread mentality of dependence, a sense of frustration and distrust in officials among people, who are frequently dominated by local elites to whom they have to leave critical decision-making.
- *Other impediments* are exposure to non-local information, ignorance of the locals, stakeholders' rights to self-organisation and lack of leaders and know-how to promote their interests.

Steps for a sound participatory planning process

Public participation should play a significant role in any sound planning process to enhance its effectiveness. Some typical steps to be undertaken include:

- *Stakeholder mapping*: grouping based on different functions, capacities and activities, including specific interests and perceptions of the situation.
- *Integrated system and problem analysis* after creating a collaborative approach with all stakeholders.
- *Development of shared vision*, goals and expected results.
- *Deficit analysis*: to cope with the mid-to-long-term impacts identified, necessary (primarily remedial) actions should be defined – also with the help of a developed set of indicators for sustainability.
- *Development of tools and solutions*: management tools (addressing present and prospective pressures and drivers acting on the system) and innovative solutions (including the application of new soft/hard technologies) should be discussed and assessed against alternatives.
- *Monitoring success/failure*: criteria/parameters should be developed to monitor future development, including qualitative and quantitative success against goals and expected results.

Connections

This section suggests some elements based on the issues raised in Part IV. In essence, children have a unique *insider's* perspective that makes them experts in their own lives, and thus, they are uniquely placed to voice their desires and needs with the support and encouragement of adults. Actively involving children in decision-making becomes an empowering process, leading to increased confidence and raised self-esteem that children can copy to other decision-making processes, surpassing the scope of tourism planning and development. Following these underlying concepts, we have sought to develop some connections for readers as follows:

- For students, we pose some questions which may assist the connections between teaching and learning.
- For researchers (graduate or professional), we suggest some guidelines for child-centred research, with children as active partners in the research and not mere objects of it.
- For practitioners, we raise matters of concern for their facilitation and creation of child-friendly environments.

Teaching and learning

When discussing the issue of children's involvement in the participatory process of tourism destination development, there are several aspects that students can comment upon. Here are a few key points to consider:

a   Importance of inclusivity: students can highlight the significance of including children in the decision-making process of tourism destination development. They may discuss how children, as stakeholders, can provide valuable insights and perspectives that adults might overlook. Involving children can lead to more diverse, sustainable and community-focused tourism development plans.

b   Educational opportunities: students can explore how children's involvement in the participatory process offers unique learning experiences. They might discuss how engaging children in discussions about tourism development will help them develop a deeper understanding of their local environment, cultural heritage and the potential impacts of tourism. This involvement fosters their sense of ownership and responsibility towards their community.

c   Environmental and cultural preservation: students can emphasise the role of children in advocating for the conservation of the environment and cultural heritage. They could discuss how children, when allowed to participate, may voice concerns about sustainable practices, conservation efforts and the protection of cultural identities. Their involvement helps shape tourism development plans prioritising resource protection and sustainable use.

d   Empowerment and social inclusion: students can explore how involving children in the participatory process of tourism destination development empowers them and promotes social inclusion. They may discuss how children's voices and ideas should be valued and respected, helping them develop a sense of agency and confidence. This inclusion could also foster a sense of community cohesion and bridge the generation gap.

Guidelines for researchers

Overall, researchers should approach children's involvement in tourist destination development with sensitivity, respect, and a commitment to ethical research practices. By considering the following important factors, researchers can conduct studies that contribute to the well-being and empowerment of children and inform sustainable and inclusive tourism practices. When dealing with the issues of children's participation in the process of tourist destination development, researchers should consider the following:

a   Ethical considerations and informed consent: researchers must prioritise the ethical treatment of children and obtain informed consent from both children and their parents/guardians. This involves providing specific information about the research project, its objectives, potential risks and benefits, and ensuring that children and their parents have sufficient time to consider participation.

b   Rationale for inclusion: researchers should clearly articulate the rationale for including children in the study. This includes explaining why their participation is necessary and how their perspectives and experiences can contribute to understanding tourist destination development.

c   Meaningful children's engagement: viewing children as equal partners in decision-making (rather than as passive subjects) is important. Researchers should involve children in developing programmes and activities, seeking their input and valuing their perspectives.

d   Consideration of child development: researchers must consider children's developmental stage and capabilities when designing research methods and activities. Ensuring that the research process is age-appropriate and does not cause harm or undue stress to the children involved is essential.

e   Well-being and safety: The well-being and safety of children should be a top priority. Researchers should establish protocols to protect children from harm or exploitation during the research process. This may involve obtaining approvals from institutional review boards and adhering to set guidelines and regulations.

f   Collaboration with relevant stakeholders: researchers should collaborate with relevant stakeholders such as parents, educators, community leaders and policy-makers to ensure that the research aligns with the needs and interests of the children and the broader community. Engaging these stakeholders can help researchers gain valuable insights and ensure the study has a positive impact.

Keynotes for practitioners

When dealing with the issues of children's participation in tourist destination development, practitioners should review several essential points. These points can help ensure that children's needs and perspectives are considered and that their involvement is meaningful and beneficial. The guidelines below enable practitioners to foster a more inclusive and child-centred approach to tourism development, ensuring that children's voices are heard, their needs are met and their rights are respected throughout the process:

a Legal frameworks and policies: practitioners should review the existing legal frameworks and policies related to children's participation in tourism development. This includes understanding children's rights, such as those outlined in the United Nations Convention on the Rights of the Child (UNCRC), and ensuring that these rights are respected and upheld throughout the development process.

b Child-friendly environments: it is important to review tourist destinations' physical and social backgrounds to ensure they are child-friendly. This involves considering aspects such as safety and accessibility, and providing appropriate amenities and facilities for children. Creating a welcoming and inclusive environment can encourage children's participation and engagement.

c Education and awareness: practitioners should review the educational opportunities and awareness-raising initiatives available to children in the context of tourism development. This includes providing information and resources that help children understand the benefits and challenges of tourism, as well as their rights and responsibilities as participants. Education and awareness can empower children to engage in decision-making and actively contribute their ideas and perspectives.

d Consultation and participation mechanisms: reviewing the consultation and participation mechanisms is crucial. Practitioners should assess whether children have opportunities to express their views, opinions and suggestions regarding tourism development. This can involve conducting child-friendly consultations, establishing youth advisory boards or committees, and ensuring children's voices are considered in decision-making.

e Capacity building and empowerment: practitioners should review the capacity building and empowerment programmes available to children in tourism development. This includes training, skills development and support to enable children to participate and contribute to the process actively. Building children's capacity and empowering them can enhance their confidence, skills and knowledge, allowing them to play a meaningful role in shaping the development of tourist destinations.

f   Monitoring and evaluation: practitioners should review the monitoring and evaluation mechanisms to assess the impact of children's participation in tourism development. This involves regularly evaluating the effectiveness and outcomes of children's involvement, identifying areas for improvement and ensuring that their participation leads to positive and sustainable changes.

PART V

The future of tourism – with children, for children

INTRODUCTION TO PART V

This part discusses the Positive Youth Development (PYD) framework. The PYD framework provides a suitable toolkit for modelling children's quality of life. It explores the integration of PYD theory with sustainability theory and advances the development and application of the PYD toolkit to make a child-friendly tourism destination. In addition, the aim of this chapter is to provide up-to-date and comprehensive contributions from the PYD framework for future research, interventions and policy recommendations concerning children living and working in tourism cities.

In Chapter 13 we review how building skills, fostering agency, building healthy relationships, strengthening the environment and transforming systems are a requisite to make youth more positive. A toolkit that may help develop children's positivity is to be found in the Positive Youth Development framework. The framework is valuable in preparing children for the realities of climate change, answering global issues and challenges, empowering them as change agents and engaging them in post-crisis decision-making. Concerning tourism, opportunities to engage in tourism planning and development may benefit children's well-being, as this gives the sense that they contribute equally to the present and future community development and are valued members of society. Hence, we discuss sustainable tourism development linked to the model, aiming at foreseeing child-friendly tourist communities.

In Chapter 14, we promulgate the view that "children are the future". Excluding "the future generation" from the decisions made for "the future generations" is simply unacceptable. Participatory approaches to research *with* and not merely *on* communities are ideologically grounded and underpinned by theoretical interests linked to social justice and democratic principles, which enable a critical or transformative worldview. By empowering children's voices, understanding their lived realities with perceived anxieties and prospects

DOI: 10.4324/9781003374299-22

regarding future tourism development will inevitably help advance critical tourism scholarship by focusing solely on socio-cultural aspects of tourism impacts. In addition, this chapter presents innovative research methods that are yet to be embraced by tourism scholarship. These include deliberative youth panels aiming to empower children's voices and contribute to social justice and delivering a child-led model for sustainable tourism development underpinned with qualitative and quantitative conceptual values.

In Chapter 15 we summarise the Key Concepts and Critical Factors in the two preceding chapters, as well as examine the most appropriate Connections for students, researchers and practitioners.

13
POSITIVE YOUTH, POSITIVE FUTURE

Introduction

The approach to sustainable development *for children with children* resulted in children being actively involved in improving healthcare (RCPCH, 2010, 2015), research (Canosa et al., 2016; Kellet, 2004; Small, 2008) and as activists to prevent climate change (Burke et al., 2018; Löfström et al., 2021; Marris, 2018). By perceiving children as agents of change and the generation that will not only be exposed to the results of the malpractices of the previous generations but also as torchbearers of positive improvements, we need to reflect on current practices of children's involvement and participation and develop processes for greater empowerment and inclusion.

One of the frameworks that can build a positive future through positive children is the so-called Positive Youth Development framework (hereinafter PYD). PYD approaches are broadly designed to build skills, foster agency, build healthy relationships, strengthen the environment and transform systems (Catalano et al., 2019). The PYD framework provides a toolkit suitable for modelling children's quality of life (Qi et al., 2022). Thus, many scholars showed that the principles of PYD theory are valuable in preparing children for the realities of climate change (Sanson et al., 2019; Sanson & Bellemo, 2021; Olenik, 2019), engaging them in answering global issues and challenges (Olenik, 2019), empowering them as change agents and engaging them in the post-crisis decision-making (Arnold, 2020; Frasquilho et al., 2018).

Concerning tourism, evidence shows that opportunities to engage in tourism planning and development may benefit well-being, as this gives the sense that children are equally contributing to the present and future community development and are being valued (Koščak et al., 2023). However, to date, tourism literature in general and research on resident attitudes towards tourism are yet

DOI: 10.4324/9781003374299-23

to be introduced to the PYD framework. Thus, we intend to explore the integration of PYD with sustainability theory and advance the development and application of the PYD toolkit to make child-friendly tourism communities. In addition, we aim to provide up-to-date and comprehensive contributions from the PYD framework for future research, interventions and policy recommendations concerning children living and working in tourism communities.

Positive Youth Development

Theoretically, the PYD framework is influenced by three different theories: the theory of human development, the theory of context and community influence, and the theory of context and community change. Several PYD models have been proposed in the scientific literature, such as social-emotional learning (Zins & Elias, 2007), Benson's model on external and internal developmental assets (Benson et al., 2011), Catalano's 15 PYD constructs (Catalano et al., 2002) and the Five Cs Model of PYD (Lerner et al., 2005). With the proliferation of all these models, one vulnerability was exposed, and that is the lack of a shared set of constructs among models (Tolan, 2014; Ciocanel et al., 2017; Leman et al., 2017; Lerner et al., 2018; Shek et al., 2019). Thus, recently, Catalano et al. (2019) proposed the integration of constructs from different models, organising PYD constructs into four domains:

1.   Assets – exposure to education or training, interpersonal skills, recognition of emotions and self-control.
2.   Agency – positive identity, self-efficacy, ability to plan, perseverance, positive feelings about the future.
3.   Contribution – engagement in civil society and with adults.
4.   Enabling environment – bonding, prosocial opportunities, support, prosocial norms, values, recognition, gender-responsive, physical and psychological safety.

Assets

Assets refer to the necessary resources, skills and competencies of children to achieve desired outcomes. Children must develop interpersonal skills (i.e. social and communication), higher-order thinking skills, self-control, recognising emotions and building empathy and academic achievement facilitated through formal education and training.

Formal education and training enable skill building specific to vocation, employment or financial capacity (e.g. money management, business development and marketing). Also, academic achievement is necessary, including knowledge and mastery of academic subjects such as mathematics, written and spoken language, sciences, history and geography.

Interpersonal skills are linked to children's ability to interact with others, including verbal and non-verbal communication and social listening, building assertiveness, knowing how to resolve conflicts and negotiating. These skills help integrate thinking, feeling and actions to achieve specific social and inter-personal goals.

Higher-order thinking skills lead to reasoned conclusions that children reach based on their ability to evaluate varied information gathered from multiple sources for the problem they recognised needed solving. Recognising the emo-tions and feelings of others is based on one's ability to build empathy and positively respond to oneself and others. This is also related to self-control, which means children learn to delay gratification, control their impulses, focus and be attentive, and control their emotions and behaviours.

Agency

Agency refers to children perceiving and being able to employ their assets and aspirations to make decisions or influence them regarding improving their lives and setting their own goals. The agency also includes acting upon decisions regarding their lives to achieve desired outcomes.

Therefore, the agency is about having a positive identity and beliefs about the future, self-efficacy, perseverance or diligence and the ability to plan and set goals. Children should hold positive attitudes, beliefs and values about them-selves and their future but also be optimistic about their future potential, goals, options, choices and plans. These are all crucial elements of the agency. More-over, children should be confident, believe in their abilities to achieve many different things and sustain efforts and interests in long-term projects despite difficulties. Therefore, children should be motivated and stimulated to make plans and act towards meeting their goals.

Contribution

Contribution refers to children being the agents or sources of change they wish to see for themselves and the community. The child-led approach enables planners, policy-makers and researchers a unique "insider" perspective: children are experts in their own lives, and actively involving children in planning, developing or research becomes an empowering process. Kellet (2010, p. 197) states that the child-led approach makes "a virtuous circle of increased con-fidence and raised self-esteem, resulting in more active participation by children in other aspects affecting their lives".

Children's contribution should be meaningful; that is, it should rest on an inclusive, intentional,

mutually respectful partnership between them and adults who see their power equally shared. Moreover, contributions from children should be valued and respected, and their ideas and perspectives should be respected and incorporated into programmes, policies, strategies, etc. Children should be able to design and deliver the latter by having their skills and strengths recognised, stimulated and integrated.

Moreover, the contribution is about meaningfully engaging in challenging and changing the existing system, practices and power structures so that children can exhibit their recognition as experts in their own lives, thus building their leadership capacities.

Enabling environment

A positive future and positive children need a supportive environment that enables bonding opportunities for prosocial involvement and promotes prosocial norms, values and recognitions, encouraging children's positivity. Such an environment develops and supports their assets, agency and access to services, such as youth- and gender-responsive services. Moreover, the environment that strengthens children's ability to avoid risks and stay safe and secure through youth-friendly laws and gender-responsive policies prioritises their physical and psychological safety.

The term "environment" should be interpreted broadly, and it should be considered as a social (e.g. relationships with peers and adults), normative (e.g. attitudes, norms and beliefs), structural (e.g. laws, policies, programmes, services and systems) and physical (e.g. safe, supportive spaces) space. Such space establishes and promotes emotional attachment and commitment to the family, peers, teachers and/or community that signal to children that they are cared for and supported. The latter is also a prerequisite for positive interactions and participation in family, peer groups, at schools and in the community.

Implementation of PYD on children in tourism communities

Positive and empowered children can contribute to the development and sustainability of tourism in their communities. However, there are also many challenges and barriers to that. Tourism development is benefiting from children because they:

- Provide valuable insights and perspectives on their needs, preferences and expectations as tourists or hosts.
- Enhance their skills, knowledge and confidence by engaging in tourism activities and projects.
- Foster a sense of ownership, responsibility and stewardship for their natural and cultural heritage.
- Promote intergenerational dialogue and cooperation among different stakeholders in tourism.

Some of the challenges and barriers that hinder children's participation in tourism planning are a lack of:

- Access to information, education and training on tourism issues and opportunities.
- Efficient decision-making structures, platforms and mechanisms that facilitate children's involvement.
- Recognition and respect for children's rights, opinions and contributions by adults.
- Resources, support and incentives for children's participation.
- Protection and safety measures for children from potential risks and harm associated with tourism, such as child labour, exploitation, abuse and violence.

To overcome these challenges and barriers, some of the recommendations for enhancing children's participation in tourism planning are to:

- Provide children with relevant information, education and training on tourism issues and opportunities.
- Establish effective decision-making structures, platforms and mechanisms that enable children's involvement.
- Recognise and respect children's rights, opinions and contributions as legitimate and valuable.
- Allocate sufficient resources, support and incentives for children's participation.
- Implement protection and safety measures for children from potential risks and harms associated with tourism.

Children are claimed to be the longest-serving stakeholders in society (Badham, 2002). However, in today's culture of transparent and participatory planning (Lloyd, 2008), where citizens are encouraged to participate in community development, Matthews (2002) contends that children remain outside the developmental processes and form a section of society with little or no influence over decision-making. Indeed, it may be argued that the community may make benign decisions based on ignorance of children's wishes or needs, and at worst, they may be simply ignored.

Viewing children as agents of change and advocates of positivity may contribute new ideas to sustainable tourism development. The involvement of young people within the planning process not only addresses children's rights and interest in participating in decisions that affect their lives, but it also helps broaden the types of voices within the process. Hence, complementing existing developmental practices with the PYD toolkit helps children experience, learn, evaluate and improve their ability to act in their environment and take responsibility.

PYD also has a close philosophical and theoretical bond to Hart's (1997) "Ladder of Children's Participation", specifically to child-initiated and shared decisions with adults (the top rung). In educational terms, Hart (1997) suggests that children can learn to appreciate democracy and a sense of their capability and responsibility to participate in a democratic society. Notably, he further suggests planning, designing, monitoring and managing the enabling environment to provide an ideal realm for the active practice of children's empowerment and involvement. This opens up the potential for a better understanding of how children might be encouraged to appreciate their communities, mainly through their planning, development and management.

BOX 13.1 CASE STUDY: BREŽICE YOUTH COUNCIL AND PARTICIPATIVE BUDGET FOR YOUTH

The municipality of Brežice always placed great emphasis on young people in its work, as evidenced by the newly acquired Youth Friendly Municipality certificate. In 2022, during the European Year of Youth, the municipality also adopted the strategy for young people in Brežice 2022–2030. The strategy was co-designed and co-created with its youth. At the same time, there was also an initiative to establish the Youth Council. Membership in the Youth Council is voluntary for citizens of Brežice (with permanent or temporary residence) between the ages of 13 and 30. The municipality supported the initiative and offered young people a budget, where all finances (approximately 7,000 EUR) are intended only for youth projects. In their first year of establishing the Youth Council, all three voted projects (i.e. Sports Tourism on the Sotla River, Street Work, Escape Room and Weight Cage) were successfully implemented. In 2023, the Youth Council met for the second time and deliberated on the four project ideas. As a result, three projects (i.e. Traktoriada and Diary of Young People, Graffiti Workshop and International Tambura Festival) received votes, and the municipality will support their implementation with 8,000 EUR.

Challenges of involving children in research and different processes

Children can be considered as the agents of research, i.e. partners or participants – respondents. Involving children as research partners enables "democratisation" of the whole process as the power relations in the research process are challenged, and the researcher reinvents "definitions and practices of authority" (Dentith et al., 2012, p. 16).

On the other hand, one of the research's most challenging aspects is engaging children in the participatory process. Given the complexities around adult–child power relations in such contexts, children were intentionally not approached through schools, which would likely have positioned the researcher in a role of authority (Hart, 1992; Kellett, 2004). However, recruiting children through community groups helped ensure they were not in a context where they might feel obligated to participate in the research. Conversely, this impacted recruitment considerably, given that children today are increasingly pressured by multiple out-of-school activities, leaving little spare time for involvement in research. Also, multiple layers of adult gatekeepers often preclude children from participating in research projects (Graham et al., 2013). With this in mind, Beazley et al. (2009, p. 374) argue that when recruiting participants through community groups, gaining access to children separate from parents is "likely to be problematic". Powell and Smith (2009, p. 136) similarly argue that the "biggest barrier to children's participation is the need in every case for an adult to consent to their participation". This is potentially why we still witness the lack of research on children's attitudes towards tourism.

Working with children demands more time and patience from researchers, policy-makers and managers than what they would usually need when working with adults. This means that every phase of the research and programme process will likely need more time than initially planned or considered. Also, people engaged in child-led approaches also need to be trained and build the capacity to work with children. In addition, working with children may require special permissions from different ethical boards, organisations, schools, parents and children. Flexibility for pivoting research processes and children as partners/participants can be challenging and not appealing. Hence, many wish not to engage with children and instead build/ develop for them based on their adult experience and knowledge.

Self-reporting challenges

Children's knowledge, attitudes, perceptions and behaviours are often surveyed through self-reports. The latter is collected through written questionnaires, online surveys, or in-person interviews. One of the challenges is the problem of reporter bias. Children can often overstate what they learned, how helpful a training or a programme was, and how they will use the knowledge and skills acquired, especially immediately after the training/programme/process. However, children may not know "what they don't know" at the beginning and may, thus, overestimate their knowledge, which can result in underestimating the impact of a training/programme/process. In addition, children, especially very young ones, may not comprehend or understand the questions or even feel awkward or uncomfortable answering them.

Selecting a study design and appropriate data collection methods

A mixed methods approach using qualitative and quantitative strategies is often the ideal design because it provides a balanced and more affluent analysis of the problem. Using both qualitative and quantitative methods yields richer, more practical and reliable insights into children's lives in tourism communities. However, we acknowledge that mixed methods may not suit all research aims equally. Researchers, practitioners and professionals may be well equipped with the knowledge to plan and apply qualitative, quantitative or mixed methods to their investigation with children.

When considering indicators and study design through a PYD lens, it is essential to understand that while children are the focus, they should not be the only data source. Including other stakeholders in the research process using the PYD framework is equally important to ensure that the analysis is more accurate and comprehensive, i.e. triangulated. Any divergences may be more easily detected if the data collection process includes triangulation measures. Triangulation may also include verifications from independent and/or objective sources, such as direct observation, video and photo fixation and geotagging.

References

Arnold, M.E. (2020). America's moment: Investing in Positive Youth Development to transform youth and society. *Journal of Youth Development*, 12 (2), 16–36.

Badham B. (2002). Faith in young people in regeneration. *Childright*, 190, 10–11.

Beazley H., Bessell S., Ennew J., *et al.* (2009). The right to be properly researched: Research with children in a messy, real world. *Children's Geographies*, 7 (4), 365–378.

Benson, P.L., Scales, P.C. & Syvertsen, A.K. (2011). The contribution of the developmental assets framework to Positive Youth Development theory and practice. In Lerner, R.M., Lerner, J.V. & Benson, J.B. *Advances in Child Development and Behavior*. Elsevier, 197–230.

Burke, S.E., Sanson, A.V. & Van Hoorn, J. (2018). The psychological effects of climate change on children. *Current Psychiatry Reports*, 20 (5), 1–8.

Canosa, A., Moyle, B. & Wray, M. (2016). Can anybody hear me? A critical analysis of young residents' voices in tourism studies. *Tourism Analysis: An Interdisciplinary Journal*, 21 (2), 325–337.

Catalano, R.F., Berglund, M.L., Ryan, J.A.M., Lonczak, H.S. & Hawkins, J.D. (2002). Positive Youth Development in the United States: Research findings on evaluations of Positive Youth Development programs. *Prevention & Treatment*, 5 (1), 98–124.

Catalano, R.F., Skinner, M.L., Alvarado, G., Kapungu, C., Reavley, N., Patton, G.C., *et al.* (2019). Positive Youth Development programs in low- and middle- income countries: A conceptual framework and systematic review of efficacy. *Journal of Adolescent Health*, 65 (1), 15–31.

Ciocanel, O., Power, K., Eriksen, A. & Gillings, K. (2017). Effectiveness of Positive Youth Development interventions: A meta-analysis of randomised controlled trials. *Journal of Youth and Adolescence*, 46, 483–504.

Dentith, A.M., Measor, L. & O'Malley, M.P. (2012). The research imagination amid dilemmas of engaging young people in critical participatory work. *Forum Qualitative Sozialforschung/Forum: Qualitative Social Research*, 13 (1), 22–44.

Frasquilho, D., Ozer, E.J., Ozer, E.M., Branquinho, C., Camacho, I., Reis, M., *et al.* (2018). Dream Teens: Adolescents-led participatory project in Portugal in the context of the economic recession. *Health Promotion Practice*, 19 (1), 51–59.

Graham, A., Powell, M.A., Taylor, N., Anderson, D.L. & Fitzgerald, R.M. (2013). *Ethical Research Involving Children*. UNICEF Office of Research – Innocenti. www.childethics.com.

Hart, R.A. (1992). *Children's Participation: From tokenism to citizenship.* UNICEF Innocenti Research Centre.

Hart, R.A. (1997). *Children's Participation: The theory and practice of involving young citizens in community development and environmental care.* Earthscan.

Kellett, M. (2004). 'Just teach us the skills please, we'll do the rest': Empowering ten-year-olds as active researchers. *Children & Society*, 18 (5), 329–343.

Kellett, M. (2010). Small shoes, big steps! Empowering children as active researchers. *American Journal of Community Psychology*, 46 (1–2), 195–203.

Koščak, M., Knežević, M., Binder, D., Pelaez-Verdet, A., Işik, C., Mićić, V., Borisavljević, K. & Šegota, T. (2023). Exploring the neglected voices of children in sustainable tourism development: A comparative study in six European tourist destinations. *Journal of Sustainable Tourism*, 31 (2), 561–580.

Leman, P.J., Smith, E.P., Petersen, A.C. & SRCD Ethnic-Racial Issues and International Committees (2017). Introduction to the special section of child development on Positive Youth Development in diverse and global contexts. *Child Development*, 88 (4), 1039–1044.

Lerner, R.M., Almerigi, J.B., Theokas, C. & Lerner, J.V. (2005). Positive Youth Development: A view of the issues. *The Journal of Early Adolescence*, 25 (1), 10–16.

Lerner, R.M., Tirrell, J.M., Dowling, E.M., Geldhof, G.J., Gestsdóttir, S., Lerner, J.V., et al. (2018). The end of the beginning: Evidence and absences studying Positive Youth Development in a global context. *Adolescent Research Review*, 4, 1–14.

Lloyd, G. (2008). *Planning Reform in Northern Ireland: Independent report to the Minister for the Environment.* http://www.planningni.gov.uk/index/about/about-reform-independentexpert-report.pdf.

Löfström, E., Richter, I. & Nesvold, I.H. (2021). Disruptive communication as a means to engage children in solving environmental challenges: A case study on plastic pollution. *Frontiers in Psychology*, 16 (12), 635448.

Marris, E. (2018). *Why the World Is Watching Young Climate Activists.* https://media.nature.com/original/magazine-assets/d41586-019-02696-0/d41586-019-02696-0.pdf.

Matthews, H. (2002). Children and regeneration: Setting an agenda for community participation and integration. *Children & Society*, 17 (4), 264–276.

Olenik, C. (2019). The evolution of positive youth development as a key international development approach. *Global Social Welfare*, 6, 5–15.

Powell, M.A., & Smith, A.B. (2009). Children's participation rights in research. *Childhood* 16 (1), 124–142.

Qi, S., Hua, F., Zhou, Z., et al. (2022). Trends of Positive Youth Development publications (1995–2020): A scientometric review. *Applied Research Quality Life*, 17, 421–446.

RCPCH (2010). *A Guide to the Participation of Children and Young People in Health Services.* https://www.rcpch.ac.uk/sites/default/files/RCPCH-not-just-a-phase-2010.pdf.

Sanson, A., & Bellemo, M. (2021). Children and youth in the climate crisis. *BJPsych Bulletin*, 45 (4), 205–209.

Sanson, A.V., Van Hoorn, J. & Burke, S.E.L. (2019). Responding to the impacts of the climate crisis on children and youth. *Child Development Perspectives*, 13 (4), 201–207.

Shek, D.T., Dou, D., Zhu, X. & Chai, W. (2019). Positive Youth Development: Current perspectives. *Adolescent Health, Medicine and Therapeutics*, 10, 131–141.

Small, J. (2008). The absence of childhood in tourism studies. *Annals of Tourism Research*, 35 (3), 772–789.

Tolan, P. (2014). Future directions for positive development intervention research. *Journal of Clinical Child & Adolescent Psychology*, 43 (4), 686–694.

Zins, J.E., & Elias, M.J. (2007). Social and emotional learning: Promoting the development of all students. *Journal of Educational and Psychological Consultation*, 17 (2–3), 233–255.

14

THE FUTURE FOR CHILDREN IN TOURISM

Introduction

The ultimate goal of the 2030 Agenda for Sustainable Development is to transform the world and make our society a collaborative partnership that improves lives and changes the world for the better. Tourism is one of the social forces suggested as having the potential to contribute, directly or indirectly, to all Sustainable Development Goals set in the 2030 Agenda. Tourism has been hailed as a force for change that can be used to improve quality of life, promote inclusivity, create jobs and advance knowledge (WTO & UNDP, 2017), while studies are ceaselessly demonstrating its social, economic and cultural benefits to the quality of life of individuals and the well-being of communities (Moscardo, 2012; Šegota et al., 2022; Uysal et al., 2016). Hence, many local and national governments favour tourism as a community development tool.

However, more importantly, children are being recognised as "torchbearers of the 2030 Agenda" (United Nations, 2018, p. 6), making them essential partners in global sustainable development efforts. The UN highlights that:

> youth are at the heart of sustainable development. Their active engagement is key to achieving sustainable, inclusive and stable societies and to avert the most serious future challenges to sustainable development, including the impacts of climate change, conflict, gender inequality, forced migration, poverty and unemployment.
>
> *(United Nations, 2018, pp. 6–7)*

Moreover, studies have shown that they can influence their parents, teachers, peers and, most importantly, their communities and local and national governments (Asian Development Bank and Plan International UK, 2018).

DOI: 10.4324/9781003374299-24

Still, very little is known about how children perceive tourism. Children are one of the most neglected social groups concerning how their opinions and perceptions are gathered and considered in planning, policy-making and governance in general – and in tourism in particular (Koščak et al., 2023; Lugosi et al., 2016; Poria & Timothy, 2014; Small, 2008; Thornton et al., 1997). A handful of studies gathered children's perceptions of tourism, with Koščak et al. (2023) bringing perspectives of children in six different European destinations. When asked whether they wished to be included in tourism planning and development, children were happy to voice their opinions about current and future tourism development (Koščak et al., 2023). If the governments listened to and included children's views on tourism development, they would step towards an inclusive and just society.

However, "there is a gap between the appealing conceptual idea of sustainable tourism and its alarmingly slow penetration of action and practice" (Mihalič, 2016, p. 462). For tourism to exercise its regenerative role and encourage sustainable development, it must include all voices (Šegota et al., 2017). And excluding "the future generation" from the decisions made for "the future generations" is simply unacceptable.

Children as active participants in transforming our world

The United Nations (2018) showed that children are partners in the social transformation of our world; as such, they always need to be considered equal, not only when needed. For example, during the Covid-19 pandemic, children were perceived as a social group that needed to take responsibility in a "once in a lifetime situation". Many scientists and practitioners who were serving as vaccine advisers to governments (such as the UK, the US, Israel and the EU) called for children to be vaccinated to protect themselves from the virus but also to help protect vulnerable adults and stop the spread (Larcher & Brierley, 2020; Ledford, 2021). As a result, children as young as 12 years old were actively called upon to get vaccinated. In the case of their parents opposing or refusing to vaccinate them, children were asked to act upon their right to freedom of choice and get vaccinated despite parental opposition. This suddenly positioned the children as partners, i.e. active and crucial members in society's fight against the virus (Larcher & Brierley, 2020). Therefore, if we are suddenly finding ways of recognising their vital responsibility in the community, why do we not give them the same importance in making decisions concerning their imminent future?

In support of this concept of partnership and participation, Article 12 of the UNRC requires children to be informed and consulted over matters that concern them and that their views be given due weight following their age and maturity (Archard, 2004; United Nations, 1989). Moreover, in recent years, the approach for children with children resulted in children being actively involved in improving healthcare (RCPCH, 2010), research (Canosa et al., 2016; Kellet,

2005; Small, 2008) and as activists to prevent climate change (Burke et al., 2018; Löfström et al., 2021; Marris, 2018).

Research on children is well suited within the Positive Youth Development (PYD) framework when examining and promoting children's well-being and engagement. As seen in the previous chapter, the PYD approaches are broadly designed to build skills, foster agency, build healthy relationships, strengthen the environment and transform systems (Catalano et al., 2019). These approaches must be explored further to help increase children's involvement and consultation over issues that affect them.

Unlocking the potential of invisible children in tourism

Evidence shows that opportunities to engage in tourism planning and development may benefit well-being, as this gives the sense that children are equally contributing to the present and future community development and are being valued (Koščak et al., 2023). However, to date, tourism literature in general and research on resident attitudes towards tourism are yet to be introduced to the PYD theory. This is because tourism practitioners and academics still neglect children's voices.

For example, there are only 15 studies that directly elicited children's perceptions of tourism spaces (e.g. Buzinde & Manuel-Navarrete, 2013; Canosa et al., 2017, 2019; Koščak et al., 2023; Ohashi et al., 2012; Seraphin & Green, 2019), tourists (e.g. Canosa et al., 2017; Koščak et al., 2023; Miller & Beazley, 2022; Molero et al., 2003), perception of themselves (e.g. Gamradt, 1995; Koščak et al., 2018) and impact of tourism on their health (e.g. Anderson-Fye, 2004; Dancause et al., 2011; Leatherman et al., 2010, Yang et al., 2023). Moreover, as Small (2008, p. 773) argues, youth involvement in research should go "beyond the commercial incentive". In other words, youth is often perceived as not significantly contributing to tourism businesses and development. However, ending the silence of marginalised community members and increasing the interest in child-centred research will be possible with better advocacy of critical scholarship (Canosa et al., 2016).

One of the ways to advance critical scholarship is through empowering children's voices in tourism development. Tourism and its transformative and disruptive powers over host communities made it a social force many welcomed with open arms (Higgins-Desbiolles, 2006). Residents have learned how to live with tourism and its "powers" in many ways (McKercher et al., 2015). They adapt, avoid, support, oppose and continue leading their lives as residents of tourism destinations. While the experiences and lived realities in tourism destinations are as diverse as there are residents, the literature, on the other hand, seems to be in a state of arrested development (Nunkoo et al., 2013; Šegota et al., 2022; Woosnam & Ribeiro, 2022). It is unanimous in demonstrating that the more residents benefit from tourism, the more they will positively perceive tourism impacts and continue supporting tourism. And vice versa (Deery et al., 2012; Sharpley, 2014; Woosnam & Ribeiro, 2022).

Unfortunately, this prevalent "truth" wades into the resident attitudes studies on the premises of the social exchange theory (Gursoy et al., 2019; Woosnam & Ribeiro, 2022). Although the theory has been criticised for downgrading the resident–tourism relationship to financial exchanges (Joo et al., 2021; Maruyama et al., 2019), it has explanatory value for understanding multiple aspects and dimensions of the relationship. However, exploring social and cultural interactions between residents and tourism is limited.

By empowering children's voices, understanding their lived realities with perceived anxieties and prospects regarding future tourism development will inevitably help advance critical tourism scholarship by focusing solely on socio-cultural aspects of resident–tourism exchange. Since children are not perceived as financial beneficiaries of tourism development until adulthood (Small, 2008), their power is to help understand other-than-financial tourism relationships. For example, previous commentaries (e.g. Khoo-Lattimore, 2015; Poria & Timothy, 2014; Yang et al., 2020) have indicated that the majority of research has explored the objective dimension of tourism impacts, but limited attention has been focused on host-children satisfaction with tourism impacts on their lives or their subjective well-being. However, exploring experiences in tourism destinations directly from children, rather than relying on adults' or experts' assumptions, is essential in advancing tourism scholarship and knowledge of the sector.

At the same time, such research can contribute to developing a more inclusive view of tourism and its impacts (Poria & Timothy, 2014) and help expand the researcher's capacity to conceptualise tourism's socio-cultural and environmental constructs (Carr, 2011). To achieve that, the research on children as residents/hosts can renounce conceptualisations dominating the literature on resident attitudes towards tourism, leading towards the exploration of research not bounded by the premises that the more residents economically benefit from tourism, the more supportive they will be of its development (Sharpley, 2014).

Asking questions about tourism and findings answers from children

The following section will discuss how to fill the lacuna of neglected children's voices in sustainable tourism development. Hence, we will present a conceptualisation of the three-year project *Empowering the neglected voices of children in tourism development* (code J5–50162), which was selected for funding by the Slovenian Research and Innovation Agency.

It is rather unusual to present a project; however, throughout this book, we have seen that research on children is very scarce. And even more so, practice-led exemplars of including children in tourism development are sparse. Hence, with the presentation of this project, we wish to stimulate students, academics and professionals to think about the needs, problems and expectations of youth regarding tourism and its impacts on the quality of life. In other words, the project's outlines should be a source of information for decision-makers about how to address tourism as a social force for communities from the perspective of its "future for future". Next are specific steps used in holistically approaching child-led research in tourism. We will also present the case of Slovenia, where the project is based.

Creating a roadshow of tourism impacts on the community

Tourism affects collective life in the community and creates conditions for community development (Ahn et al., 2002). It creates foundations for and exposes the community to different types of place change. To better understand these changes, one must first analyse demographic trends and characteristics specific to the community, such as seasonality, stage of economic development, type of tourism activities, level of tourism development, etc. These trends and characteristics are external to residents and are used to differentiate between communities (Williams & Lawson, 2001) as they represent "characteristics of the location with respect to its role as a tourist destination" (Faulkner & Tideswell, 1997, p. 6).

Analysing demographic trends and tourism-led community characteristics helps provide a state-of-the-art roadmap, aiming for detailed insight into communities. More importantly, the roadmap must include and combine analyses of various community characteristics instead of focusing on only a selected number. An example of the roadmap is combining analyses of community demographic profiles, tourism data, climate change indicators, CO_2 footprint and vulnerability, and tourism work conditions and practices.

BOX 14.1 CASE STUDY: SLOVENIA – SMALL STATE WITH RICH DATA

Slovenia represents a unique environment for studying and recognising the importance and value of children in sustainable tourism development. Firstly, the Slovenian government is not an exception in embracing tourism as a community development tool. Over the last six years, the national government has been susceptible to promoting the country as a green boutique tourism destination (METS RS, 2017, 2022) that unifies satisfied residents, motivated employees, enthusiastic visitors and care for future generations.

Slovenia is home to 220 municipalities that span four macro tourism regions which focus on distinct visitor experiences – the Mediterranean region with sun and sea and culinary experiences, the Alpine region with mountain, sport and outdoor experiences, the Thermal Pannonian region with wellness and rural experiences, and Ljubljana and Central Slovenia with cityscapes, events and cultural experiences (METS, 2017). These different tourist experiences also reflect the region's ability to mitigate tourist seasonality (Šegota & Mihalič, 2018), one of the key economic indicators guiding destinations' development.

Slovenia is known to have an excellent system of capturing statistical data on the level of municipalities. The Statistical Office of the Republic of Slovenia conducts various surveys in the economic, demographic, social and environmental fields. The data is published promptly and transparently and following rigorous methods. The open access to these data and using them for a detailed analysis at the municipality (i.e. community) level provide an opportunity to map tourism impacts and enable micro-level state-of-the-art analysis.

Surveying children's perceptions of tourism

In general terms, each community is different in how it is affected by tourism. Some communities can represent the so-called flagship destinations. Tourism in those communities inevitably affects children's socialisation process, shaping their quality of life (Poria & Timothy, 2014; Yang et al., 2020). On the other hand, children living in communities less visited by tourists may not be equally affected by tourism. A study by Koščak et al. (2023) shows that children in mature tourist destinations (i.e. those with a long history of tourism development and frequently visited by tourists) might accept tourist activity as part of the everyday. In contrast, in destinations with fewer tourists, children are much more attentive to the activity impacting daily life. However, the study shows that regardless of the destination's development, children exhibit negative emotions towards tourists and perceive them to have greater power to manage their lives than local communities (Koščak et al., 2023). However, comparative studies of such interest and importance are very scarce.

Hence, to establish a baseline for potential community comparisons (e.g. geographical, methodological, time-wise), there must be a big enough pool of studies on children's attitudes towards tourism. This pool needs to be inundated with central assumptions that children are not a homogenous group and that their attitudes are structured along the lines of different socio-economic factors but also the characteristics of tourism communities.

Empirical research using a survey-based approach offers a general overview of children's perceptions of tourism. The unique stronghold of these surveys is in scratching the surface of children's attitudes towards tourism and offering a loop into differences in attitudes linked to the community's development stage. Hence, such surveys should be developed and conducted around the following questions:

- How do children perceive tourism and hospitality business in general?
- What specific economic, environmental and socio-cultural tourism impacts are noticeable in their communities?
- What are tourism's effects on a family's life?
- How involved are children in decisions related to tourism planning and development?

BOX 14.2 CASE STUDY: SLOVENIA – CHILDREN'S WAY OF EXPERIENCING TOURISM IMPACTS

Many tourism destinations in developed countries have suffered from staff shortages in hospitality and tourism in the recent decade. Moreover, with the collapse of international travel, the Covid-19 pandemic worsened the already affected sector by risking more than 100 million jobs (UNWTO, 2022; WTTC, 2022). As a result, the sector's recovery is questionable, with many employees taking up new opportunities outside of tourism and hospitality. Hence, a gap in the market is being created between the current and future number of available personnel and the expected supply of jobs. Likewise, Slovenia is not exempt from this alarming forecast. Hence, the government has listed tourism and hospitality professions as deficit occupations (Dostop.si, 2023), enabling prospective students to become eligible for the deficit scholarship. Such financially incentivised activities are hoped to encourage youth to pursue careers in tourism and hospitality. However, a recent survey-based study by Koščak et al. (2023) has shown that young people from Kranjska Gora, one of the top Slovenian tourist destinations, were reluctant to work in the industry. In general, the study found that children recognise that the industry creates employment opportunities, but at the same time, it is perceived as labour-intensive with meagre wages, demanding all-day commitment with negative effects on family life (Koščak et al., 2023). Such perception certainly does little to change the perception of tourism becoming a desired life orientation. More worryingly, a study by Koščak et al. (2023) shows that children's perceptions and feelings towards tourism in Slovenia are not as positive as expected, with many perceiving tourism as too disruptive for local communities. Hence, if they perceive tourism as a disruptive force, they will likely become dissatisfied residents who deliver poor guest experiences (Šegota et al., 2022), jeopardising the government's sustainable tourism strategy.

Understanding children's lived realities in tourism destinations

Scratching the surface and getting an overall view of the sentiment of children's attitudes is an excellent starting point for further research. One of the limitations of such studies is their plastic portrayal of the complex combination of characteristics, impacts and responses in a community. However, the social experiences and lived realities in tourism destinations are multidimensional. To understand them, combining objective and subjective analyses would shed light on resident feelings and emotions, an insight-deprived topic (Hadinejad et al., 2019). It was stressed that "integrating the tools of qualitative and quantitative approaches enables the verification of facts as well as the investigation of complex and multidimensional reality" (Nunkoo et al., 2013, p. 19).

To provide an informed, evidence-based understanding of children's everyday experiences and engagements with the local environment, including tourism, one needs to sidestep from positivism into the phenomenology and utilise its methods, such as focus groups, interviews, (n)etnography, etc. to get a deep insight into children's sense of spatial attachment, belongings, and discourses, informing their understanding of tourism and hospitality. In this way, one can critically reflect on broader cultural and social processes affecting their everyday practices and discourses.

In line with previous steps, the principles of community studies (Crow, 2002) must be followed. They assume that locality and community research remain crucial in explaining the nature and characteristics of contemporary social change. Despite the general acceptance that one indeed lives in a globalised, digitally mediated and mobile world, the research should foreground the salience of place, local communities and residential processes for outcomes in the areas of lifestyle cultures, health and well-being, and political alignments (Savage et al., 2005). Hence, to explore the experience of children from differing socio-economic backgrounds, specific attention must be paid to reference frames within which children narrate their experiences.

BOX 14.3 CASE STUDY: SLOVENIA – EDUCATION IS BOURDIEURISTIC

Each project needs to have a population and a sample, and the project we are presenting here focuses on high school students aged 14 to 18 attending vocational and high schools (i.e. gymnasiums). Hence, the project also philosophically follows the argument of Bourdieu and Passeron (1977/2000) that the educational system contributes to reproducing social structure or class relations in societies. The three aspects of the tourism lived experiences of children will be examined using focus groups:

a *Place attachment and belonging in a digitally mediated world.* By employing a spatially sensitive but non-reductive account of social practice, the interest is in children's social relationships and elective belongings to understand how they might feel they belong in different contexts simultaneously.

b *Local regimes of hospitality and symbolic boundary making.* The aim is to unravel children's understandings of the role of locals as hosts in guest–host relationships and their attitudes towards incomers/non-locals/tourists, potentially challenging the dominant hospitality regimes (moral ownership over the place, "we do not serve you" paradigm).

c *Perceived anxieties and prospects of tourism futures.* The focus is on grasping their take on the occupational prestige of professions in tourism and, in this sense, gaining insight into their classification schemes. Accounts of how they perceive work in tourism, assess tourism professions and envision their professional trajectory and work culture will be valuable for further explaining the discourses surrounding their career choices.

Deliberative panels "for future, with future"

The current youth is a generation with greater political awakening and aware-ness than previous generations, which is not afraid of political consumerism, signing petitions or public mobilisation (Lavrič et al., 2020), and shows excep-tionally high levels of environmental awareness and concern for climate change (Gorenc et al., 2020). This generation is about to sidestep into adulthood to co-create the futures of their communities by participating and making decisions about their development. With all its attendant socio-economic changes, they will inhabit the present and future tourism development, making them receptive to how tourism affects lives in their communities (Koščak et al., 2019). The recognition that children should not be mistaken for *muted* or *silent* social groups (Burke et al., 2018; Löfström et al., 2021; Marris, 2018) leads to con-sidering children as active co-creators of the future. One way of hearing the children talk about their future is through public deliberative problem-solving to identify limits children are willing to accept regarding tourism's economic, environmental and socio-cultural impacts.

While there are numerous previous accounts of deliberative citizen panels, the area of involving children needs consideration on to what extent and how the approach should be adapted to fit the needs of young people. Here, the condi-tion is to go beyond deliberative pedagogy (i.e. where children are considered chiefly as learners) and towards including creative approaches (for example, dramatic vignettes introduced in youth citizen juries by Coleman et al., 2018).

Hence, youth deliberations (citizen juries and citizen panels) as methods of inclusion of children can help identify tourism-related public issues (i.e. desti-nation management and sense of place, environmental issues linked to climate change, and working conditions). Discussing the future with the future enriches academic knowledge and professional practice: it considers children as active co-creators. It goes beyond considering children as objects of research or as only "future citizens" but as having essential contributions to democracy here and now (e.g. Nishiyama, 2017).

BOX 14.4 CASE STUDY: SLOVENIA – PARTNERING UP WITH THE NATIONAL YOUTH COUNCIL

The National Youth Council of Slovenia is an umbrella organisation linking all national youth organisations irrespective of their interests and ideological or political orientations. Its key purpose is to defend the interests of young people and promote their participation in policy-making in the fields that significantly impact their lives and work.

The National Youth Council is known for assisting in organising the National Children's Parliament. The latter is a yearly event where 132 children meet in the national parliament to deliberate on a selected general topic. In 2022, the event was organised for the 32nd year by the Slovenian Association of Friends of Youth. The aim is to plan the deliberative methods of the project and provide a handbook on the deliberative inclusion of young people in local destination development.

The project will implement three youth citizen panels on destination management in cooperation with the National Youth Council of Slovenia. The intended topics are tourism and climate change, destination management and youth's sense of place, and working conditions in tourism and hospitality.

Developing a children-led model for sustainable tourism

Any tourism destination sees its use of resources negotiated within the resident–tourism exchange process (Uysal et al., 2016). This negotiation is often approached positively, with many individuals and communities warmly embracing tourism (Dioko, 2017). But not all community members are equally involved in the exchange (Šegota et al., 2017), resulting in tourism being subject to judgements by its impacts (Uysal et al., 2016). As a result, positive and negative tourism impacts are felt differently at the individual and community levels, with not all community members benefiting from tourism (McGehee & Andereck, 2004; Andereck et al., 2005; Šegota et al., 2017, 2022). Hence, children, as often deprived of the possibility to participate in making decisions about tourism development (Canosa et al., 2016; Yang et al., 2020), may view the use of community resources differently from others. However, their opinions on the limits of community development through tourism have not been sought.

Proposing a multi-criteria evaluation model, assessing tourism-related decisions and how they affect children's quality of life, should be based on children's perceptions of the use of community resources and their limits. The model should be based in the previously described steps and associated with a handbook for community developers, managers and policy-makers, enabling evaluating, ranking and comparing strategies, policies, programmes and decisions affecting tourism impacts on children's quality of life. The aim is to support communities' transition towards sustainable tourism development with a formal benchmarking methodology. The explicitly defined criteria, weights and hierarchies would facilitate understanding children's voices, needs, priorities and rights.

Such a multi-criteria evaluation model development approach is most appropriately based on Multi-Criteria Decision Methodology (MCDM). An overview of MCDM and the development of this methodology is available in many seminal and current studies (e.g. Fishburn, 1967, Keeney & Raiffa, 1976; Keeney & Fishburn, 1974; Keeney, 1982; Chankong & Haimes, 1983; Fülöp, 2005; Bohanec et al., 2013; Kolios et al., 2016). The main characteristic of MCDM is that the decision problem is broken down into sub-problems and individual option characteristics, which are easier to define or measure than a significant, complex problem (Krause et al., 2015).

BOX 14.5 CASE STUDY: SLOVENIA – QUALITATIVE IS QUANTIFIED

As sustainable development issues include many qualitative variables, the project will use the Decision Expert (DEX) as the central evaluation model development methodology. DEX combines elements of expert systems and the MCDM. Values of decision option attributes in DEX are expressed in qualitative values – descriptive classes rather than numbers, for instance, "low", "appropriate" and "excellent". Qualitative values are used in decision problems where the criteria cannot be precisely measured, i.e. quantified, such as evaluating development strategies and managing environmental issues. In addition, the DEX methodology uses simple if-then rules, by which experts may find easier to express their knowledge and understand than mathematical models (Rozman et al., 2009; Žnidaršič et al., 2008). Moreover, DEX methodology is particularly suitable for solving complex decision problems, which typically involve many (< 15) attributes, many options (< 10), prevalently qualitative reasoning rather than numerical evaluation, inaccurate and/or missing data and group decision-making, which requires communication and explanation.

References

Ahn, B., Lee, B. & Shafer, C.S. (2002). Operationalizing sustainability in regional tourism planning: An application of the limits of acceptable change framework. *Tourism Management*, 23 (1), 1–15. https://doi.org/10.1016/S0261-5177(01)00059-0.

Andereck, K.L., Valentine, K.M., Knopf, R.C. & Vogt, C.A. (2005). Residents' perceptions of community tourism impacts. *Annals of Tourism Research*, 32 (4), 1056–1076.

Anderson-Fye, E.P. (2004). A "coca-cola" shape: Cultural change, body image, and eating disorders in San Andres, Belize. *Culture Medicine and Psychiatry*, 28 (4), 561–595.

Archard D. (2004). *Children: rights and childhood*. Routledge.

Arnold, M.E. (2020). America's moment: Investing in positive youth development to transform youth and society. *Journal of Youth Development*, 12 (2), 16–36.

Asian Development Bank and Plan International UK (2018). "What's the evidence?" Youth engagement and the sustainable development goals. https://www.adb.org/sites/default/files/publication/466811/youth-engagement-sdgs.pdf (accessed 13 December 2022).

Benson, P.L., Scales, P.C. & Syvertsen, A.K. (2011). The contribution of the developmental assets framework to positive youth development theory and practice. In Lerner, R.M., Lerner, J.V. & Benson, J.B. *Advances in Child Development and Behavior*Elsevier, 197–230.

Bohanec, M. (2014). DEXi: Program for multi-attribute decision making, user's manual, version 4.01. IJS Report DP-9989. Jožef Stefan Institute. http://kt.ijs.si/MarkoBohanec/pub/DEXiManual401.pdf (accessed 23 November 2019).

Bohanec, M., Aprile, G., Costante, M., Foti, M. & Trdin, N. (2013). *Decision support model for the assessment of bank reputational risk*. Proceedings of the 16th International Conference Information Society IS, Ljubljana, Slovenia, 7–11 October, 11–14.

Bohanec, M., Cortet, J., Griffiths, B., Žnidaršič, M., Debeljak, M., Caul, S., ... Krogh, P.H. (2007). A qualitative multi-attribute model for assessing the impact of cropping systems on soil quality. *Pedobiologia*, 51 (3), 239–250.

Bohanec, M., Rajkovič, V., Bratko, I., Zupan, B. & Znidarsič, M. (2013). DEX methodology: Three decades of qualitative multi-attribute modelling. *Informatica*, 37, 49–54.

Bohanec, M., Rajkovič, V., Semolič, B. & Pogačnik, A. (1995). Knowledge-based portfolio analysis for project evaluation. *Information and Management*, 28 (5), 293–302.

Bourdieu, P., & Passeron, J.-C. (1977/2000). *Reproduction in Education, Society and Culture*. Sage Publications.

Burke, S.E., Sanson, A.V. & Van Hoorn, J. (2018). The psychological effects of climate change on children. *Current Psychiatry Reports*, 20 (5), 1–8.

Buzinde, C.N., & Manuel-Navarrete, D. (2013). The social production of space in tourism enclaves: Mayan children's perceptions of tourism boundaries. *Annals of Tourism Research*, 43, 482–505.

Canosa, A., Graham, A. & Wilson, E. (2019). My overloved town: The challenges of growing up in a small coastal tourist destination (Byron Bay, Australia). In Milano, C., Cheer, J.M. & Novelli, M. *Overtourism: Excesses, discontents and measures in travel and tourism*. Routledge, 190–204.

Canosa, A., Moyle, B. & Wray, M. (2016). Can anybody hear me? A critical analysis of young residents' voices in tourism studies. *Tourism Analysis: An Interdisciplinary Journal*, 21 (2), 325–337.

Canosa, A., Wilson, E. & Graham, A. (2017). Empowering young people through participatory film: A postmethodological approach. *Current Issues in Tourism*, 20 (8), 894–907.

Carr, N. (2011). *Children's and Families' Holiday Experience*. Taylor & Francis.

Catalano, R.F., Berglund, M.L., Ryan, J.A.M., Lonczak, H.S. & Hawkins, J.D. (2002). Positive youth development in the United States: Research findings on evaluations of positive youth development programs. *Prevention & Treatment*, 5 (1), 98–124.

Catalano, R.F., Skinner, M.L., Alvarado, G., Kapungu, C., Reavley, N., Patton, G.C., *et al.* (2019). Positive youth development programs in low- and middle- income countries: A conceptual framework and systematic review of efficacy. *Journal of Adolescent Health*, 65 (1), 15–31.

Chankong, V., & Haimes, Y. (1983). *Multiobjective Decision Making: Theory and methodology*. North-Holland.

Ciocanel, O., Power, K., Eriksen, A. & Gillings, K. (2017). Effectiveness of positive youth development interventions: a meta-analysis of randomised controlled trials. *Journal of Youth and Adolescence*, 46, 483–504.

Coleman, S., Pothong, K. & Weston, S. (2018). Dramatising deliberation: A method for encouraging young people to think about their rights. *Journal of Public Deliberation*, 14 (1), Art. 2.

Crow, G. (2002). Community studies: Fifty years of theorisation. *Sociological Research Online*, 7 (3), 82–91.

Dancause, K.N., Dehuff, C., Soloway, L.E., Vilar, M., Chan, C., Wilson, M. & Garruto, R.M. (2011). Behavioral changes associated with economic development in the South Pacific: Health transition in Vanuatu. *American Journal of Human Biology*, 23 (3), 366–376.

Deery, M., Jago, L. & Fredline, L. (2012). Rethinking social impacts of tourism research: A new research agenda. *Tourism Management*, 33 (1), 64–73.

Dioko, L.A.N. (2017). The problem of rapid tourism growth – an overview of the strategic question. *Worldwide Hospitality and Tourism Themes*, 9 (3), 252–259. https://doi.org/10.1108/WHATT-02-2017-0005.

Dostop.si (2023). Kateri deficitarni poklici bodo v 2023/24 prejemali štipendije?https://www.dostop.si/kateri-deficitarni-poklici-bodo-v-2023-24-prejemali-stipendije/ (accessed 1 February 2023).

Dwyer, L. (2018). Saluting while the ship sinks: The necessity for tourism paradigm change. *Journal of Sustainable Tourism*, 26 (1), 29–48.

Faulkner, B., & Tideswell, C. (1997). A framework for monitoring community impacts of tourism. *Journal of Sustainable Tourism*, 5 (1), 3–28. https://doi.org/10.1080/09669589708667273.

Fishburn, P. (1967). Conjoint measurement in utility theory with incomplete product sets. *Journal of Mathematical Psychology*, 4 (1), 104–119.

Frasquilho, D., Ozer, E.J., Ozer, E.M., Branquinho, C., Camacho, I., Reis, M., *et al.* (2018). Dream Teens: Adolescents-led participatory project in Portugal in the context of the economic recession. *Health Promotion Practice*, 19 (1), 51–59.

Fülöp, J. (2005). Introduction to decision making methods. http://academic.evergreen.edu/projects/bdei/documents/decisionmakingmethods.pdf (accessed 26 November 2019).

Gamradt, J. (1995). Jamaican children's representations of tourism. *Annals of Tourism Research*, 22 (4), 735–762.

Gorenc, T., Carli, T., Vračko, P., Kovač, N. & Kukec, A. (2020). Znanje, stališča in vedenja mladih ter pogledi mladinskih organizacij na področje okolje-zdravje v Sloveniji. *Javno zdravje*, 7, 1–20.

Gursoy, D., Boğan, E., Dedeoğlu, B.B. & Çalışkan, C. (2019). Residents' perceptions of hotels' corporate social responsibility initiatives and its impact on residents' sentiments to community and support for additional tourism development. *Journal of Hospitality and Tourism Management*, 39, 117–128.

Hadinejad, A.D., Moyle, B., Scott, N., Kralj, A. & Nunkoo, R. (2019). Residents' attitudes to tourism: a review. *Tourism Review*, 74 (2), 157–172. https://doi.org/10.1108/TR-01-2018-0003.

Higgins-Desbiolles, F. (2006). More than an "industry": The forgotten power of tourism as a social force. *Tourism Management*, 27 (6), 1192–1208.

Joo, D., Xu, W., Lee, J., Lee, C.K. & Woosnam, K.M. (2021). Residents' perceived risk, emotional solidarity, and support for tourism amidst the Covid-19 pandemic. *Journal of Destination Marketing and Management*, 19 (January), 100553.

Keeney, R.L. (1982). Decision analysis: An overview. *Operations Research*, 30 (5), 803–838.

Keeney, R., & Fishburn, P. (1974). Seven independence concepts and continuous multi-attribute utility functions. *Journal of Mathematical Psychology*, 11 (3), 294–327.

Keeney, R., & Raiffa, H. (1976). *Decisions with Multiple Objectives*. John Wiley & Sons.

Kellet, M. (2005). *Children as Active Researchers: A new research paradigm for the 21st century?*ESRC National Centre for Research Methods. https://eprints.ncrm.ac.uk/id/eprint/87/1/MethodsReviewPaperNCRM-003.pdf (accessed 15 January 2023).

Khoo-Lattimore, C., Prayag, P. & Cheah, B.L. (2015). Kids on board: Exploring the choice process and vacation needs of Asian parents with young children in resort hotels. *Journal of Hospitality Marketing & Management*, 24 (5), 511–531.

Kolios, A., Mytilinou, V., Lozano-Minguez, E. & Salonitis, K. (2016). A comparative study of multiple-criteria decision-making methods under stochastic inputs. *Energies*, 9 (7), 566.

Koščak, M., Colarič-Jakše, L., Fabjan, D., Kukulj, S., Založnik, S., Knežević, M., ... Prevolšek, B. (2018). No one asks the children, right? *Tourism: An International Interdisciplinary Journal*, 66 (4), 396–410.

Koščak, M., Knežević, M., Binder, D., Pelaez-Verdet, A., Işik, C., Mićić, V., Borisavljević, K. & Šegota, T. (2023). Exploring the neglected voices of children in sustainable tourism development: A comparative study in six European tourist destinations. *Journal of Sustainable Tourism*, 31 (2), 561–580.

Krause, M., Cabrera, J.E., Cubillo, F., Diaz, C. & Ducci, J. (2015). *Aquarating: An international standard for assessing water and wastewater services*. IWA Publishing.

Larcher V., & Brierley J. (2020). Children of Covid-19: Pawns, pathfinders or partners? *Journal of Medical Ethics*, 46 (8): 508–509.

Lavrič, M., Deželan, T., Klanjšek, R., Lahe, D., *et al.* (2020). Mladina 2020 – Položaj mladih v Sloveniji. https://mlad.si/e-katalogi/Mladina_2020/ (accessed 5 January 2022).

Leatherman, T.L., Goodman, A.H. & Stillman, T. (2010). Changes in stature, weight, and nutritional status with tourism-based economic development in the Yucatan. *Economics and Human Biology*, 8 (2), 153–158.

Ledford, H. (2021). Should children get Covid vaccines? What the science says. *Nature*, 595, 638–639.

Leman, P.J., Smith, E.P., Petersen, A.C. & SRCD Ethnic-Racial Issues and International Committees. (2017). Introduction to the special section of child development on positive youth development in diverse and global contexts. *Child Development*, 88 (4), 1039–1044.

Lerner, R.M., Almerigi, J.B., Theokas, C. & Lerner, J.V. (2005). Positive Youth Development: A view of the issues. *The Journal of Early Adolescence*, 25 (1), 10–16.

Lerner, R.M., Tirrell, J.M., Dowling, E.M., Geldhof, G.J., Gestsdóttir, S., Lerner, J.V., *et al.* (2018). The end of the beginning: Evidence and absences studying Positive Youth Development in a global context. *Adolescent Research Review*, 4, 1–14.

Löfström, E., Richter, I. & Nesvold, I.H. (2021). Disruptive communication as a means to engage children in solving environmental challenges: A case study on plastic pollution. *Frontiers in Psychology*, 16 (12): 635448.

Løseth, K. (2018.) Knowledge development in adventure tourism businesses – the influence of serious leisure. *Annals of Leisure Research*, 21 (5), 575–591.

Lugosi, P., Robinson, R.N.S., Golubovskaya, M. & Foley, L. (2016). The hospitality consumption experiences of parents and carers with children: A qualitative study of foodservice settings. *International Journal of Hospitality Management*, 54, 84–94.

Marris, E. (2018). Why the world is watching young climate activists. https://media.nature.com/original/magazine-assets/d41586-019-02696-0/d41586-019-02696-0.pdf (accessed 15 November 2022).

Maruyama, N.U., Keith, S.J. & Woosnam, K.M. (2019). Incorporating emotion into social exchange: Considering distinct resident groups' attitudes towards ethnic neighborhood tourism in Osaka, Japan. *Journal of Sustainable Tourism*, 27 (8), 1125–1141.

McGehee, N.G., & Andereck, K.L. (2004). Factors predicting rural residents' support of tourism. *Journal of Travel Research*, 43 (2), 131–140.

McKercher, B., Wang, D. & Park, W. (2015). Social impacts as a function of place change. *Annals of Tourism Research*, 50, 52–66.

METS RS (Ministry of the Economy, Tourism and Sport) (2017). Strategija trajnostne rasti slovenskega turizma 2017–2021. https://www.slovenia.info/uploads/dokumenti/kljuni_dokumenti/strategija_turizem_koncno_9.10.2017.pdf (accessed 22 November 2022).

METS RS (Ministry of the Economy, Tourism and Sport) (2022). Strategija slovenskega turizma 2022–2028. https://www.gov.si/assets/ministrstva/MGTS/Dokumenti/DTUR/Nova-strategija-2022-2028/Strategija-slovenskega-turizma-2022-2028-dokument.pdf (accessed 22 November 2022).

Mihalič, T. (2016). Sustainable-responsible tourism discourse – towards "responsustable" tourism. *Journal of Cleaner Production*, 111 (Part B), 461–470.

Miller, A., & Beazley, H. (2022). 'We have to make the tourists happy'; orphanage tourism in Siem Reap, Cambodia through the children's own voices. *Children's Geographies*, 20 (1), 51–63.

Molero, F., Navas, M.A.S., Alemá, N.P. & Cuadrado, I. (2003). Paupers or riches: The perception of immigrants, tourists and ingroup members in a sample of Spanish children. *Journal of Ethnic and Migration Studies*, 29 (3), 501–518.

Moscardo, G. (2012). Building social capital to enhance the quality-of-life of destination residents. In Uysal, M., Perdue, R.R. & Sirgy, M.J. *Handbook of Tourism and Quality-of-Life Research: Enhancing the lives of tourists and residents of host communities*. Springer, 403–422.

Nishiyama, K. (2017). Deliberators, not future citizens: Children in democracy. *Journal of Deliberative Democracy*, 13 (1), 1–26.

Nunkoo, R., Smith, S.L.J. & Ramkissoon, H. (2013). Residents' attitudes to tourism: A longitudinal study of 140 articles from 1984 to 2010. *Journal of Sustainable Tourism*, 21 (1), 5–25.

Ohashi, Y., Ohashi, K., Meskanen, P., Hummelin, N., Kato, F. & Kynäslahti, H. (2012). What children and youth told about their home city in digital stories in "C my city!" *Digital Creativity*, 23 (2), 126–135.

Olenik, C. (2019). The evolution of positive youth development as a key international development approach. *Global Social Welfare*, 6, 5–15.

Pereira, T., & Freire, T. (2021). Positive Youth Development in the context of climate change: A systematic review. *Frontiers in Psychology*, 12, 786119. https://doi.org/10. 3389/fpsyg.2021.786119.

Poria, Y., & Timothy, D.J. (2014). Where are the children in tourism research? *Annals of Tourism Research*, 47, 93–95.

Qi, S., Hua, F., Zhou, Z., *et al.* (2022). Trends of Positive Youth Development publications (1995–2020): A scientometric review. *Applied Research Quality Life*, 17, 421–446.

RCPCH (Royal College of Paediatrics and Child Health) (2010). *Not Just a Phase. A Guide to the Participation of Children and Young People in Health Services*. https:// www.rcpch.ac.uk/sites/default/files/RCPCH-not-just-a-phase-2010.pdf (accessed 15 October 2023).

Rozman, Č., Potočnik, M., Pažek, K., Borec, A., Majkovič, D. & Bohanec, M. (2009). A multi-criteria assessment of tourist farm service quality. *Tourism Management*, 30 (5), 629–637.

Sanson, A., & Bellemo, M. (2021). Children and youth in the climate crisis. *BJPsych Bulletin*, 45 (4), 205–209.

Sanson, A.V., Van Hoorn, J. & Burke, S.E.L. (2019). Responding to the impacts of the climate crisis on children and youth. *Child Development Perspectives*, 13 (4), 201–207.

Savage, M., Bagnall, G. & Longhurst, B. (2005). *Globalisation and Belonging*. Sage Publications.

Seraphin, H., & Green, S. (2019). The significance of the contribution of children to conceptualising the destination of the future. *International Journal of Tourism Cities*, 5 (4), 544–555.

Sharpley, R. (2014). Host perceptions of tourism: A review of the research. *Tourism Management*, 42, 37–49.

Shek, D.T., Dou, D., Zhu, X. & Chai, W. (2019). Positive youth development: Current perspectives. *Adolescent Health, Medicine and Therapeutics*, 10, 131–141.

Small, J. (2008). The absence of childhood in tourism studies. *Annals of Tourism Research*, 35 (3), 772–789.

Šegota, T., & Mihalič, T. (2018). Elicitation of tourist accommodation demand for counter-seasonal responses: Evidence from the Slovenian Coast. *Journal of Destination Marketing & Management*. https://doi.org/10.1016/j.jdmm.2018.02.002.

Šegota, T., Mihalič, T. & Kuščer, K. (2017). The impact of residents' informedness and involvement on their perceptions of tourism impacts: The case of Bled. *Journal of Destination Marketing & Management*, 6 (3), 196–206.

Šegota, T., Mihalič, T. & Perdue, R.R. (2022). Resident perceptions and responses to tourism: Individual vs community level impacts. *Journal of Sustainable Tourism*, 1–19. https://doi.org/10.1080/09669582.2022.2149759.

Thornton, P.R., Shaw, G. & Williams, A.M. (1997). Tourist group holiday decision-making and behaviour: The influence of children. *Tourism Management*, 18 (5), 287–297.

Tolan, P. (2014). Future directions for positive development intervention research. *Journal of Clinical Child & Adolescent Psychology*, 43 (4), 686–694.

United Nations (1989). *UN General Assembly, Convention on the Rights of the Child*. https://www.ohchr.org/en/treaty-bodies/crc (accessed 15 January 2023).

United Nations (2018). *World Youth Report*. https://www.un.org/development/desa/youth/wp-content/uploads/sites/21/2018/12/WorldYouthReport-2030Agenda.pdf (accessed 12 December 2022).

UNWTO (2022). *UNWTO World Tourism Barometer and Statistical Annex*. https://www.e-unwto.org/toc/wtobarometereng/20/1 (accessed 15 January 2023).

Uysal, M., Sirgy, M.J., Woo, E. & Kim, H.L. (2016). Quality of life (QoL) and well-being research in tourism. *Tourism Management*, 53, 244–261.

Vargas-Sanchez, A., Porras-Bueno, N. & Plaza-Mejia, M. de los A. (2013). Residents' attitude to tourism and seasonality. *Journal of Travel Research*, 53 (5), 581–596.

Williams, J., & Lawson, R. (2001). Community issues and resident opinions of tourism. *Annals of Tourism Research*, 28 (2), 269–290. https://doi.org/10.1016/S0160-7383(00)00030-X.

Woosnam, K.M., & Ribeiro, M.A. (2022). Methodological and theoretical advancements in social impacts of tourism research. *Journal of Sustainable Tourism*, 1–17.

WTO & UNDP (2017). *Tourism and the Sustainable Development Goals – Journey to 2030*. https://www.e-unwto.org/doi/book/10.18111/9789284419401 (accessed 15 January 2021).

WTTC (2022). *World Travel and Tourism Councill Staff Shortages*. https://wttc.org/Portals/0/Documents/Reports/2022/WTTC-Staff%20Shortages-August22.pdf (accessed 15 January 2023).

Yang, M.J.H., Khoo, C. & Yang, E.C.L. (2023). An art-based inquiry into the perception of tourism impacts on their quality of life: The case of Cambodian host-children. *Journal of Travel Research*, 62 (8), 1801–1818. https://doi.org/10.1177/00472875221140414.

Yang, M.J.H., Yang, E.C.L. & Khoo-Lattimore, C. (2020). Host-children of tourism destinations: Systematic quantitative literature review. *Tourism Recreation Research*, 45 (2), 231–246.

Zins, J.E., & Elias, M.J. (2007). Social and emotional learning: Promoting the development of all students. *Journal of Educational and Psychological Consultation*, 17 (2–3), 233–255.

Žnidaršič, M., Bohanec, M. & Zupan, B. (2008). Modelling impacts of cropping systems: Demands and solutions for DEX methodology. *European Journal of Operational Research*, 189 (3), 594–608.

15

REFLECTIONS ON PART V

The Key Concepts

This section discusses and examines the Key Concepts from each preceding chapter in Part V.

Chapter 13

The Key Concepts may be categorised as follows:

- *For children with children.* This approach is the only pathway towards sustainable tourism development because it signals the inclusion of voices that have until now been neglected. So far, the approach has been used to improve healthcare and research, and prevent climate change.
- *Positive Youth Development (PYD) framework.* This provides a toolkit suitable for modelling children's quality of life. Its approaches are broadly designed to build skills, foster agency, build healthy relationships, strengthen the environment and transform systems. The PYD framework includes four domains: assets (exposure to education or training, interpersonal skills, recognition of emotions and self-control), agency (positive identity, self-efficacy, ability to plan, perseverance, positive feelings about the future), contribution (engagement in civil society and with adults) and enabling environment (bonding, prosocial opportunities, support, prosocial norms, values, recognition, gender-responsive, physical and psychological safety).
- *Tourism development benefits from children.* Children provide valuable insights and perspectives on their needs, preferences and expectations as tourists or hosts. They also foster a sense of ownership, responsibility and stewardship for their natural and cultural heritage. Children also develop

DOI: 10.4324/9781003374299-25

into skilled, knowledgeable and confident community members engaged in tourism activities and projects. This makes the quality of life and quality of visits improved. Nonetheless, they promote intergenerational dialogue and cooperation among different stakeholders in tourism.

- *Ladder of Children's Participation.* The ladder is a theoretical approach suggesting child-initiated and shared decisions with adults. The approach promotes children's learning to appreciate democracy and a sense of their capability and responsibility to participate in a democratic society. The enabling environment for such democratisation should be planned, designed, monitored and managed to provide an ideal realm for active participation in children's empowerment and involvement.

- *Methods for involving children in processes.* Viewing children as equal partners (rather than considering them passive subjects) in decision-making is essential. Researchers should involve children in developing programmes and activities, seeking their input and valuing their perspectives. A mixed methods approach using qualitative and quantitative strategies is often the ideal design because it provides a balanced and more affluent analysis of the problem. Using both qualitative and quantitative methods yields richer, more practical and reliable insights into children's lives in tourism communities.

- *Child-friendly environments.* Physical and social environments must be reviewed and reconsidered to ensure they are child-friendly. This involves considering aspects such as safety and accessibility, and providing appropriate amenities and facilities for children. Creating a welcoming and inclusive environment can encourage children's participation and engagement. Moreover, the existing legal frameworks and policies related to enabling environments should be revised. This includes understanding children's rights, such as those outlined in the United Nations Convention on the Rights of the Child (UNCRC), and ensuring that these rights are respected and upheld throughout the development process. Also, it means strengthening children's ability to avoid risks and stay safe and secure through youth-friendly laws and gender-responsive policies that prioritise their physical and psychological safety.

Chapter 14

The Key Concepts may be categorised as follows:

- *The Agenda 2030.* The 2030 Agenda for Sustainable Development reflects a transformation that would make society a collaborative partnership for improving lives worldwide. Tourism is one of the social forces seen as having the ability to contribute to all Sustainable Development Goals. The torchbearers of the agenda are children, as they were recognised as bringing fresh ideas and solutions, and their active engagement is crucial in achieving a sustainable, inclusive and stable society.

- *Covid-19 has propelled children to social partners.* The pandemic made communities and governments perceive children as social partners who needed to take responsibility in a "once in a lifetime situation". Hence, in countries such as the UK, the US, Israel and the EU, children were encouraged to be vaccinated to protect themselves from the virus and help protect vulnerable adults and stop the spread. It is striking that the age limit for deciding in favour of vaccination was 12, which means that in the case of their parents opposing or refusing to vaccinate them, children were asked to act upon their right to freedom of choice and get vaccinated despite parental opposition. Hence, we dare to ask: "If we are suddenly finding ways of recognising their vital responsibility in the community, why do we not give them the same importance in making decisions concerning their imminent future?"
- *Roadshow of tourism impacts on the community.* Analysing demographic trends and tourism-led community characteristics helps provide a state-of-the-art roadmap, aiming for detailed insight into communities. More importantly, the roadmap must include and combine analyses of various community characteristics instead of focusing on only a selected number. Such roadmaps help researchers, policy-makers and practitioners better understand place changes instigated by tourism. More importantly, such maps will enable a multilayered understanding of children's socialisation environments. Moreover, the roadmap is conceptually centred on the assumptions that children are not a homogenous group and that their attitudes are structured along the lines of different socio-economic factors but also the characteristics of tourism communities.
- *Surveying children's perceptions.* Surveys provide a general overview of children's perceptions of tourism. The unique stronghold of these surveys is in scratching the surface of children's attitudes towards tourism and offering a loop into differences in attitudes linked to the community's development. Moreover, surveys help identify segments of children and their characteristics and link their perceptions of tourism impacts to different socio-economic factors shaping their communities.
- *Understanding lived realities.* To provide an informed, evidence-based knowledge of children's everyday experiences and engagements with tourism, methods, such as focus groups, interviews, (n)etnography, etc., need to be utilised. Qualitative methods have enormous potential to enable deep insight into children's sense of spatial attachment, belongings and discourses, informing their understanding of tourism and hospitality. In this way, a critical reflection on broader cultural and social processes affecting children's everyday practices and discourses can be uncovered and understood.
- *Deliberation for greater democratisation of tourism.* Youth deliberations as methods of inclusion of children can help identify tourism-related public issues (i.e. destination management and sense of place, environmental issues linked to climate change and working conditions). Discussing the future with the future enriches academic knowledge and professional

practice; it considers children active co-creators. It goes beyond considering children as objects of research or as only "future citizens" but as having essential contributions to democracy.

- *The children-led model for sustainable tourism.* It rests on assessing tourism-related decisions and how they affect children's quality of life based on children's perceptions of the use of community resources. The model should serve as a handbook for community developers, managers and policy-makers who decide tourism development in the community, and it should enable the evaluation, ranking and comparison of strategies, policies, programmes and decisions affecting tourism impacts on children's quality of life. The model aims to support a transition towards sustainable tourism development with a formal benchmarking methodology, facilitating an understanding of children's voices, needs, priorities and rights.

The Critical Factors

The challenges of implementing PYD in tourism

Challenges and barriers that hinder child-led tourism planning and development are limited access to information, education and training on tourism issues and opportunities; inefficient decision-making structures, platforms and mechanisms that facilitate children's involvement; ignorance of and disrespect for children's rights, opinions and contributions by adults; lack of resources, support and incentives for children's participation; and failure in ensuring protection and placing safety measures in motion for children from potential risks and harm associated with tourism, such as child labour, exploitation, abuse and violence.

Well-being and safety as a top priority of development

Researchers need to consider children's developmental stage and capabilities when designing research methods and activities. Ensuring that the research process is age-appropriate and does not cause harm or undue stress to the children involved is essential. The well-being and safety of children should be a top priority. Researchers/policy-makers/practitioners should establish protocols to protect children from any harm or exploitation during the processes. This may involve obtaining necessary approvals from ethical boards and adhering to set guidelines and regulations for working with children.

Ethical considerations

Involving children in tourism research and development must rest on high ethical principles to ensure their safety, consent, confidentiality, representation and feedback. It also includes considering overcoming the barriers of power imbalance, adult bias, cultural diversity and resource constraints. Working with children can be very sensitive and time-consuming. Despite the latter, the priority must be the ethical treatment of children and obtaining informed consent from both children and their parents/guardians. This involves providing specific information about the projects and children's involvement, its objectives, potential risks and benefits, and ensuring that children and their parents have sufficient time to consider participation.

Advancing critical scholarship

Residents have learned how to live with tourism: they adapt, avoid, support, oppose and continue leading their lives as residents of tourism destinations. However, the literature seems to be under arrested development, emphasising the economic lenses of the social exchange between residents and tourists. For over five decades, academic research has been demonstrating, over and over again, that the more residents benefit from tourism, the more they will positively perceive tourism impacts and continue supporting it. Unfortunately, this prevalent "truth" downgrades the resident–tourism relationship to financial exchanges, limiting the exploration of social and cultural interactions. By empowering children's voices, understanding their lived realities with perceived anxieties and prospects regarding future tourism development will inevitably help advance critical tourism scholarship by focusing solely on socio-cultural aspects of resident-tourism exchange. This is because of children not being direct financial beneficiaries of tourism development until adulthood, meaning that other-than-financial tourism relationships can be further explored.

Connections

This section suggests some elements based on the issues raised in Part V. Following the underlying concepts from Chapters 13 and 14, we have sought to develop some connections for readers as follows:

- For students, we pose some questions which may assist the connections between teaching and learning.
- For researchers (graduate or professional), we suggest further guidelines for child-centred research.
- For practitioners, we raise questions encouraging them to implement child-friendly environment initiatives.

Teaching and learning

Developing a positive future with positive youth at its core should be high on the agenda of students as future professionals, policy-makers, professionals and researchers. Here are some points to consider:

a   The benefits and challenges of engaging children in tourism planning and decision-making include enhancing their sense of belonging, empowerment, creativity and environmental awareness, and addressing their needs, interests and rights as stakeholders and future leaders in tourism.
b   The methods and tools for facilitating children's participation in tourism include participatory action research, child-friendly consultations, workshops, games, storytelling, mapping, drawing, photography and digital media.
c   The ethical and practical issues of involving children in tourism research and development include ensuring their safety, consent, confidentiality, representation and feedback, and overcoming the barriers of power imbalance, adult bias, cultural diversity and resource constraints.
d   The case studies are best with practices of children's participation in tourism from different contexts and regions, such as rural and urban areas, developed and developing countries, cultural and natural heritage sites, and community-based and mass tourism destinations.

Guidelines for researchers

Researching with children is sensitive and time-consuming. However, it is also rewarding. Here are some elements to consider for enhancing the future of tourism research:

a   The PYD framework is yet to be introduced to tourism research and development. How should each domain (i.e. agency, assets, contribution and enabling environment) be approached to allow for the framework to be linked to tourism and what tourism-specific measures should be developed to monitor its success?
b   Mixed methods represent the ideal approach to a balanced and more affluent analysis of children in tourism communities. However, we acknowledge that they may not suit all research aims equally. Given their benefits and limitations, how can qualitative and quantitative methods yield more affluent, practical and reliable insights into children's lives in tourism communities?
c   Self-reporting bias includes overstating the initial knowledge (a priori intervention), acquired knowledge (post-intervention) and even lacking comprehension. What mechanisms or approaches must be developed to avoid or mitigate self-reporting bias in research, practice and policy-making?

Keynotes for practitioners

Practitioners may wish to review the following points:

a   How can your organisation, business or governing body create and facilitate an enabling environment for developing positive youth?

b   How do we fundamentally redesign decision-making mechanisms to enable children's contribution?

c   How do we change the *modus operandi* to contribute to the development of children's assets?

16

CONCLUDING REFLECTIONS

Introduction

The authors have through the preceding chapters emphasised the view that children are not only "residents" in tourist areas, towns and villages, but critical participants and careful observers of what occurs around them. The failure we have identified is that planners and managers will frequently ignore children or regard them as entirely subordinate to the tourism and hospitality development process. As a result, in the research conducted on tourism, there has been a noticeable lack of investment in seeking the views of children and young people about tourism and how it may impact their future lives. In other words, it would be fair to indicate that children and young people have been generally excluded from the participatory planning process that should engage in tourism communities. In other words, their access to social justice has been implicitly denied. Are they simply non-reactive objects without "social competence" in a process that may essentially and fundamentally affect their future lives?

There is little doubt from examples provided in this book that without key stimulating programmes young people are generally reluctant to enter professions in tourism and hospitality. High turnover of staff, lengthy and unsocial hours and the precarious nature of employment in tourism and hospitality are all mentioned. At the same time, it is important to see where these negative attitudes arise from, which is an element we have discussed in the preceding chapters.

The potentially negative perception of tourists that parents have is an important issue, as well as peer attitudes. Another issue is the concept of regarding tourism activity as either tangible or intangible. Mass tourism (and overtourism) is highly tangible in terms of the physical aspect of structures –

DOI: 10.4324/9781003374299-26

hotels, guest houses and related tourism facilities – as well as in the over-whelming level of impact tourism has on the socio-economic environment. It is also tangible in the organisation and deployment of tourists; they arrive in groups, they make visits in groups and conduct social activities in groups. They are an overwhelmingly tangible and demonstrable feature.

Sustainable tourism, however, tends towards a far lower profile with smaller groups from one to 20. Carrying capacity policies for sustainable and heritage tourism sites acts in depressing or capping groups by visitor size and volume. Thus, sustainable tourism is differentiated in terms of a less tangible profile and impact on the host communities.

We have also in the preceding chapters expressed the view that a critical concept is distancing ourselves from the ideology of seeing tourism destinations only in an economic and financial sense and measuring all activity in terms of value added or financial market inputs. We are even more aware of the fact that sustainable tourism, to a degree, rejects consumerism and the commoditisation of tourism products. It inherently seeks to protect and preserve fragile environments, which inevitably must have a profound impact on children and their future.

1 Sustainability

We have sought to propose that moving towards sustainable, ethical and respon-sible tourism implicitly engage us in transformational development strategies, despite the problems of the post-pandemic environment. The market for sustain-able tourism appears to be in a period of general slow economic growth with the challenges of inflation, wars in Ukraine and the Middle East as well as the ongoing energy crisis. All of these factors affect and impact on advanced economies, which tend to provide the major market for sustainable and ethical tourism.

Nonetheless, the momentum to create more resilient, sustainable and inclu-sive tourism is neither diminished nor abandoned. We are additionally required to face the problem of how tourism should re-focus economically, socially and environmentally to meet the Sustainable Development Goals. We see that tour-ism communities are frequently in the front line in terms of negative aspects of modern tourism relating to their cultural and environmental fragility. Impor-tantly, an ultimate and critical issue must be where children fit into locally oriented tourism that meets all long-term sustainability requirements.

Key Concepts

The immediate issues may be seen as:

i Understanding that pre-Covid global tourism developed at a rate above the actual growth of the global economy.
ii During the pandemic between 2020 and 2022, there was strong growth in an alternative tourism model.

iii The post-pandemic new challenges were either finding the "new normal" or slipping back to the "old normal".
iv Rethinking sustainability.

This then gave rise to a rethinking during the pandemic and immediate post-pandemic period of the approach that tourism held, in general terms, regarding sustainability. It may be suggested that the following concepts were defined and explored:

i New development paradigms which acknowledging the fragility of tourism.
ii The constant process of managing uncertainty.
iii The essential promotion of human capital development.

In the wake of the recovery from the effects of Covid-19, the attention of the tourism industry was shaken by the new realities that began to emerge. This included not only agents of the post-pandemic recovery but a set of new macro-economic challenges (e.g. inflation, rising interest rates, lowering consumer confidence) and the direct effects of the war in Ukraine (disruption of energy supplies and massive increases in energy costs). The effects may be seen as:

i The appearance of a "rocky road" towards macro-economic recovery with increasing cost sensitivity impacting on tourism consumers and providers.
ii Interest rate pressures on small-scale tourism enterprises, which in turn creates cost challenges for creating sustainable tourism.
iii The impact of endogenous shocks on the Green Recovery concept and its development.

Serious questions are thereby posed as to the extent of tourism's commitment towards a Green Recovery. Clearly there are:

i Failings in attainment of the UN Sustainable Development Goals.
ii Increasing problems of degradation in tourism communities and the effect on children with concomitant effect of economic downturns on children and young people – financially and in terms of their safety.
iii The role of children in sustainable tourism destinations and the longer-term effects of climate change for future generations.

Critical Factors

This leads to the potential for isolating Critical Factors in the development and management of an enhanced sustainability process for tourism that is inclusive of important groups such as children and young people:

• Identifying the long-term strategic issues and developing a resilient model.

- Boosting the role of communities, children and young people in the sustainable development process.
- Realising that sustainability comes at a cost while avoiding any form of degradation.

2 What is tourism doing for children?

We have uncovered and evaluated some critical "incidents" where tourism should promote socially *just* transformations as an alternative to a focus on purely economic achievements. The relationship between communities and tourism is complex, and requires a deviation from a unidimensional perspective. If we can understand how tourism affects life in a community, from the youngest to the eldest, we should also ensure that the momentum to create *just* tourism is the prerequisite of the future. Furthermore, we must embrace our ignorance or disinterest in knowing about tourism's influence on family life and actively work on assessing the impacts, refreshing the perspectives and improving strategies to address tourism impacts holistically.

Key Concepts

These Key Concepts may be categorised as follows:

i Understanding that the economic-centric tourism paradigm continues to be prevalent.
ii Regrettably we see that child exploitation and abuse are implicit for some children in global tourism, yet we recognise that tourism is omnipresent in the socialisation of children living in tourist destinations.
iii Children's attitudes towards tourism are influenced by their parents, teachers, peers and the community.

These initial concepts may then be explored in terms of the following:

i Children may exist in an environment of intense tourist activity, which has a potentially profound effect on family life and relationships; there is no apparent knowledge of how children perceive tourism impacts, as they are viewed as passive objects of the socialisation process carried out by adults.
ii How children perceive the economic, environmental and socio-cultural impacts of tourism when the possible benefits of tourism's economic impacts must be balanced against uncertainty and a lack of well-being.

Critical Factors

These factors may be viewed in the following terms:

- Challenges to family life and difficulty in observing the positive transformative power tourism might have where tourism is stress – both negative and positive as others enter the communal space.
- *Us* versus *them* – an implicit challenge to a community's symbolic value, uniqueness and cultural unity and the quality of life of host children – the great unknown, which society may not have fully comprehended.
- The problems of avoiding the delineation caused by information communication technology.

3 What are children doing for tourism?

There are a number of critical "incidents" linked to child labour, tourism seasonality and employment. We inevitably view tourism as a generator of jobs, whilst ignoring a substantial and often terrifying dark side, which requires to be revealed. Tourism is frequently home to child labour, as well as health and safety malpractice for children and young people. Questionable social practices will tend to be hidden from tourists. By uncovering the malpractices of the sector, we open the potential to create *just* tourism. The long-term trends are not impressive, but by examining these unjust practices and shedding light on them, we may be able to assist in creating a greater sense of global awareness so that such malpractice is addressed early and strategies for mitigation are put in place.

Key Concepts

The initial Key Concepts may be seen as:

i Child labour numbers are alarming, while child labour is geographically omnipresent, not just in underdeveloped countries but also in advanced economies.
ii Natural and institutional seasonality are inter-related given that tourism seasonality has both positive and negative outcomes.
iii We require taking account of the concept of "not in my bed" (NIMB), where children develop negative sentiments towards their beds and their home being used for accommodating tourists.
iv Children's rights are important and require balancing the potential for school-age children to work part-time against the requirements of UN Article 32 on the rights of the child.

At the same time, we should take account of the fact that tourism is a sector of employment opportunities with labour shortages in many key markets. In the European Union, 16% of employees in tourism and hospitality are aged between 16 and 29 years of age. This requires the management of the child/young person labour market between exploitation and positive development.

Critical Factors

The following Critical Factors may be identified, which affect the place of children within tourism communities:

- In many areas of high tourism activity, there is a massive problem, with housing for young people in general and for those working in tourism in particular. Much of this problem is driven by second home ownership and/or Airbnb-type accommodation.
- "Living with strangers" through having tourists in the family home has inherent dangers for young people that are not fully comprehended.

Furthermore, we should realise that in many tourism destinations, post-pandemic recovery has resulted in the same overtourism problems that existed in 2019. At the same time, we need to realise that the dual crisis of population ageing in advanced economies coupled with the potential ravages of climate change imposes a frightening threat to the ability of tourism to continue at its current levels.

4 What can children do for tourism?

In essence, children have a unique *insider* perspective that makes them experts in their own lives, and thus, they are uniquely placed to voice their desires and needs with the support and encouragement of adults. Actively involving children in decision-making becomes an empowering process, leading to increased confidence and raised self-esteem that children can copy to other decision-making processes, surpassing the scope of tourism planning and development. The issue must be how we manage and support that process in the unique situation that tourism creates.

Key Concepts

The Key Concepts can be viewed in terms of what tourism may do regarding empowerment. It is a prerequisite for sustainable tourism development and a multidimensional concept. Social empowerment in tourism can create community cohesion, whilst psychological empowerment emboldens the sense of pride. At the same time political empowerment enables residents of tourism communities to regain their voice in the community's government.

This thereby leads us to avoid the disregarding of the conceptual role of participatory planning in terms of the view that:

i   While public engagement is a central component of sustainability, this should include children in participatory planning.
ii Managing a participatory planning process implies the creation of a favourable discussion and identification of the solution using different viewpoints.
iii Utilising the *Ladder of Citizen Participation* – a metaphorical ladder representing increasing levels of citizen agency, control and power whilst valuing the importance of local community participation in tourism development.

Critical Factors

It is appropriate to suggest that the following factors have significant importance:

- Empowerment, tourism and children – empowering children in environments with intensive tourist activity and not neglecting their voice.
- Structural and personal elements of strengthening the community, as no participatory planning equals no sustainable development.

This leads to considering the benefits of participatory planning as important and Critical Factors in potential success for tourism communities through the important factors of coverage, efficiency, effectiveness, adoption of innovations and sustainability.

Lack of participation and failure to engage, even where innovative approaches or processes are applied, can occur due to poor strategy, effective management objectives and communication, or where the project is complex and lacks full participation at an early stage. Very often, citizens do not take part in decision processes because of local political conditions or power structures, a lack of funding, legislative and administrative obstacles and a widespread mentality of dependence, frustration and distrust.

5 The future of tourism – with children, for children

This requires the inclusion of children's voices, which appear to have been neglected so far. In that sense the Positive Youth Development framework has the capacity to provide a toolkit suitable for modelling children's quality of life. Undoubtedly tourism development benefits from children's valuable insights and perspectives on their needs, preferences, and expectations as tourists or hosts; this involves methods for involving children in processes by viewing them as equal partners in decision-making and not passive subjects.

Key Concepts

The following developments are important steps:

i 2030 Agenda for Sustainable Development reflects a transformation that would make society a collaborative partnership for improving lives worldwide and engage children

ii Covid-19 propelled children to social partners – the pandemic made communities and governments perceive children as social partners who needed to take responsibility in a "once in a lifetime situation".

iii Roadshow of tourism impacts on the community – analysing demographic trends and tourism-led community characteristics helps provide a state-of-the-art roadmap, aiming for detailed insight into communities.

iv Surveying children's perceptions – surveys provide a general overview of children's perceptions of tourism.

v Understanding lived realities – to provide an informed, evidence-based knowledge of children's everyday experiences and engagements with tourism.

vi Deliberation for greater democratisation of tourism – youth deliberations as methods of inclusion of children can help identify tourism-related public issues.

vii The children-led model for sustainable tourism – resting on assessing tourism-related decisions and how they affect children's quality of life based on children's perceptions of the use of community resources.

Critical Factors

These may be seen as follows:

- The challenges of implementing PYD in tourism.
- Well-being and safety as a top priority of development.
- Ethical considerations.
- Advancing critical scholarship.

Without doubt the opinions of children and young people about tourism and regarding their possible employment in tourism is a neglected concept. This tends to suggest that the push towards greater sustainability is incomplete as those who will be participants in future tourism, as the climate crisis unfolds, will not have a developed sense of understanding what sustainability implies. As we have already stated, those young people must have a voice in the planning of tourism development in their destinations, and that voice must be heard.

Without any delay we urgently need to access the views of children and young people who live, work or are observers in the tourism industry. These are neglected areas in tourism research, which may, in turn, challenge and expand current theorising within the sociology of childhood. We are mistaken to neglect young people's views and attitudes towards tourists, because these are the basis for the future development of tourism activities.

INDEX

Printed in the United States
by Baker & Taylor Publisher Services